Analyzing Activity Areas

An Ethnoarchaeological Study of the Use of Space

Susan Kent

University of New Mexico Press: *Albuquerque*

Library of Congress Cataloging in Publication Data

Kent, Susan, 1952–
  Analyzing activity areas.

  Bibliography: p.
  Includes index.
    1. Ethnoarchaeology.   2. Spatial behavior.
3. Room layout (Dwellings)   4. Navajo Indians.   5. Anthropo-
geography—Southwest, New.   6. Southwest, New—
Antiquities.   I. Title.
CC79.E85K46   1983   304.2   83-14492
ISBN 0-8263-0718-3
ISBN 0-8263-0719-1 (pbk.)

Manufactured in the United States of America.
International Standard Book Number (clothbound)
0-8263-0718-3
International Standard Book Number (paperbound)
0-8263-0719-1
Library of Congress Catalog Card Number 83-14492.
First Edition

Designed by Emmy Ezzell

To my friends,
without whose help
none of this would have been accomplished
or been as worthwhile.

Contents

Contents

Figures

Tables

Acknowledgments

There are many people without whose comments and encouragement this book, which represents a substantial revision of my dissertation, would never have been written. Although not every one of the following people agreed with all my interpretations, all did make substantive and thoughtful comments that helped me clarify my thinking. I sincerely thank Lewis Binford, David Brugge, and my dissertation committee, M. E. Shutler, Fekri Hassan, and William Lipe. Other people who contributed by providing valuable comments on various rough drafts of this manuscript include Patricia Gilman, Charlotte Frisbie, Patricia Draper, Frederick Gorman, Theodore Frisbie, Judy Rose, Beth Hadas, Chip Stanish, and Don Rice. I would also like to thank Judy Rose and Arlene Miller for their support during the collection and analysis of data. However, I, of course, take *full* responsibility for the contents of this book.

I will never forget the people with whom I lived, and who so generously allowed me to share a part of their lives. To my Navajo friends I say *"ahéhee,"* to my Spanish-American friends, *"muchas gracias,"* and to my Euroamerican friends, many thanks. I would also like to thank the Tribal Council of the Navajo Nation for granting me permission to work on the reservation.

I thank my archaeology crew, who often had to endure the most arduous conditions, including extreme heat, severe windstorms, and numerous rattlesnakes, in order to excavate the archaeological sites. Thanks also go to Linda Wheelbarger and Ray Druian for their aid in the bone-gnawing experiment, including the use of their dogs.

Thanks also go to Eric Blinman, who drafted all figures except those in chapter 5, which were drawn by Chris Brown, and those in chapter 4 and figures 2, 4, 10, 11, and 16, which were drafted by June Lipe. Figures 84–87 were originally published as Figures 4–7 of my article "The Dog: An Archaeologist's Best Friend or Worst Enemy—The Spatial Distribution of Faunal Remains," in the *Journal of Field Archaeology* 8 (1981):367–72. They are reprinted here with the permission of the publisher. The archaeological sites were excavated as part of the Navajo Indian Irrigation Project, Block II, New Mexico State University Cultural Resource Management Division, Las Cruces, New Mexico.

1

Method and Theory

A number of non-archaeological models, probably most efficiently derived from ethnographic study, must always be used in archaeology, or else our logical, imaginative, and possible premises and hypotheses may well turn out to be subjective and ethnocentric, and will have little to do with conditions of the non-western, non-industrial, small-scale societies. . . . (Stanislawski 1973:378)

The use of space is an integral part of every human being's daily life. Every day, we make subliminal and conscious decisions concerning the locations at which a diverse range of activities will be performed. Such decisions are based on the spatial patterning that is learned in childhood through socialization. For example, most Euroamerican youngsters are taught that activities that may be performed in the kitchen are not always appropriate in the bathroom or bedroom. The culturally determined use of space is so ingrained that people often express vague feelings of uneasiness and disorientation in situations where the spatial behavioral patterns differ from those to which they are accustomed. Such feelings are part of the culture shock experienced by many people upon arrival in foreign communities.

This book is concerned with a particular aspect of spatial behavior—the use of activity areas. The term *activity area* is used here to describe the locus at which a particular human event occurred. Specifically, my research was designed to test the assumptions made by archaeologists attempting to delineate activity areas. These usually implicit assumptions include the presumption that activity areas can be discerned at an archaeological site by the content and patterning of artifact and faunal remain assemblages and that the activities performed at such areas are generally both sex specific and monofunctional. In an attempt to evaluate the cross-cultural validity of these assumptions, I lived with Navajo, Euroamerican, and Spanish-American families and excavated twentieth-century Navajo archaeological sites.

My study is designed to evaluate commonly used assumptions, to suggest different ways to approach archaeological data, and to stimulate discussion. Although nonconventional, it endeavors to complement existing attempts to examine and interpret patterns in the archaeological record. Some of my research may be controversial, but certainly the past was complex enough and our knowledge of it incomplete enough that we should not limit ourselves to viewing it only in established ways. To quote Binford and Sabloff, "Paradigm change is brought about and implemented . . . by seeking out new perspectives" (1982:150). The following is an attempt to provide another productive approach to understanding the past and the processes that were a part of it.

My research was conducted in order to test three usually implicit assumptions as hypotheses. They are that: (1) activity areas can be discerned from the content and spatial patterning of artifact and faunal remain assemblages, (2) most activity areas are sex specific, and (3) most activity areas are monofunctional. Corollaries of these hypotheses are: (a) artifacts and faunal remains are abandoned at the locus where they are used, (b) the refuse abandoned at an activity area permits inferences regarding the area's function(s), (c) males and females do not usually use the same activity loci, and (d) activities relating to different functions are performed in separate areas.

In order to test the validity of these hypotheses, it was necessary to conduct my own ethnographic research, because ethnographers have not traditionally gathered the kind of data necessary for assessing archaeological method and theory. Karl Heider has described the problem: "Studies of housebuilding and pottery-making are all very well, but for the archaeologist the emphasis should be on function and disposal rather than on manufacture: how are houses and pots used, and what happens to them afterwards . . ." (1967:63). The dearth of appropriate ethnographic data available for the archaeologist was also recognized by L. H. Robbins (1973:209):

The [ethnographic] reports seldom, if ever, tell us (1) the number of individual items present in a specific inhabited settlement or dwelling area, (2) the distribution of items according to specific human activity areas, (3) percentages of kinds of raw materials used by the inhabitants for their artifacts, and (4) what happens to the contents of the residence when it is abandoned. Instead of providing such detailed quantitative information, traditional ethnographic reports generalize about the material culture of an entire society. While these broad pictures best suit the research needs of ethnographers, they do not provide archaeologists with much systematic information that is useful.

Fortunately, this situation is rapidly changing, thanks to the work of Ascher (1962), Binford (1978a, 1978b, 1979a, 1979b, 1980), Crystal (1974), Matson (1974), D. E. Thompson (1974), Yellen (1977a, 1977b), and others. However, detailed studies of activity area usage are still relatively rare. One notable exception is Roberts's (1965) description of the use of space in three Zuni households. Unfortunately, he probably obtained more data regarding formal and ideal behavior than real behavior since he did not actually live with each family he studied. He spent only 10 to 15 hours in each household, primarily observing rather than participating in their activities on what may or may not have been a typical day.

The Use and Development of Ethnoarchaeology

Ethnographic data are being used more and more to formulate and test archaeological hypotheses and models. This technique, usually called ethnoarchaeology, has experienced a florescence during the last fifteen years. The goals and conduct of ethnoarchaeological research depend upon the general theoretical orientation of the investigator. As a result, there are as many different reasons for carrying out ethnoarchaeological research as there are paradigms in archaeology. To deny one in favor of another would only inhibit the field and limit our understanding of the past.

The first anthropologist to use the term *ethnoarchaeology* in print was Fewkes (1900:578). For almost 60 years after

Fewkes's publication, anthropologists discussed the value of ethnoarchaeological research, although little such research was actually conducted (e.g., Bauxar 1957a, 1957b; Bullen 1947; Kleindienst and Watson 1956; Meggers and Evans 1957; R. Thompson 1956).

Early ethnoarchaeological research was done both by archaeologists and by ethnographers. Their studies were diverse, including, among others, the observation of the life history of contemporary communities (Ascher 1968), the investigation of an Apache wickiup (Longacre and Ayres 1968), and the observation of the breakage rate of utilitarian pottery in a Mexican village (Foster 1960). Pioneering ethnoarchaeological research also attempted to evaluate traditional archaeological reconstructions. For example, J. P. White (1967) exposed potential fallacies in such reconstructions when he compared traditional archaeological functional classification systems for lithic artifacts to those classification systems used by modern New Guinea Highlanders (in other words, emic or folk classifications versus etic or analytic classifications). Fallacious reconstructions of archaeological sites were, according to Heider, the result of assumptions that "are derived from common sense and a passing acquaintance with the ethnographic literature, and are generally very reasonable. Unfortunately for the archaeological process, cultures are generally quite unreasonable" (Heider 1967:52).

The years 1969–79 witnessed a burgeoning interest in ethnoarchaeology, and a concomitant confusion as to its nature. The extent of this confusion is indicated by the variety of definitions of ethnoarchaeology offered during this period by such anthropologists as Adams (1976), Gould (1974, 1978a, 1978b), Kramer (1979), Oswalt (1974), Schiffer (1976, 1978), and Stiles (1977).

There have been several interesting areas of research in ethnoarchaeology during the past fifteen years. One includes the assessment of the applicability and usefulness of the technique itself and the reevaluation of traditional archaeological approaches. Studies such as those by Bonnichsen (1973), Cranstone (1971), David (1971), and Stanislawski (1973) offer "cautionary tales" concerning traditional archaeological inferences. They attempt to point out some of the pitfalls archaeologists may encounter when reconstructing sites—pitfalls such as overestimating site populations and the prevalence of extended families, misidentifying cultural material, and misinterpreting area functions and intrasite artifact and activity area patterning and relationships.

Another pursuit of ethnoarchaeologists is to document the role of scavengers, including the domestic dog, in the preservation of faunal remains at archaeological sites (see Binford 1981; Binford and Bertram 1977; Casteel 1971; Crader 1974; Kent 1981; Lyon 1970; Pastron and Clewlow 1974). A third area of interest is the evaluation of different facets of traditional lithic artifact analysis. These studies include a discussion of the procurement, use, and discard of lithic raw material (Gould 1978c), as well as assessments and suggestions for lithic artifact classification systems (e.g., Ebert 1979; J. P. White and Thomas 1972). Perhaps the most popular endeavor has been the investigation of various aspects of the manufacture, use, and disposal of pottery (e.g., DeBoer and Lathrap 1979; Friedrich 1970; Furst 1972; Hardin 1979; Longacre 1974; Ochsenschlager 1974; Sharon and Donnan 1974; Stanislawski 1969, 1974, 1978).

In addition, numerous ethnoarchaeological undertakings do not fit into any of the above major categories. An example is the investigation of corporate groups as an archaeological unit (Hayden and Cannon 1982). Studies range from analyses of the items taken by Nunamiut Eskimo men on 47 trips away from their village (Binford 1976) to examinations of British mortuary practices (Pearson 1982) to the discovery that archaeological site variations between two adjacent ecological zones in Australia represent seasonal migrations of the same group (C. White and Peterson 1969). Other well known ethnoarchaeological studies include Binford's (1978b) evaluation of assumptions about such things as site variability through an examination of the hunting, storage, and consumption of meat and the use of bones by the Nunamiut, Hole's (1978, 1979) identification of pastoralists' sites in Iran, Solecki's (1979) test of Naroll's area and population equation with Kurds occupying Shanidar Cave, and Yellen's (1977a) work on activity area locations among the !Kung Bushmen and his appraisal of general archaeological methodologies. Geographical location of ethnoarchaeological research has also been varied. Studies have ranged from southwestern Alaska (e.g., Ackerman and Ackerman 1973) to Cyprus (Sallade and Braun 1982) to Tasmania (R. Jones 1978), from Mesopotamia (Yoffee 1979) and Iran (Kramer 1982; Watson 1978, 1979) to Costa Rica (Lange and Rydberg 1972), and from Ethiopia (Clark and Kurashina 1981) to Arizona (Kelley 1982; Schiffer, Downing, and McCarthy 1981).

The topical and spatial scope of these ethnoarchaeological studies is a reflection of the applicability of the approach to diverse problems and geographical regions. However, the research conducted thus far has only begun to exploit the full potential of the approach. Although not without its problems (see Chapter 5), ethnoarchaeology can aid archaeologists in their interpretations and understanding of bygone peoples by reducing the tendency to create a mythical past by using ethnocentric and/or overly simplistic models.

Current Intrasite Spatial Studies

Spatial research is another area in which anthropological interest is rapidly growing. Early spatial studies tended to concentrate on the use of space by animals and on cross-cultural descriptions of personal space (Hall 1963, 1966, 1968; O. M. Watson 1970, 1972). Early spatial studies in archaeology were, for the most part, concerned with regional spatial investigations (e.g., Willey 1956). Settlement pattern analyses have been and currently are of interest to many archaeologists (e.g., Chang 1968; D. L. Clark 1972; Hodder and Orton 1976; Hodder 1978; Reher and Witter 1977; Sterud 1979; Thomas 1972; Trigger 1968; and others). There also are several recent ethnoarchaeological studies on symbolism and the use of space (e.g., Donley 1982; Kent 1982a; Moore 1982).

The investigations of the location and use of activity areas within a site, such as those conducted by both ethnographers and archaeologists, are of more importance to the present research. Many ethnographies contain brief references to the location and/or use of activity areas (e.g., for the Navajos, see

Kluckhohn and Leighton 1962; Lamphere 1977; Kluckhohn, Hill, and Kluckhohn 1971). Such references on the Navajos include descriptions of the use of space during ceremonies and discussions of the sexual division of space within hogans. However, there are few detailed descriptions or analyses of activity areas for any one group. There are some exceptions which include Bourdieu's (1973) article on the reflection of the male/female opposition in the Berber use of houses, and Cunningham's (1973) analysis of the symbolism behind the use of the Indonesian Atoni house. Other exceptions include Douglas's (1972) warning to archaeologists that not all groups use space in the same manner and that the differences that do exist are not always the result of environmental factors, Hugh-Jones's (1979) structuralist analysis of the use of Amazonian Indian houses, and Rapoport's (1969) cursory cross-cultural description of the use of space within dwellings.

Several ethnoarchaeological studies have been devoted, some completely and others in part, to investigating the location and/or use of activity areas (e.g., Binford 1978a; Bonnichsen 1973; Portnoy 1981; Yellen 1977a). Some archaeologists have attempted to discern activity area location and/or usage at their sites (e.g., Anderson 1974; Blake 1976; Breternitz 1982; Brugge 1980; Hammack 1969a, 1969b; Schiffer 1976; Watson, LeBlanc, and Redman 1971). For example, Flannery and Winter (1976:43) identified male and female work areas within an early Mesoamerican house:

even these early households had "objects owned and used by men" and "objects owned and used by women," and the distribution of these within the house might well have been patterned. Thus, early houses could have been "conceptually divided" into work areas with men's tools and male-related features, work areas with women's tools and female-related features, and areas of overlap due to family interaction.

Various concentrations of artifacts and features located at an Archaic Cochise site in the American Southwest were interpreted as sex specific: "male-produced items at the Lone Hill Site appear to be spatially segregated from female-produced or female-related items such as milling stones and hearth

concentrations" (Agenbroad 1978:68). According to Binford and
Binford (1966:29; original emphasis), "The basic assumption
allowing us to deal rationally with archaeological assemblages
is: *The form and composition of assemblages recovered from
geologically undisturbed context are directly related to the
form and composition of human activities at a given location.*"

These and other important studies concerned with discern-
ing and interpreting activity areas at a site enhance our understanding of the past and the processes that were part of it.
Some of these interpretations are based on the assumptions
concerning activity areas that are evaluated in this research.

The first assumption—that activity areas can be discerned
from the content and spatial patterning of artifact and faunal
remain assemblages—is implicit in most activity area delineation.

The basic assumption is that the vertical and horizontal distribution
of all material making up an archaeological site is as important as
the material itself, because that distribution reflects patterned human cultural activity just as much as do the form, style, and manufacturing technique of the artifacts.
This emphasis on spatial relationships implies that we can delimit
activity areas by plotting tool types or other artifacts against precise
provenience with respect to ground matrix, architectural features,
or each other. (Watson, LeBlanc, and Redman 1971:117)

The second assumption—that most activity areas are sex
specific—is also widely held and can be seen in Price's interpretation (1978:19–20) of activity areas at a Mesolithic site in
the northern Netherlands:

Wood/bone working appears to be a major focus of activity in the
southeast half of the site, concentrated in three areas (A, B, and C),
while more cutting activities are found in the northwest.
These differences may be related to locations of male and female
activity. The presence of points and backed blades (hunting tools)
and blade cores (tool manufacture) in Area E suggests that this area
may be dominated by male-specific tasks. The scrapers, borers, and
notched pieces concentrated in the southern portion of the site may
be associated with female-specific tasks. . . .

According to DeGarmo, who interpreted a small pueblo in the southwestern United States, the conclusions he reaches

imply that the distribution ought to make sense instead of nonsense. That they make sense because they represent a systematic, spatial division of male labor in the settlement may be an *obvious interpretation* of the data. (DeGarmo 1975:295; emphasis added)

Similar assumptions are clearly manifested in the work of many other researchers, among them Longacre (1968:97), Gillespie (1976:95), and Hill (1970:58, 63).

The third assumption—that most activity areas are monofunctional—underlies the interpretation of different loci identified at archaeological sites. According to Watson, LeBlanc, and Redman (1971:119):

Various members of a single culture may perform different activities in different parts of the same site at about the same time. The resulting horizontal distribution of cultural debris and features might indicate or delineate butchering, cooking, sleeping, and toolmaking activity areas, which the archaeologist would probably interpret correctly as different activities of the same people.

An example of the use of this assumption is from Davis (1978:79–81), who delineated function specific activity areas on the Oldowan floors:

Because of evidence which indicates that many debitage flakes were utilized as tools, together with the fact that faunal remains comprise an important part of the high density areas, it was suggested earlier that the ellipses represent activity areas devoted to the preparation and consumption of games.

The "stone circle" at DK suggests that some form of shelter or windbreak may have been constructed in Oldowan camps. . . . These areas may have been the loci of dwellings or sleeping quarters which were deliberately cleared of occupation debris. . . . In this interpretation, dwellings or sleeping quarters were situated around the peripheries of the living sites, adjacent to "kitchen areas." The latter were areas of intensified activities connected with the final stages of preparation and/or more fragmentary bone refuse, together with a complement of lighter flakes. . . . Because of the closer spatial relationships between choppers and UTH on the one hand, and larger and more complete faunal remains on the other, it is possible that these were primary butchering areas, in which larger animals were initially dismembered before they were finally consumed in the "kitchen areas."

Ohel concluded that the different concentrations of small bone fragments, debitage, larger bones, and tools he delineated on the floor of Oldowan and Lower Acheulean sites at Olduvai tentatively suggest that "the elongated concentrations reflect 'food-processing areas' while the circular ones indicate 'consumption areas'" (Ohel 1977:423). Another example of assumed monofunctionality of loci is the interpretation of both function-specific and sex-specific activity areas in pithouses excavated along the Snake River in Washington:

> Primary food preparation and primary lithic reduction were consistently accomplished at loci immediately east of the structure. . . .
> Internally, the southeast quadrant of the house was devoted to secondary food processing and cooking. . . .
> The northern half of the structure was probably devoted to hide working, basket manufacture, and possibly some minor wood working. Secondary lithic reduction was accomplished on the southern floor but infrequently. The western sector of the house may have been devoted to storage and sleeping.
> The domestic activity network of House 5 was dominated by female-oriented tasks. Was this a result of sampling error, or was a men's house present nearby where the men did their work? (Brauner 1976:294–95)

These examples by no means exhaust the many activity area descriptions and analyses present in the ethnographic and archaeological literature, but they do indicate the type and focus of many of these kinds of studies.

Probably because the spatial patterning of behavior is often subliminal, anthropologists have tended to neglect the subject in favor of, for example, ceremonial, kinship, and subsistence behavior. Nevertheless, anthropologists are beginning to recognize that activity area analyses can sometimes provide information not available from other studies. My research attempts to determine whether people from different cultures use space in the way archaeologists assume they do, and then to ascertain why they do or do not. The resulting conclusions have implications for all anthropologists.

A Model of the Interrelationship
of Culture, Behavior, and Cultural Material

Attempting to understand the behavior behind the use and disposal of material culture and the distribution of activity areas is an exciting new frontier in archaeology. According to Binford (1980:5; original emphasis):

the archaeological record is the *product* or derivative of a cultural system such that it is symptomatic of the past. We cannot hope to understand the causes of these remains through a formal comparative study of the remains themselves. We must seek a deeper understanding. We must seek to understand the relationships between the dynamics of a living system in the past and the material byproducts that contribute to the formulation of the archaeological record remaining today. In still more important ways we seek to understand how cultural systems differ and what conditions such differences. . . .

Michael Schiffer has also recognized the necessity to understand the human behavior that created the archaeological record.

Because archaeologists seek to offer diverse inferences about past behavioral systems, they require a correspondingly varied set of laws which cover all aspects of the functioning of sociocultural systems as they impinge upon or relate to material phenomena that are potentially present in the archaeological record. Thus, not only must we acquire laws governing manufacture, use, and even discard of particular artifact classes, but we must also obtain more basic principles relating to the general functioning of material culture. (Schiffer 1978:242)

Other anthropologists who have discussed this relatively recent focus of archaeology include Gould (1978a) and David (1971). Most of the endeavors specifically designed to investigate such matters are ethnoarchaeological studies (e.g., Ascher 1968; Binford 1976, 1978a, 1978b, 1980; O'Connell 1979; Stanislawski 1973, 1974, 1978; Yellen 1977a, 1977b).

With relatively few exceptions, activity area use is described only cursorily in the anthropological literature. Research has often been restricted to the explanation of how activity areas and their associated material culture were used, neglecting the more important question of *why* they were used in the observed manner. Although it is difficult to answer the question *why*, the difficulty does not diminish the importance of such a question. It does, however, make conclusions more tentative because they are often inferred rather than observed. Henry Glassie justifies the speculations he makes in his structural analysis of historic houses in Virginia by writing, "An interpretation of the house's meanings and functions, its possible extensions in context, is at its most controlled, an act of pure courage. But hypothesis and a bit of scholastic over-reaching are better than nothing" (Glassie 1975:117). Speculation, as long as it is labeled as such, is vital for archaeologists and ethnographers interested in understanding what they are describing. Much of the present work is admittedly speculative, but it represents an attempt to integrate behavior with culture and cultural material in order to view a whole entity.

Culture has been variously defined throughout the anthropological literature (e.g., Geertz 1973; Kroeber and Kluckhohn 1963; Wagner 1975). In this study, culture is viewed as a shared system of meaning and symbols. Behavior is defined as social actions interpreted within a system of meaning (culture being that system of meaning—see chapter 6 for a more complete discussion). Cultural material comprises the tangible products of behavior—artifacts and, in some cases, faunal and botanical remains.

Culture, behavior, and cultural material are not discrete entities independent of one another. Behavior, social actions interpreted within a system of meaning, is not separate from culture, a system of meaning and symbols, or from cultural material, the tangible products of behavior, any more than culture and cultural material are separate from behavior or from one another. They can be separated only analytically in order to examine parts of the whole. I have devised a model (fig. 1) to take into account not only the behavioral aspects of the use of activity areas, but the cultural and cultural material dimensions as well. Like all models, this one is only an explanatory tool. Models have been defined as "theories which explicitly direct attention to certain resemblances between the theoretical entities and the real subject-matter. With this usage in mind, models have been defined as 'scientific met-

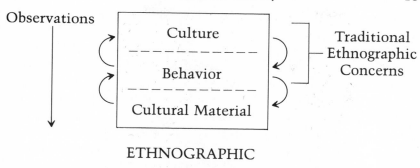

Figure 1. Model of the interrelationship of culture, behavior, and cultural material.

aphors.'. . . . The scientist recognizes similarities that have pre-viously escaped us, and systematizes them" (Kaplan 1964:265).

Although culture, behavior, and cultural material are inter-related, they are not interchangeable. Some archaeologists have, however, confused them. Classic examples of confusing cul-tural material with behavior are statements that a certain pottery style "migrated" somewhere or that a specific projec-tile point type became "restricted" to a particular area (e.g., "Tularosa Black-on-white, developing in the Little Colorado, began its expansion south to establish the Salado culture. . ." [McGregor 1965:344]). Pottery types do not expand south or migrate, and projectile points do not become restricted to an area—people do, and in these cases, cultural material is being confused with the behavior of people. As will be seen in the following chapters, archaeological assumptions concerning the use of space often result from a similar confusion between behavior and culture. It is only through the recognition of the differences among culture, behavior, and cultural material, and of their interrelationships, that such confusions can be avoided.

Because it is not possible to reduce all aspects of a group's culture or behavior to quantitative terms, it is necessary to compare a group with others in order to place it within a general context (see Hsu 1979:528). For example, an anthropologist cannot measure the strength or strictness of the division of labor of a single group by itself. Instead, the group must be compared to others to see that the divison of labor in Group A, for instance, is stronger or stricter than that in Group B, but is less than that in Group C. Such comparisons are usually made implicitly. According to Hsu (1979:526):

> There is another reason why the anthropologists should seek systematic understanding of their own culture. No matter what single society (or village) anthropologists study, they cannot help but make some sort of comparison with the society and culture whence they came. They will necessarily view the other ways of behaving, thinking, and feeling through the filter of their own.

Band-level societies, for example, are usually considered to be egalitarian, but egalitarian compared to whom? They are egalitarian compared to groups with a different level of social and political complexity, like Euroamericans. Because no culture or behavior can be characterized in absolute terms, similarities and differences between groups need to be plotted on a continuum. The position of a group on the continuum represents a specific location only in relation to other groups.

The various levels in the model—culture, behavior, and cultural material—are difficult to discern in the archaeological context as a result of the usually fragmentary nature of archaeological assemblages and the complication of postdepositional disturbances (see Schiffer 1976). Because culture, behavior, and cultural material must be inferred from archaeological data, some anthropologists have hesitated to go beyond the description of cultural material or behavior. There are, however, some exceptions, such as Deetz (1968) and Hill (1970). Anthropologists who are empirically oriented share an epistemological bias that differentiates them from other anthropologists, who, though recognizing that empirical observations are vital for gathering most types of data, do not consider empirical "proof" a necessity in the formation of anthropological models and theories.

The need to examine the nonempirical aspects of culture within an archaeological context has been discussed by Brugge (1980:3): "The features that we investigate on the ground are static physical objects, but the heritages to which they relate are living dynamic forces. They are not less real because they exist in the minds of people, nor do they lack the power to influence events in the physical world." Such an approach does not advocate ignoring the physical environment; rather, the environment receives less emphasis than in most archaeological research, for as Sahlins states, "Culture is not merely nature expressed in another form. Rather the reverse: the action of nature unfolds in terms of culture; that is, in a form no longer its own but embodied as meaning" (Sahlins 1976:209).

Selection of the Ethnographic Study Groups

To study the use of activity areas, I lived with three groups of people—Navajos, Euroamericans, and Spanish-Americans (fig. 2). A cross-cultural approach was essential to ensure against a bias resulting from dependence on data drawn from only a single culture's use of space. Criteria for choosing which specific families to observe varied somewhat. I tried to maintain consistency by studying families that had both mother and father and at least two children living at home. There were two notable Navajo exceptions, which are discussed further in the next chapter—one household contained only a single individual and another lacked a male head of the household. In another attempt to maintain consistency, I selected Euroamerican and Spanish-American families that occupied similar types of houses. Each house was a rectangular structure with three bedrooms, Euroamerican manufactured furniture, and a television set located in the living room. Only one home (Spanish-American) deviated from this pattern in that the house contained four bedrooms.

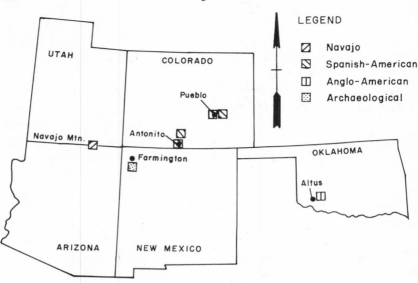

LEGEND

▨ Navajo
▧ Spanish-American
▥ Anglo-American
▦ Archaeological

UTAH

COLORADO

Pueblo

Navajo Mtn.

Antonito

OKLAHOMA

Farmington

Altus

ARIZONA   NEW MEXICO

Figure 2. Map of study areas for each ethnographic group observed and the archaeological sites investigated.

THE NAVAJOS

I chose the Navajos as my primary study group for several reasons. The life-styles of Navajo families still range from traditional to nontraditional, a situation particularly conducive to a study of the effects of culture change on the use of space. Those families who still maintain a traditional life-style speak mostly in Navajo and live in aboriginal dwellings. The more isolated parts of the Navajo Reservation are so remote that contacts with Euroamericans and their use of space are rare; thus I was able to observe the traditional use of activity areas in non-Euroamerican-manufactured structures. In addition, I was able to live with families whose older members had little or no formal education. Even today in the remote parts of the reservation such education is available only at boarding schools where the children are subjected to Euroamerican modes of spatial patterning. The less traditional families I observed had more experience with Euroamerican conventions. The observation of these less traditional Navajos' use of space, when compared with that of the more traditional families, provided an opportunity to study the effects of culture change on the use of activity areas.

Another factor in my selection of the Navajos as the major study group is that they do not emphasize the differences between the sexes the way Euroamericans do, and the sexual division of labor that does exist is not rigid. This meant that my being a woman did not interfere with my observation of and participation in most activities. Lamphere has noted the same phenomenon (1977:14):

> Being a woman was an advantage among the Navajo for this type of study. On one hand, the Navajo division of labor is extremely flexible so that Navajo women (and by analogy the female anthropologist) can participate in a wide variety of productive tasks. . . . Thus I was barred from relatively few activities . . . and I had easy access to activities that would have been more difficult for a male to observe.

THE EUROAMERICANS

The Euroamerican group was chosen for comparison with the Navajos. I selected both rural and urban families in an attempt to ascertain differences in their use of space, and I chose households belonging to different socioeconomic classes in an attempt to discern possible sources of variation in the spatial patterning of the group.

THE SPANISH-AMERICANS

Various terms have been used to designate Spanish-American people living in the United States; these include *Spanish-Americans, Chicanos, Mexicans, Mexican-Americans,* and *Hispanics.* Although it may be a bit confusing when contrasted with the term *Euroamerican,* I chose to use *Spanish-American* to refer to these people, because that is the term used by the families with whom I lived. These families were strongly opposed to the terms *Chicano* and *Mexican-American.*

I selected the Spanish-Americans in order to contrast their use of space with both the Euroamericans and the Navajos. I

felt that a group which typically occupied rectangular mul-
tiroomed houses similar to those of the Euroamericans would
make an interesting comparison for assessing the importance
of structure shape and size on activity area usage. The two
Spanish-American families with whom I lived belonged to
different socioeconomic classes. One of them belonged to the
same class as one of the rural Euroamerican families with
whom I also lived. This facilitated the evaluation of the influence of socioeconomic class on spatial patterning.

Other factors that influenced my decision to choose the
Spanish-Americans for comparison were that I speak Spanish,
had the necessary contacts, and, having grown up with Spanish-Americans, was somewhat familiar with their life-style.
All of this helped me establish rapport with the families and
hastened their acceptance of me.

The Ethnographic Research

The ethnographic fieldwork was conducted by participant-
observation and concomitant informal interviews. I was quickly
incorporated into three of the Navajo families I lived with and
rapidly assumed the role and responsibilities of a daughter. In
other families my status was that of a close friend. One reason
for my relatively rapid acceptance was that I actually lived
with the families (except for those I visited only once or twice
for a few hours at a time).

I usually slept with the Navajo and Spanish-American children. However, I had my own room and bed in all of the
Euroamerican houses at which I stayed. The families were
willing to help me learn my chores, stumble through their
language in the case of the Navajos, and understand their
beliefs and practices.

I was completely open about my age (25 years old when I
began the research), my purpose in living with the people, and
my research, but because of my youthful appearance and because I was unmarried and was a student, people often viewed
me as a high school student, approximately 16–18 years old.
This had both advantages and disadvantages. Because I was
thought to be young, I was not considered a threat and readily

fit into the role of daughter or close friend. This enabled me to observe real as opposed to ideal behavior—a great help to any researcher. For example, in Euroamerican culture, people may eat at the kitchen or dining-room table when guests are visiting in order to conform to cultural ideas of where people should dine (ideal behavior); but when just the family or a close friend is present, they will eat in the living room, in front of the television set (real behavior).

Since I wanted to observe both ideal and real spatial behavior, it was imperative for me to assume the role of family member or close friend. However, my role did not always permit me to go where I wanted or do everything I would have liked to do. At one Navajo household, for example, my chores sometimes kept me inside the hogan, preventing me from shearing sheep or performing other outdoor activities. Nevertheless, I did succeed in observing and/or participating in all major activities, and informal interviews aided in filling in any gaps in my own observations. I took copious notes on the location, performance, participants, and so forth of each activity observed. Observations from each day were compiled and contrasted with those obtained on other days and/or with different families.

The Archaeological Research

In order to contrast the ethnographic data with archaeologically derived information, I excavated historic Navajo sites as part of the Block II Navajo Indian Irrigation Project mitigation study under the auspices of the Cultural Resource Management Division at New Mexico State University, Las Cruces, New Mexico. The sites were actually excavated prior to the ethnographic fieldwork. I investigated a total of seven sites with Navajo components; however, only the five most appropriate to the present study are included here (see table 1). The sites investigated were arbitrarily assigned to me from the total sample of Block II Navajo sites that were examined in the course of a larger project.

The individual site research designs varied according to the amount of time allotted for the investigation, the type of site,

Chapter 1

Table 1. Archaeological sites investigated. (See chapter 4 for a more complete description of each site.)

Site Number	Description
2-1-01	Single-component site with a burned hogan, no features, and little cultural material
2-1-03	Very large multicomponent site with four hogans, numerous features, and extensive cultural material
2-54-28	Large multicomponent site with four hogans, many features, much cultural material
2-C6-14	Small site with one hogan, few features, and little cultural material
2-C6-18	Medium-sized site with one hogan, several features, and some cultural material

the number of artifacts and features present, and the equipment available. Nevertheless, several key foci remained the same. These included the attempt to determine the date and duration of occupation(s), the economic status and subsistence base of the inhabitants, and the spatial relationships between hogans, other features, faunal remains, and artifacts. In addition, I was concerned with ascertaining the occupants' degree of departure from traditional culture, identifying the function(s) of specific features, and, when a site had more than one hogan, determining whether or not the hogans were inhabited contemporaneously. Another focus was to attempt to determine whether or not relationships existed between features and specific artifact categories such as corrals and artifacts connected with animal husbandry. My excavation strategy, though modified as circumstances necessitated, is summarized in figure 3.

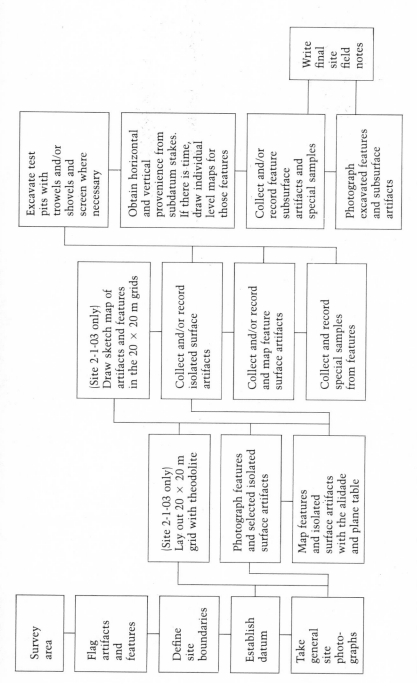

Figure 3. Idealized scheme of the methodological procedures employed at the archaeological excavations.

2

Individual Ethnographic
Residence Descriptions

Since we construct the past inferentially we cannot use our constructions to test the accuracy of the premises that provided the basis for the characteristics constructed. . . .

Since we cannot use the inferred characteristics of the past to test the basis for our inferential procedures, how do we develop reliable means for knowing the past? The answer . . . is that we must engage in middle-range research, which consists of actualistic studies designed to control for the relationship between dynamic properties of the past about which one seeks knowledge and the static material properties common to the past and the present. . . . (Binford 1981:29)

The Navajos

Most of the Navajo households studied were located in the Navajo Mountain area. Exceptions included one located at Shonto, another located west of Tuba City, and a third in the Kaibito area (see fig. 4). However, both the Shonto and Tuba City families were originally from Navajo Mountain, and they spent much time there.

THE NAVAJO MOUNTAIN COMMUNITY

The Navajo Mountain community, located on the border of Utah and Arizona, was chosen as the study area because it was, at the time of this research, one of the most conservative parts of the Navajo Reservation. Nevertheless, within the widely dispersed community and at relatively nearby Shonto, there also live semitraditional and semi-nontraditional Navajos. The Navajo Mountain community is remote and so isolated that most residents can identify (occasionally from the sight of a truck alone) visiting outsiders, be they Navajos or Euroamericans. During my stay in the late 1970s, the telephones at

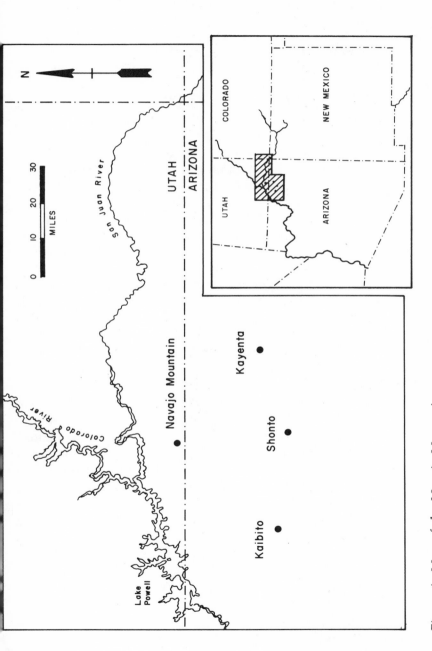

Figure 4. Map of the Navajo Mountain area.

the trading post and school were out of order more often than not, and mail was delivered to the trading post once a week in winter, if the roads were passable, and twice a week in summer. Approximately two years before my research, the trading post–school complex was hooked up to a rural electrical line. Prior to that time, a generator had been used.

At the time of the research, only six non-Indians were living at Navajo Mountain—the trader who had spent over 40 years in the area, the Headstart and first grade teacher who was about to retire after 15 or 20 years of teaching at Navajo Mountain, a man married to a Navajo, a nurse practitioner who worked at the clinic, a nurse practitioner trainee who arrived during the last week of my stay, and the pastor's wife. All but the pastor's wife, who resided at the mission, lived at the trading post–boarding school complex. Euroamerican doctors, usually from Page, Arizona, flew in once a week to spend a few hours at the clinic.

The physiography of the area has been described as "alternations of slopes and cliffs caused by different rates of erosion of the resistant and weak sedimentary beds. Resistant beds forming ledges, cliffs, or rock benches are separated by slopes, valleys, and badlands carved on the weaker intervening materials" (Cooley 1958:27).

The Navajo Mountain region receives average annual rainfall of 12 to 16 inches, and temperatures range from 10° to 25° F in the winter to 80° to 88° F in the summer (Shepardson and Hammond 1970:11). The major vegetation at Navajo Mountain is Utah Juniper (*Juniperus osteosperma*), pinyon (*Pinus edulis*), sagebrush (*Artemisia tridentata*), and Mormon tea (*Ephedra* sp.; Little 1971, 1976). The top of Navajo Mountain is more moist than the canyon bottoms, except near ephemeral streams, and the vegetation changes accordingly.

Camps (defined by Shepardson and Hammond 1970:45, as households or clusters of households that make up a residence unit, always a clearly defined territorial entity) are widely dispersed in the study area. Many are located a mile or more from their closest neighbors. Most of the households (defined by Shepardson and Hammond 1970:46 as the occupant[s] of a single hogan and typically, but not necessarily, a nuclear family) are either matrilocal or neolocal with one patrilocal exception. Previously, clans were reported to have been more important at Navajo Mountain than they were during the time of this research (Collier 1966). In 1960–61, the community's population was characterized by Shepardson and Hammond (1970:13) as

581 individuals, that is, 116 men, 126 women, and 339 children (154 boys and 185 girls) under the age of eighteen. This count includes all Indians, Navajo, and Paiute, maintaining residence at Navajo Mountain during 1960 and 1961. Paiute residents number 18— 5 men, 5 women, and 8 children. Population density of the area is 0.84 persons per square mile as compared to 1.6 for the Western Navajo region and 3.2 for the Reservation as a whole.

Navajos have traditionally lived in hogans, which are built according to several styles. The most common types present in the Navajo Mountain area are the forked-stick and many-legged varieties, although cribbed-log and nontraditional hogans made of cement, plasterboard, and tarpaper can also be found (stone-wall hogans are extremely rare in the study area). Most Navajos agree that the conical forked-stick hogan, which basically consists of three large converging support posts that interlock at the top, with smaller supporting posts, are the oldest known Navajo dwellings (see Kluckhohn, Hill, and Kluckhohn 1971:145, Figure V). Many-legged hogans are more recent structures and have vertical walls with a converging cribwork roof (see fig. 6). They seem to be most common on the north-northwestern part of the Navajo Reservation. Cribbed-log hogans, generally the most common hogan on the rest of the reservation, consist of horizontally laid logs that form the walls, with a cribwork roof (see Kluckhohn, Hill, and Kluckhohn 1971:146, Figure 107.e). All three types of hogan are covered with earth. The reasons for the distribution of these different types of hogan are not well understood, although regional variation and conservatism are often cited. The Navajo Mountain area is the most conservative and remote part of the reservation, which, according to Jett and Spencer (1981:221), accounts for the fact that it has the most forked-stick hogans still in use.

Chapter 2

THE FAMILIES

I lived with and/or observed a total of nine Navajo households (fig. 5). Time spent with the individual families varied from one month (e.g., the Many Sheep and Bitter Water households) to a few hours (e.g., the Red Cliff and Yazzie households). (All personal names in this study have been changed to protect the anonymity of the informants, and I have described them in the ethnographic present for the most part.) I visited several other households, but not long enough to map their camps, hogans, or ramadas, or to note the locations of a variety of activities.

I divided the households into four categories: traditional, semitraditional, semi-nontraditional, and nontraditional. Only the last category was not represented in the sample of households observed (table 2). The different categories were based on the subsistence activities of the household, the number of traditional crafts manufactured at the camp, the types of dwelling(s) inhabited (hogans and ramadas versus Euroamerican-style houses), the practice of certain customs (such as mother-in-law avoidance), the ceremonies performed (such as baby's First Laugh ceremony), and the adherence to specific beliefs (witchcraft and others). The designations were applied primarily to the heads of the households since all the older children had attended boarding schools where they had been forced to deviate from their traditional culture.

An example of the traditional category is the Many Sheep household (see fig. 5). The oldest male of this traditional household does not speak English; his wife knows only a few words. Neither had ever attended school or lived in anything but aboriginal-style abodes. Although they are nominally Christians, the family hold many traditional beliefs—including witchcraft and the existence of werewolves—and observe such customs as the First Laugh ceremony, mother-in-law avoidance, and the *Kinaaldá* (girl's puberty ceremony). In other words, the baseline or reference point for the designation *traditional* is Navajo culture and behavior as of the first part of the twentieth century. (This is discussed in much more detail in Kent in press.)

The oldest male of the semitraditional Bitter Water house-

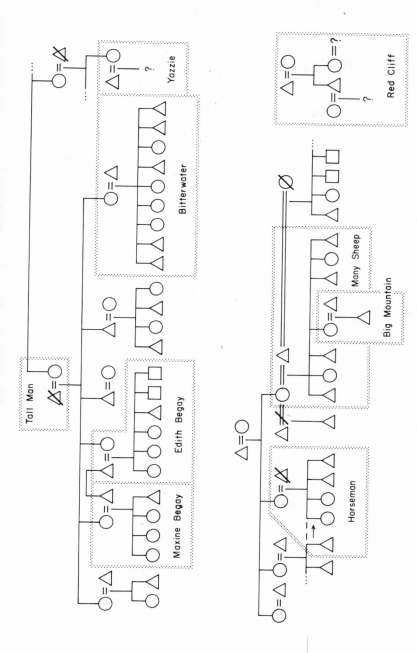

Figure 5. Schematic view of the genealogical relationships of the Navajo households observed.

Table 2. Navajo households observed, grouped by departure from traditional culture categories.

Departure from Traditional Culture Category	Households Observed
Nontraditional	None observed
Semi-nontraditional	Horseman Household Tall Man Household Maxine Begay Household
Semitraditional	Bitter Water Household Big Mountain Household Edith Begay Household Red Cliff Household
Traditional	Many Sheep Household Yazzie Household

hold speaks some English and has had a few years of formal education. His wife's formal education ended with the second grade; she does not speak English. In the past he has been employed in a few unskilled jobs. The family lived for a time south-southwest of Shonto, where he grew up. During the summer, the Bitter Water household drives every week or so to a Euroamerican town, such as Page or Flagstaff, Arizona. The family lives in a tarpaper-and-plasterboard hogan with an adjacent ramada in the summer, and a one-room rectangular stone house during winter. They have a herd of sheep and goats and several corn fields. Their fear of witchcraft is strong. During my stay with them they sponsored several traditional ceremonies. In general, their beliefs, attitudes, and overall life-style are more traditional than nontraditional.

Households assigned to the semi-nontraditional category included at least one head of household who was employed as a full-time wage laborer and had had at least a fifth grade or higher formal education. Semi-nontraditional households live in Euroamerican-style houses during the winter, summer, or year round (one exception being Lucy Tall Man who had moved from a rectangular house when her husband died in 1970 to a Bureau of Indian Affairs–built "hogan" with both electricity and indoor plumbing). Most are familiar with Euroamerican centers such as Phoenix, Arizona, and Farmington, New Mexico, as well as closer towns such as Flagstaff and Page, Arizona. The heads of these households speak English fairly well, although Navajo is invariably the language they use when speaking to other Navajos. Nevertheless, most still believe in witchcraft and werewolves, and they occasionally perform traditional subsistence activities, such as herding and limited horticulture, in addition to their salaried jobs.

I observed no completely nontraditional households. Such a household would be one that no longer adhered to the traditional beliefs and customs, performed traditional subsistence activities, manufactured crafts, or lived in aboriginal houses. Nontraditional Navajos belong to an emerging modern Navajo culture that differs from both Euroamerican and traditional Navajo cultures.

Traditional: The Many Sheep Household

The Many Sheep household is the most traditional one I observed. The family lives approximately three hundred meters east of the camp belonging to the mother and sisters of Bah, the female head of the household. The Many Sheep household had lived at Bah's mother's camp about fifteen years ago, prior to the death of one of Bah's children. After the death, they abandoned the hogan, as is consistent with traditional customs, and moved to their present location. Although they are nominal Christians, the family adheres to many traditional beliefs (such as mother-in-law avoidance and fear of witchcraft) and conducts traditional rites of passage ceremonies, such as the *Kinaaldá*. Bah weaves saddle blankets (*'ak'idahi'niłi*) and baskets, both the coiled "wedding" basket (*ts'aa'*) and the pitched water basket (*tóshjeeh*). Chee, her husband, makes rawhide quirts (*bee 'atsxis*). Neither has had any formal education or has ever been exposed to Euroamerican spatial patterning (e.g., in a boarding school or elsewhere). Bah is the only person in the household who understands or speaks a few words of English. They do not use an automobile nor do they know how to drive.

Twelve people compose the Many Sheep household, not all of whom resided with Bah and Chee at the time of my research. Chee was 73 years old and had been married once before. His

first wife, who had been from the Shonto area, died. Approximately 23 years ago Chee married Bah and moved to Navajo
Mountain. He does not maintain close contact with the children from his first marriage, most of whom are 30 or more
years old and live in the Shonto area.

   Bah is 51 years old and has lived all her life at Navajo Mountain. She also has been married before; her children do not
know the reason why the marriage ended. She has, by her first
husband, one son, Les, who at the time of this research was
24 years old, married, with one son. He works as a carpenter
apprentice in Farmington, New Mexico, and comes home every
few months for a weekend visit. Bah's second child, and Chee's
first with Bah, is Gene, age 22, who has spent some time in
the U.S. Marines. At the time of my research he worked as
an apprentice construction laborer in a tribal program building
Euroamerican-style houses. Although he worked in the Navajo
Mountain area, he spent little time at home, beyond sleeping
there.

   Betty, 20 years old, attends a small junior college in Phoenix,
Arizona. Having just graduated from high school, Randy, age
19, plans to attend a small vocational-technical school in Utah.
Elsie is 17 years old. She dropped out of high school in her
sophomore year when she became pregnant. Elsie and her
husband, Teddy Big Mountain, 19 years old, live outside Tuba
City with their three-month-old son when they are not at the
Many Sheep camp. They make inexpensive necklaces and sell
them at a roadside stand on the Flagstaff-Page highway. The
younger children—Willy, age 13, Sally, age 11, and Tommy,
age 9—all attend Shonto Boarding School and are home only
during the summer vacation (mid-June to late August) and one
or two weekends a month during the winter.

   The Many Sheep camp consists of a wood-and-earthen many-
legged hogan; a wooden ramada; ash, wood-chip, and storage
areas (areas of artifact concentrations); a horse corral; two
sheep corrals; and two small corn fields (figs. 6 and 7). The
camp is located near good grazing land, which permits year
round habitation. Nevertheless, the sheep and goat herd is
taken up to Navajo Mountain for a month or two during some
summers, depending on the local availability of water.

   The hogan is occupied during the winter. It is used mini-

Figure 6. Exterior of the Many Sheep hogan. The horse corral is on the left.

mally, mostly for storage, during the summer, when the ra-mada is inhabited. As is true at most Navajo camps, water is hauled from tribal wells. There is no outhouse. Chee has a secluded sweat house situated 200–250 meters north-north-west of camp.

Traditional: The Yazzie Household

I spent only about three hours at the Yazzie camp and, con-sequently, know relatively little about it. The household is related to Lucy Tall Man through her oldest sister and her daughter (fig. 4). The camp is located in the Kaibito area, in the general vicinity of where Lucy grew up.

I tentatively placed the Yazzie household in the traditional category, although they may, in fact, be more accurately classi-fied as semitraditional. They inhabit a large many-legged ho-gan, which contains a butane stove in addition to a center-split oil-drum stove. The location of activities within the ho-

Figure 7. The Many Sheep ramada with horse corral left background.

gan during my visit appeared to follow traditional patterns, however.

Semitraditional: The Big Mountain Household

The Big Mountain camp consists of Elsie, Bah Many Sheep's daughter; her husband, Teddy; and their three-month-old son. When not staying at the Many Sheep camp at Navajo Mountain, they live in a tarpaper-and-plasterboard hogan located at Teddy's mother's camp, about three miles west of Tuba City. Teddy dropped out of high school in his junior year and helps Elsie run their small jewelry stand on the Page-Flagstaff highway. He is a peyotist, in addition to adhering to the traditional Navajo religion; according to him the two are compatible.

Semitraditional: The Bitter Water Household

The Bitter Water camp is composed of a single household located near a house belonging to the mother of Lisa, the female head of the family. Lisa is 39 years old and, although she attended a Euroamerican school through the first or second grade, she does not speak English. Lisa cards and spins her own wool, which is sold to the trading post. Her 42-year-old husband, Johnny, knows a little English and for a brief time was employed as an unskilled laborer.

Their oldest child, Joe, age 19, has just graduated from high school and has no plans for the future. George, 17 years old, lives in Phoenix with a maternal uncle and only occasionally comes home for brief visits. Laurie, age 16, has just graduated from the eighth grade at Shonto Boarding School and plans to enter high school in the fall. The younger children, except for 3-year-old Frank and year-old Jamie, all attend Shonto Boarding School. They are Janet, 13 years old, Nancy, 12 years old, Sammy, 10 years old, and Alice, 9 years old. Alice stays home much of the year because she does not get along well with the other children at school.

The Bitter Water summer camp consists of a tarpaper-and-plasterboard eight-sided hogan with an adjacent wooden ramada. There are also storage, wood-chip, and ash areas, a horse corral, trash areas, sheep corrals, and an outhouse (figs. 8 and 9). The sheep corral was moved twice during my month-long stay, once for ceremonial reasons (as prescribed by a singer) and once because it was located near the hogan and the odor became offensive in the warm weather. The Bitter Water household has occupied their summer camp for approximately three years. Their winter camp contains a rectangular stone one-room house; a forked-stick hogan used solely for storage; trash areas; wood-chip, ash, and storage areas; and four corrals. The winter camp had been inhabited for five years prior to my research; the family usually spends approximately six months at each camp. Before the move to their present winter camp five winter seasons ago, they lived in a forked-stick hogan located just east of Lisa's mother's house.

Semitraditional: The Red Cliff Household

I spent approximately six hours over the course of several visits observing this household, which included a woman about 80 years old and her daughter of about 40. Consequently I know relatively little about either of them or about the family, and they are only tentatively assigned to the semitraditional

Figure 8. Storage area 3 and the water storage area at the Bitter Water camp. In the background on the left is storage area 6, and on the right is wood pile 4, where butchering occurred.

category. Neither woman speaks English, and both are at least nominal Christians. The daughter weaves rugs as did the older woman in her younger days.

The older woman's son, who usually drives to Navajo Mountain once or twice a month to visit, is semi-nontraditional, or possibly nontraditional, and works in Window Rock, Arizona. His wife lives and teaches at Shonto Boarding School.

The Red Cliff camp consists of, as far as I was able to determine, a partially covered ramada and a two- or three-room rectangular cement house.

Semi-nontraditional: The Edith Begay Household

The Edith Begay camp consists of an extended family. Billy, the male head of the household, has his father residing with them year round, but his mother stays with them only during the summer, and lives at Tec Nos Pos, Arizona, with another child during the winter. This somewhat unusual arangement

Figure 9. The Bitter Water sheep corral.

is, in part, due to the fact that Billy's mother, Sally, is virtually blind and requires constant care.

While I was at Navajo Mountain, an Enemyway ("Squaw" dance) was held for Sally in an attempt to help her regain her eyesight. A few months before, she had been flown to the Public Health Hospital in San Francisco, California, but the doctors had not been able to provide any help. The entire household believes in the effects of witchcraft. They agree that they have been the target of its evil on several occasions, after which they have held the appropriate ceremonies.

Billy, in his forties, is a wage laborer and speaks some English. His wife, Edith, who is the sister of Lisa Bitter Water (fig. 5), also understands English, although only Navajo is spoken at home. Of their seven children, only three were living at home during my stay. Nancy, 18 or 19 years old, had just graduated from high school; Diana, 17 years old, had finished her sophomore year at Tuba City High School, and Tommy, about 4 years old, had not yet begun school. Two young maternal cousins from Tec Nos Pos were also living with them for the summer, during my stay at the camp.

The Edith Begay summer camp consists of a one-room rectangular cement house, a wooden ramada, outhouse, corrals, a one-room rectangular stone house, and an abandoned many-legged hogan. A sweat house, no longer used, is located northeast of the camp. Billy's father at one time started to construct a many-legged hogan north of the camp, but he never completed it. I was told that their winter camp includes hogans and no nontraditional houses, but I never visited it.

Semi-nontraditional: The Tall Man Household
Lucy Tall Man, 69 years old, lives by herself in a Bureau of Indian Affairs–built hogan at Navajo Mountain Boarding School. It is similar to the one occupied by Maxine Begay during the winter. Lucy is employed as a cook for the boarding school. Having begun working as a cook in 1958, she has also cooked at Inscription House, Shonto, and Kaibito boarding schools. Lucy graduated from the sixth grade and speaks English well. She was born and raised near Kaibito, where some of her sisters still live. Lisa Bitter Water, Edith Begay, and Maxine Begay are all her daughters, and another daughter lives in Norman, Oklahoma, with her Seminole Indian husband and their two children. Lucy's two sons are wage workers in Phoenix, Arizona. She is only nominally Christian, and attends Enemyway ceremonies ("Squaw" dances) whenever she has the opportunity.

She moved to the hogan at the school after her husband, George, died in 1970. Prior to his death, the couple occupied a two-room rectangular stone house near the Bitter Water camp. Associated with the house, which Lucy visits every few weeks, or more frequently if she can find a ride, are wood-chip areas, a small corn field, corrals, and a forked-stick hogan formerly inhabited by the Bitter Water household. Lucy uses the house solely for storage, although she expresses vague plans of moving back in a few years after she retires.

Semi-nontraditional: The Horseman Household
The Horseman household consists of a female head of the household, Christy, her children, and an adopted nephew. The

household is part of a camp that includes Christy's parents and two of her sisters. Bah Many Sheep, her older sister, lived at the camp until her child died. Christy, age 43, had a third-grade Euroamerican education, and understands some English. In 1969 she attended the first of four years of Navajo adult Bible school in Flagstaff. After her husband drowned driving across a flooded arroyo, Christy married his brother, but he soon left her. She became a Christian and today regularly attends church and prayer meetings at the mission.

Mary, Christy's oldest child, is 23, a junior at the University of Northern Arizona in Flagstaff. She has been majoring in police science, but does not plan to return to school in the fall. Instead, she is trying to obtain a job as a supervisor at an electrical plant located outside Page. Twenty-year-old Ruth is a sophomore at the University of Northern Arizona, majoring in dental hygiene. She was primarily raised by her maternal grandmother, now 79 years old. During the summers, she works as a receptionist and interpreter at the local health clinic. Tony, age 19, has just graduated from high school and is going to attend a vocational-technical school in Utah in the fall. Frank is about 16 years old and a junior in high school. Joey, 8 years old, is Christy's sister's son but she, at her own request, has informally adopted him. He has completed first grade at the Navajo Mountain school and will be entering Shonto Boarding School in the fall. His biological brother, 6-year-old Alfred, often plays with him at the Horseman house.

The Horseman house is one of the clearest examples of a semi-nontraditional family dwelling I observed. It consists of a cement hogan which has glass windows and is attached to a rectangular one-room house. Euroamerican manufactured furniture and appliances, such as a couch, chairs, table, butane stove, and refrigerator, are located in the house. The hogan contains trunks, a wood-burning heater, and Euroamerican manufactured beds. The camp is occupied year-round; during the summer, however, Christy's sister often takes the camp's communal herd up on Navajo Mountain for a month or two, and her parents move to a ramada several miles south of their camp. The Horseman household has its own ramada; a corral (not used during my stay); a small garden; wood-chip, storage, ash, and trash areas; and an outhouse. It is difficult in some cases to differentiate the Horseman household's wood-chip and ash areas from those of the other households that make up the camp.

Semi-nontraditional: The Maxine Begay Household

The least traditional household I observed, the Maxine Begay household, occupies a home in the tract housing project provided for employees of the Shonto Boarding School. All the houses are multibedroom rectangular stucco dwellings. John, the brother of Billy Begay (fig. 5), is the male head of the household, which consists of a nuclear family. He is a night groundsman and guard at the school. Although he speaks English well, and his wife Maxine, who is a high school graduate, also has a good command of English, Navajo is spoken at home. They have four children—Janice, 12 years old; Janie, 9; Joanie, 8; and Fred, about 2—all of whom, except Fred, attend Shonto Boarding School.

Maxine is the daughter of Lucy Tall Man and the sister of Lisa Bitter Water and Edith Begay. She works as an aid at the Navajo Mountain Boarding School in the winter, during which time she and Fred live in a Bureau of Indian Affairs–built hogan located on the school premises. In addition, they own a rectangular one- or two-room house in the Navajo Mountain area, which they rarely use, except for weekend visits.

Their camp at Shonto consists of a three-bedroom rectangular house with an attached one-car garage. The backyard is surrounded by a chain-link fence. The Bureau of Indian Affairs hogan Maxine occupies during the winter at Navajo Mountain Boarding School has electricity, indoor plumbing, a stove, a refrigerator, and other Euroamerican manufactured articles. Their Euroamerican-style house in the Navajo Mountain area has two rooms and contains a bed, boxes, a few chairs, and a butane stove. A corn field is situated within sight of the house. I was not at their Navajo Mountain camp long enough to note any other outdoor or indoor features.

The Euroamericans

The rural Euroamerican households I observed are both located in Jackson County, southwest Oklahoma (fig. 10). The

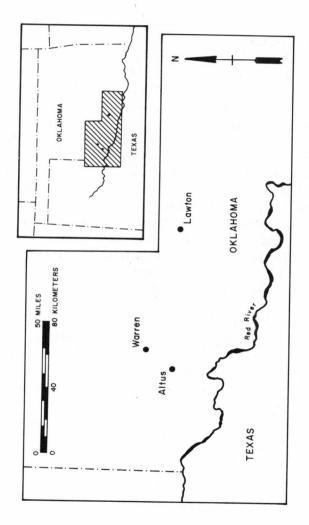

Figure 10. Map of Jackson County, Oklahoma study area.

urban family I stayed with live in Pueblo, Colorado (fig. 11). None of the families are related to one another.

JACKSON COUNTY, OKLAHOMA

Jackson County, Oklahoma, was selected as a study area because I had contacts in the area who were able to help locate rural Euroamerican families with whom I could stay.

The major topographical relief in Jackson County is provided by the Wichita Mountains. The average precipitation is almost 64.75 centimeters (26 inches), most of which falls between April and November. Temperatures average 82° F in the summer and 43° F in the winter. Tornadoes occasionally pass through but do not usually inflict extensive damage (however, 1979 was an exception). Agriculture is the major economic activity in the county. The main crops are wheat, cotton, sorghum, and alfalfa, but peanuts and pecans are also cultivated. About 25 percent of the cropland is irrigated with water from streams and wells (Bailey and Graft 1961:1). Cattle are raised in addition to agricultural plants. The natural vegetation in the study area includes netleaf hackberry (*Celtis reticulata*), black willow (*Salix nigra*), post oak (*Quercus stellata*), and other trees.

Neither of the two rural households I observed is located near a major metropolis. The Smith household is approximately seven miles from Altus, Oklahoma, which has a population of 23,302, making it the largest town in Jackson County. The Joneses live about twenty-four miles outside of Altus and four miles from the small town of Warren, which is not incorporated, and has an estimated population of 200–300 persons.

PUEBLO COUNTY, COLORADO

Pueblo County was chosen as the study area for the urban Euroamerican family (and one rural Spanish-American household; see the following section), because of the contacts I had, which facilitated locating informants. Pueblo, with a population of 110,668, is the largest city in the county and in southeastern Colorado in general (fig. 11). It is the shopping

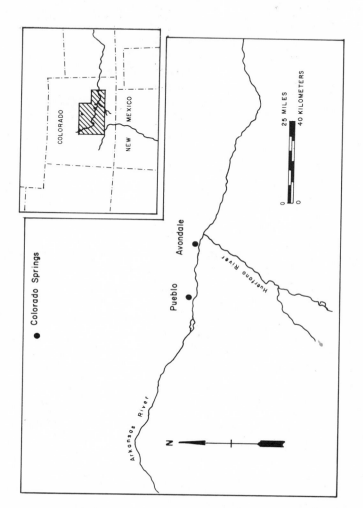

Figure 11. Map of Pueblo County, Colorado study area.

and medical center for most of southeastern Colorado. Pueblo's primary industry is the Colorado Fuel and Iron steel mill, the largest of its kind west of the Mississippi River. A small university and the state mental hospital are also located in Pueblo. The county is characterized by low gently rolling foothills lying west of a much larger area of native prairie. Pueblo County averages 29.64 centimeters (11.67 inches) of precipitation a year, much of which comes in the form of snow. The mean temperature is 50.8° F and varies between −25° F in the winter and 97° F in the summer. The relatively low amount of precipitation results in a native vegetation primarily consisting of sand dropseed (*Sporobolus cryptandrus*), tumblegrass (*Schedonnardus paniculatus*), rabbitbrush (*Chrysothamnus nauseosus*), and sagebrush (*Artemisia ludoviciana*).

THE FAMILIES

Euroamerican society is characterized by social (and usually concomitant economic) strata called classes. Usually classes are achieved rather than ascribed, although upward mobility is often difficult, especially for minority groups. The nature of the elements that constitute a class and the definitions of the various classes continue to provoke heated methodological debates in sociology. Such debates are beyond the scope of my research. Nevertheless, I have adopted the class concept because it provides convenient labels by which to compare the different Euroamerican and Spanish-American families with whom I lived. The definitions presented below represent a synthesis of two classic works on the subject by Warner and Lunt (1941) and by Kahl (1957).

Upper upper classes and lower upper classes. Old aristocratic families with inherited wealth and nouveau riche families (usually very successful businessmen and physicians) make up the two upper-class strata. I did not live with a family from these socioeconomic classes, owing both to research time and money constraints and to lack of contacts.

Upper middle class. This class is composed of professionals, such as college professors and moderately successful businessmen. The people who belong to this class are mostly "white"

Table 3. The observed Euroamerican and Spanish-American households listed by socioeconomic class

Socioeconomic Class	Households Observed
Upper upper class	None observed
Lower upper class	None observed
Upper middle class	Johnson Household
Lower middle class	Jones Household
Upper lower class	Smith Household Martínez Household
Lower lower class	García Household Sánchez Household

and American born. The males are career oriented and most are college graduates. They stress achievement and accomplishment. Upper-middle-class families live in comfortable apartments in cities or in single-family houses in the suburbs. The Johnson household is assigned to this class (table 3).

Lower middle class. The less successful businessmen and professionals and more successful manual workers constitute the lower middle class. Education is highly valued, and parents, most of whom have at least a high-school diploma, have a strong desire for their children to attend college. Lower-middle-class families tend to live in small abodes or multiple-family houses. They emphasize respectability and tend to be religious, "probably the most regular churchgoers in our society" (Kahl 1957:203). The Jones family belongs to this class.

Upper lower class. The men from this stratum include semi-skilled, factory, and other laborers. They usually do not complete high school and often drift from one job to another. The upper-lower-class laborer usually views his job only as a means to obtain money and rarely derives pleasure from his work, unlike some members of the other classes. Both the Smith and Martínez households are assigned to this class.

Lower lower class. These people tend to have the least money and education of all of the six classes. They also are not as interested in education. Lower-lower-class families usually live in substandard housing, often without indoor plumbing or other modern conveniences, and work irregularly at semi-skilled and unskilled jobs. Many subsist solely on welfare and social security payments. Large families are common because they represent a source of security in times of need. According to Kahl (1957:216), "they usually have not gone beyond grammar school (and often have not finished it), their family life is unstable, their reputations poor, and their values are based on apathy or aggression for they have no hope." The García and Sánchez households belong to this class.

One difficulty in assigning the Spanish-American families to socioeconomic classes is that, beyond their associated economic position, classes are based on Euroamerican ideas and values. This problem is accentuated when viewing the Navajos, whose cultural values and standard of wealth differ substantially from Euroamerican ones. Thus the class distinctions are more useful as a comparative index for the other groups than for the Navajos, who are not assigned to any socioeconomic class. Nevertheless, with the exception of two semi-nontraditional households that probably belong to the upper lower class, all the Navajos I stayed with can tentatively be assigned, based on Euroamerican economic criteria alone, to the lower lower class.

The Rural, Upper-Lower-Class Smith Household

The Smith household is composed of a nuclear family living approximately seven miles from Altus, Oklahoma. Three years prior to this research, and before they bought their present house, they owned a used furniture store and lived in Altus. Tim, the 41-year-old male head of the household, has shifted among a variety of jobs. At the time of my stay, he was an insurance salesman, but was contemplating leaving this employment to become the night manager of a small gas station and grocery store. His 39-year-old wife, Lillian, is a nurse at the county hospital in Altus and works the 3-to-11-P.M. shift. Both Tim and Lillian were raised in southwestern Oklahoma and attended a small local college. Tim did not graduate and, after dropping out, began his long series of assorted jobs. Lillian cans fruits and vegetables at home, does the housework, and, with some help from Tim, does most of the outdoor chores, such as feeding their many animals.

Their oldest daughter, Linda, age 18, is a nurse's aid at the same county hospital where her mother works in Altus. She also attends high school part-time; she is a senior. Mel, 16 years old, is a high-school junior. His younger brother, Don, age 11, attends the same rural school, which contains elementary, junior high, and high school classes. The youngest in the family is 8-year-old Steve, who is in the second grade.

In addition to the rectangular one-story wooden farm house, the Smiths own numerous chicken coops and houses, a pig sty and pen, a horse corral, storage and trash areas, a garage that serves as a storage area, and a combined tornado shelter and storage area (fig. 12). They raise chickens, rabbits, goats, pigs, a horse, and a cow, in addition to several cats and a dog. Two family members usually go to Altus at least once, and often more times, every day, for either work or recreation.

The Rural, Middle-Class Jones Household

The Joneses live near Warren, Oklahoma, approximately 24 miles from Altus, which they rarely visit. Harvey's father first moved to the area at the age of 12 in 1889, and Harvey, age 59 and the male head of the household, has lived on his farm all his life. He used to be a construction worker, in addition to farming his own land, until a few years ago when he suffered a major heart attack. At the time of this study, he only did some light agriculture. His wife, Betsy Sue, 52 years old, never finished high school. She takes care of the house and cans fruits and vegetables. She watches soap operas on television during the day. Both she and Harvey are very religious and attend church in Warren several times a week.

Their oldest child, Gene, 27 years old, teaches agriculture at the local rural high school. His wife is the county extension homemakers' club official. Robert, 26 years old, is a minister in a small town approximately 30 miles from the Joneses' farm. Nineteen-year-old Mark is a construction worker and welder who lives at home, except when his job is too far away for him to commute. The youngest child is 11-year-old Debbie Lynn, who attends the sixth grade at a local elementary school.

The Jones residence consists of a rectangular wooden one-story farm house (fig. 13), an old barn used mostly for storage, agricultural fields, a combined tornado shelter and storage

Figure 12. The back and west side of the Smith house.

area, and miscellaneous large pieces of farm equipment scattered near the house. They own horses and cows, which were not kept near the actual living area, and raise chickens for food. In addition they grow watermelons, hay, pecans, and peanuts.

The Urban, Upper-Middle-Class Johnson Household
The urban Johnson household is composed of a single nuclear family. The Johnsons live in a middle-class suburb of Pueblo, Colorado, where they moved two years ago from Denver, Colorado. Dale, 35 years old, graduated from Colorado State University with an accounting degree and is a certified public accountant and the controller for a business office. His 28-year-old wife, Linda, dropped out of Colorado State University after three years to get married.

They have two young children and Linda is three months pregnant with a third. The oldest child, Bob, is five years old and attends a private nursery school three mornings a week. Jenny is just under three years old. Linda spends most of her

Figure 13. The front of the Jones house.

time at home with the children, although she is active in several organizations, such as the New Comers Club and Faculty Women. She cooks, cleans, plays with the children, goes shopping, and watches television during the day.

The Johnson residence includes a rectangular two-story three-bedroom tract wood-and-stone house with an attached two-car garage (fig. 14). The fenced backyard contains a sandbox and swing-and-slide set for the children. There is a small flower garden along the driveway west of the house.

The Spanish-Americans

The rural Spanish-American families observed all reside in Colorado. One lives approximately a mile from Avondale and about 20 miles east of Pueblo, the second is located 5 miles southwest of Antonito, and the third is approximately 3 miles south of La Jara and 11 miles north of Antonito (fig. 15).

Figure 14. The Johnson house.

PUEBLO COUNTY, COLORADO

One of the Spanish-American families observed lives a mile
outside Avondale, a small farming community with a population of approximately 2,600, which is located about 20 miles
east of Pueblo, the largest city in the county. Crops grown
around Avondale include corn for grain and silage, alfalfa, truck
garden vegetables, and vine crops such as melons for seed
(Fitzsimmons 1979: personal communication).

CONEJOS COUNTY, COLORADO

The other Spanish-American families live in Conejos County,
Colorado, which is part of the San Luis Valley. The western
half of the county, where the families I observed lived, is composed of gently rolling to sometimes steep foothills and mountains with elevations that range from 2,377 meters (7,800 ft.)
to 3,200 meters (10,500 ft.).

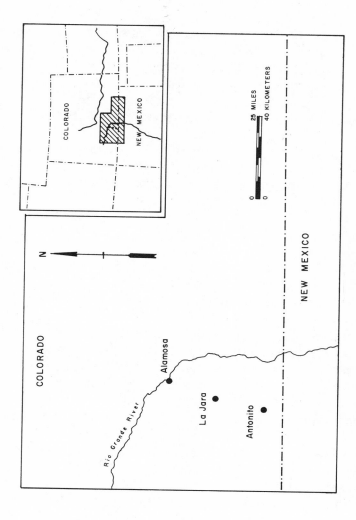

Figure 15. Map of Conejos County, Colorado, study area.

The average winter temperature is 21.7° F and, although the daily average minimum is 4° F, the year of my fieldwork was unusually severe and temperatures dropped well below zero during my February stay. The average summer temperature is 61.5° F and the average daily maximum is 79.6° F. Average rainfall is about 20.32 centimeters (8 in.) and snowfall is 71.12 centimeters (23 in.). Agriculture and livestock are the primary sources of income in the county. Irrigated crops include potatoes, barley, alfalfa, and oats. Both cattle and sheep are raised. The native vegetation in the county varies with topography and includes quaking aspen (*Populus tremuloides*), gambel oak (*Quercus gambelii*), and Utah serviceberry (*Amelanchier utahensis*).

The population of Alamosa, Colorado, the largest city near Conejos County, is 8,000. Antonito, the largest town in the county, has a population of 1,100. La Jara's population is 800.

THE FAMILIES

In this research, I use the term *Spanish-Americans* for mestizos who have lived in the United States for generations, currently receive few influences from Mexico or Spain, and are unaware of any relatives in either country. Though they do not believe they are direct descendants of the conquistadores, they speak Spanish, consider themselves ethnically different from other groups living in the United States, and share a common set of beliefs and customs, not all of which are the same as those of other Americans.

The term *Mexican-American* more appropriately describes people who are still influenced by the Mexican culture and often have close relatives living in Mexico. They usually live along the United States–Mexico border or in large city barrios. Most can trace their family history to Mexico. Although popular among the younger people, the term *Chicano* has activist and other political connotations. In fact, the Martínez children are not permitted to use the term by their parents, although some of their relatives refer to themselves as Chicano. The name *Hispanic* refers to people living in northern New Mexico who are direct descendants of the Spanish conquistadores (and can sometimes genealogically demonstrate their affinity with them), speak a Spanish dialect containing many archaic words and a different intonation pattern from that of other Spanish speakers, and have not, for the most part, intermixed physically or culturally with Indians or with later immigrants from Mexico.

Consequently, the term *Spanish-American* is the most appropriate for the group of people with whom I lived. It is also the term they themselves use most frequently, especially the older generation.

The Rural, Upper-Lower-Class Martínez Household

The Martínez residence, a single household, consists of a nuclear family. They live a mile from Avondale and 20 miles from Pueblo, Colorado. The whole family, including Félix, the 46-year-old male head of the household, speaks English well, in addition to Spanish. Félix has a fifth-grade education and for 20 years has been a semiskilled laborer for a Pueblo-based company—a job that entails numerous trips to rural areas located within Pueblo County. His wife, Rosa, is approximately 40 years old and is a receptionist at a local health clinic. Their residence is located next to Rosa's sister's and near her mother's houses.

Their oldest child, a son, died at the age of 21, approximately four months before my visit. He was married and living in Salt Lake City, Utah. Their second oldest child, Chris, is 20 years old and has dropped out of her senior year in high school after becoming pregnant and marrying Juan, who is 25 years old. They have a one-year-old daughter, Juanita. Chris lives with her parents while Juan works in Denver. He visits every weekend, and they plan to move to Denver as soon as he is able to find an inexpensive apartment. George is 17 years old and in his last year of high school, but has no plans for after graduation. He works weekend evenings as a dishwasher at a Pueblo restaurant. His younger brother, Joe, age 15, is a sophomore in high school. The youngest child, Ann, is in the sixth grade at a local junior high school.

The Martínez residence consists of a rectangular three-bedroom stucco house with indoor plumbing and electricity. A small flower garden is located in front of the house.

The Rural, Lower-Lower-Class García Household

The García residence consists of a single household comprising a nuclear family and an informally adopted grandchild. They live five miles southwest of Antonito, Colorado. Juan, the 63-year-old male head of the household, understands very little English and speaks none. After spending some time in the Marines during World War II, he was a sheep herder until he broke his leg in an accident 17 years ago, which left him disabled (at the time of this research, however, he walked with only a slight limp). María, his wife, is 58 years old and speaks English well. She completed the eighth grade. Neither Juan nor María is employed or owns a car, so both stay home most of the time.

They have ten children. Four daughters live in Denver, all of them on welfare; two are widowed, one is married, and one is living with a boyfriend. Another daughter, Juana, age 24, is married and lives in a trailer in Antonito, where her husband is a semiskilled laborer. They have a daughter, who is almost 3 years old, and an 8-year-old son. Rosa, 21 years old, is mentally retarded and lives at home. She attends a day school for the handicapped in Alamosa, Colorado, located approximately 35 miles to the north. The next oldest child living at home is Anita, age 16. She dropped out of her sophomore year of high school and usually spends the day at home. José, 14 years old, and Félix, 13 years old, attend the junior high school in Antonito. The youngest child, Melinda, age 12, attends the elementary school, also located in Antonito. Juan and María's grandchild, Martha, age six, lives with the Garcías. She seldom sees her mother, who lives in Denver. Martha sometimes attends a Head Start program in Conejos, located approximately 10 miles northwest of the García home.

Their residence consists of two rectangular multibedroom stucco houses (fig. 16). The smaller house is used solely for storage, although the boys occasionally play there. The Garcías occupied the smaller house until approximately six months before my visit, when the larger house was vacated after the death of Juan's older brother. Prior to his brother's death, Juan and his family spent winters in a rented house in Antonito and summers at their present location, which they now inhabit year round.

Figure 16. The García house. A storage shed is west (right of the house), and an abandoned house is west-northwest of the house (on the far right).

The house has electricity, but no indoor plumbing; water is hauled from a nearby well. Heat is provided by two wood-burning heaters and the wood-burning kitchen stove. Their residence also contains a wood-chip area, a storage shed, two outhouses, a dog house, and a rabbit pen and hutch.

The Rural, Lower-Lower-Class Sánchez Household

Virgil Sánchez is the brother of María García and lives about 3 miles south of La Jara, Colorado, and 11 miles north of Antonito. He lives by himself and is a commercial sheep herder. He speaks some English. His rectangular two-room house is provided by his employer and contains electricity, a gas heater, and a wood-burning stove, but no indoor plumbing. A large sheep corral is located near his house. I spent only two hours at his house, and therefore know little else about him or his residence.

Ethnographic Observations
on the Usage of Activity Areas

> A pattern *does* underlie the spatial distribution of specific ac-
> tivities; the location or locations in which an activity takes place
> are not scattered at random, and the byproducts from many
> kinds of activities do form clusters that one can distinguish on
> the ground. (Yellen 1977a:95; original emphasis)

This chapter describes the activities during a typical day at
one household from each category of the groups observed, as
an illustration of the patterning and use of activity areas among
the various households. The single events that occur each day
are not of interest to this study; rather it is the series of events
that is important, because that is where patterns can be discerned.

A typical day is defined here as a twenty-four-hour sequence
in which no unusual activity or weather occurs. A day has
been described elsewhere as "a twenty-four hour period which
is bound on either side by a period of sleep at a designated
spot (excluding naps)" (Topper 1972:63). In reality, of course,
there is no such thing as a typical day, for at least one atypical
event occurs during almost every twenty-four-hour period.
Therefore I have combined parts from several days in order to
illustrate a relatively typical day. As a matter of narrative style
I have used the past tense in describing these days rather than
the ethnographic present employed in chapter 2.

Saturdays and Sundays are atypical days for Euroamericans
and Spanish-Americans in that they are the only time both
the children and the working members of the household are
potentially home all day. Therefore, because they are different
from the rest of the week, weekend activities are not considered typical and are described separately in the discussion
sections. Special activities and events such as ceremonies,
trips into town, and the presence of visitors also often affect

the use of space. The special events that occurred are also described in the discussion sections.

An activity area is defined in this study as any locus at which a particular human event has occurred. This can be a single incident performed by one individual or multiple activities conducted by a number of people, either at one point or over a period of time.

Navajo Spatial Patterning

A DAY IN THE LIFE OF THE TRADITIONAL MANY SHEEP HOUSEHOLD

The day began at 5:30 A.M. when Chee, the male head of the household, chopped wood at wood-chip area 1 (fig. 17). After reviving the fire in the split-oil-drum stove (fig. 18), he lay down again on his sheepskin bed in the southeastern portion of the hogan. His wife, Bah, got up around 6:30 A.M. and swept the eastern half of the hogan floor. The large trash was picked up and disposed of in the fire or at a trash area out-of-doors; the smaller refuse was merely swept out the door. Bah then used a shovel to clean out the ashes in the split-oil-drum stove and tossed them into ash area 1 (fig. 19). Chee again got up and added water from the storage tanks (located outdoors, southwest of the hogan) to the metal pots on the stove. At about 7:00 Bah began to prepare breakfast; it was ready by 7:30.

Breakfast consisted of the leftovers from dinner—fry bread, mutton, and coffee. Food was consumed in the southwestern portion of the hogan between the stove and Gene's bed (fig. 18). The family sat on the dirt floor to eat breakfast. A folded cardboard box functioned as a table. After the meal, Bah stored the leftover food in the boxes and food cabinet located along the northeast wall. The cardboard box that served as the table was returned to its storage area next to the food cabinet. Dishes and utensils, including those from the day before, were then washed by Bah in a large metal pot in the northern part of the hogan. The pot usually was kept on the stove all day.

Gene left for work around 8:00 A.M. Chee, leaning on his

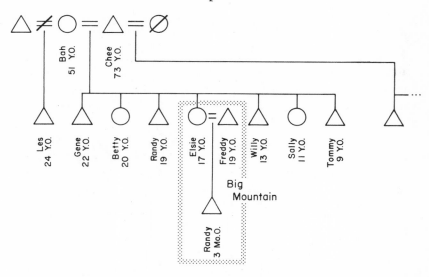

Figure 17. The composition of the Many Sheep and Big Mountain households.

rolled-up sheepskin bed in the southeastern portion of the hogan, worked on braiding a partially completed leather quirt. Bah meanwhile lay down on her goatskin bed located next to the north-northwest wall.

Elsie changed her baby's disposable diaper on the Euroamerican manufactured double bed next to the northwest wall. She later wrapped the infant on a cradleboard and gave him a bottle of Similac baby formula. Following a brief discussion with Bah, Chee went outside to the horse corral, where he saddled his horse, while Bah walked over to sheep corral 1 and separated the kids and lambs that she did not want to go out to graze that day from the rest of the herd. They were put in the nearby lambing pens. A tin-can rattle permanently stored at the corral was used to separate the young lambs from the older sheep, as well as to move the herd in the direction Chee wanted it to go. Chee, on horseback, took the herd out to graze at approximately 9:30. Bah returned to the northwestern quadrant of the hogan, between her goatskin bed and the stove, and began to weave a coiled wedding basket (ts'aa'; see fig.

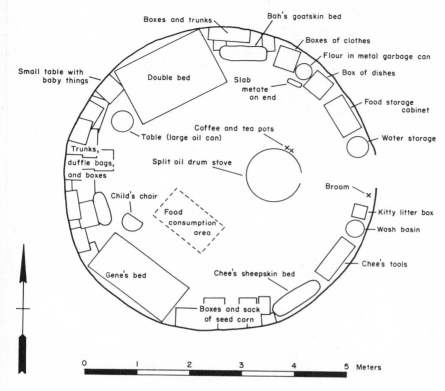

Figure 18. The Many Sheep hogan.

20). She used a large knife to scrape the branches smooth, a bowl of water to soak them in, and a metal icepick with a wooden handle as a punch. These objects were stored along the northern wall just east of her bed when not in use and the dyed branches were kept in a bundle hanging from the east-southeastern wall. Like Chee's rawhide strips, other branches were buried in a pit located out-of-doors near wood-chip area 2 in order to prevent them from drying out and to keep the dogs from disturbing them. A shovel used to uncover the pits was kept over them in order to mark their location, which was north of the hogan. Elsie watched her mother weave the basket and talked with her while sitting on the double bed.

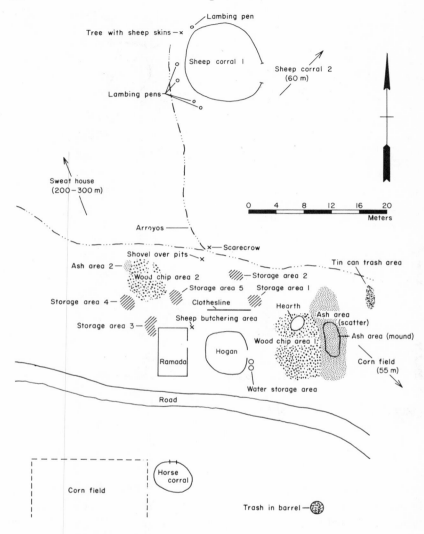

Figure 19. The Many Sheep camp.

Elsie, after sitting on the bed for about an hour, washed the baby in a metal washtub on a small child's chair in the western part of the hogan. All of the baby's things (shampoo, diapers, canned formula, and clothes) were stored along the western wall on a small table between the trunks and the northwest

Figure 20. Basket weaving in the northwestern quadrant of the hogan.

bed. Elsie wrapped the baby on a cradleboard and rocked him to sleep in the double bed. Bah meanwhile talked to Elsie while conducting a variety of activities: mending a blouse on the double bed, watching Elsie wash the baby, eating a snack of store-bought cookies with Elsie while sitting on the double bed, playing with the baby, and so on. Later Elsie, the baby, and Bah took a 10-minute nap on their respective beds. Both Elsie and Bah played with the baby when he started to cry until he fell asleep, after which they sat on their beds and talked for a while. Bah again worked for a brief time on her basket in the same area as before, while Elsie watched her mother and talked. Around noon, Bah brought in some wood, which she had chopped at wood-chip area 1, and began to prepare lunch in the northeastern quadrant of the hogan. Chee returned from herding around 12:30 P.M. and, after penning the animals in sheep corral 1, sat at his southeastern sheepskin bed until lunch was served. It consisted of mutton, *nánees-kaadí* ("tortilla bread") and coffee. Everyone ate in the southwestern quadrant of the hogan at the same place they ate breakfast (fig. 21). Chee afterward lay on his bed and pounded a piece of rawhide with a hammer on a stone anvil, while Bah put the leftover food in the northeast cabinet and placed dirty dishes in the large metal pot of water sitting on the stove. Everyone took a 15-minute nap on his or her bed. Chee then went outside to storage area 3 to scrape some pieces of rawhide with a file that is always kept at the area (see fig. 19). Bah, depending on the season, either went down to sheep corral 1 and sheared, planted corn in nearby fields, or performed other seasonal activities. Elsie meanwhile remained in the hogan and watched the baby, and Chee performed a variety of activities, such as brushing his horse in its corral, talking to Bah shearing sheep at corral 1, or planting seeds in one of the nearby cornfields. Bah returned to the hogan around 4:30 P.M., lay down on her goatskin bed, and talked with Elsie for a while. Bah then walked over to sheep corral 1 at about 5:00 P.M. to separate the animals that she wanted to remain in camp from the rest of the herd. Chee, on horseback, took the herd out (Bah herds on foot about half the time).

Gene returned home around 5:30 and worked on his car, which was parked east of the hogan. Bah wove her basket outside in the shade of the hogan wall for a while and then went inside and played with the baby on the double bed while talking to Elsie, who was also seated on the bed, stringing juniper seeds ("cedar beads"). Bah went outside to chop wood at wood-chip area 1 and brought back an armful to start the fire in the stove. She filled the pots on the stove with water from the tanks located immediately southeast of the hogan. Around 7:00 P.M., she began preparing dinner, which consisted of the same foods as lunch and breakfast, with the addition of freshly made fry bread. Chee brought the herd back between 7:30 and 8:00 and unsaddled his horse at its corral.

Dinner was served shortly thereafter and was eaten at the usual southwest food-consumption locus. After the meal, Bah, with Elsie's help, cleared the dishes from the flat folded box; leftover food was placed in the food cabinet along the northeast wall and dirty dishes were put in the pot on the stove with the lunch dishes. The folded cardboard box was returned to its storage area next to the food cabinet.

Figure 21. Mattress bed and storage area in the southwestern quadrant of the hogan. The small chair is at the food-consumption area.

Gene left camp after dinner to visit friends and did not return until early morning. Leaning against his sheepskin bed, Chee worked on his rawhide quirt. Elsie played with her baby on the double bed while Bah, who was resting on her goatskin bed, talked to both of them. Bah lit the Coleman lantern when it got dark. Chee went out to wood-chip area 1 and brought back more wood for the stove's fire. Everyone went to sleep around 9:30 or 10:00 P.M. Gene returned in the early morning and slept on his mattress next to the southwest wall (see fig. 21). The baby occasionally woke up crying during the night and Elsie spoke gently to comfort him. Chee got up to bring in the wood from wood-chip area 1 in order to rekindle the fire at approximately 5:30 A.M. and thus begin a new day.

Discussion

The hogan was used differently by the occupants according to their sex. Chee almost never ventured beyond his southeastern area in the hogan. He not only slept and ate there, but also repaired objects and made leather quirts at or near his sheepskin bed next to the southeastern wall. The oldest son living at home, Gene, stayed primarily but not exclusively in the southwestern portion of the dwelling. On the other hand, the women and younger children used the northern half of the hogan the most and the southeastern quadrant the least.

The only nontraditional beds in the hogan (the northwest double bed and Gene's southwest foam mattress) were used primarily by the children, whose behavior differed from that of their traditional parents because they had spent most of their lives in boarding schools. They used the beds to sit and sleep on. Chee and Bah slept and sat on sheepskins and goat-skins near the southeast and north-northwest walls respectively.

Food preparation always occurred in the northern part of the hogan and usually in the northeastern quadrant. Food consumption typically took place in the southwestern portion of the dwelling, between Gene's bed and the stove. The seating arrangement around the folded flat cardboard box upon which food was placed remained consistent—Chee sat on the east side of the box, Gene on the south end, Bah on the north, and Elsie (and myself) on the west.

In contrast to the sex-defined use of space within the hogan, both sexes of all ages performed activities at the same locus both out-of-doors and in the ramada. For example, different sexes of various ages chopped wood at wood-chip area 1 during the spring and at wood-chip area 2 during the summer after the move to the ramada. Wood-chip area 1 also served as a storage area where three axes, two rakes, a shovel, an enamelware wash basin, a few empty soda-pop cans, and an oil can were permanently located. Not only did both sexes use the same activity area outside the hogan, but different types of activities often occurred at the same locus. It was not unusual for Chee to scrape a rawhide strip at the same location in which Bah wove her blanket. Most outdoor activities are performed at one of the storage areas.

The Many Sheep family moved at the beginning of summer to the ramada located directly west of the hogan. Most of the furniture, such as the double bed, the food cabinet, and Chee's

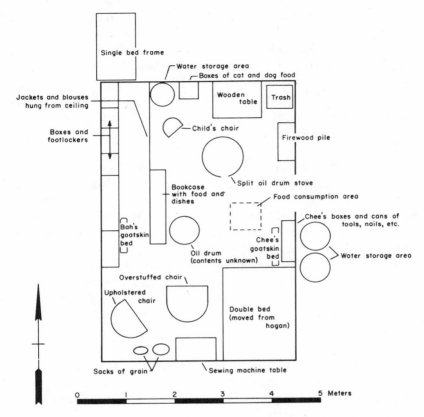

Single bed frame

Water storage area
Boxes of cat and dog food

Jackets and blouses
hung from ceiling

Wooden
table

Trash

Boxes and
footlockers

Child's chair

Firewood pile

Bookcase
with food and
dishes

Split oil drum stove

Food consumption area

Bah's
goatskin
bed

Chee's boxes and cans of
tools, nails, etc.

Chee's
goatskin
bed

Oil drum
(contents unknown)

Water storage area

Overstuffed chair

Upholstered
chair

Double bed
(moved from
hogan)

Sacks of grain

Sewing machine table

0   1   2   3   4   5 Meters

Figure 22. The summer arrangement of objects in the Many Sheep ramada.

and Bah's skin beds, was taken with them. The hogan was still used minimally, but mostly for storage. The use of space within the ramada differed dramatically from that in the hogan. Although Chee slept and ate in the east-southeastern quarter of the ramada as he had in the hogan, he used other parts of the ramada, including the southeast and northern parts (fig. 22). Bah and the children also used most of the ramada, seemingly without any restrictions. Both chairs and the double bed were used by each family member regardless of sex or age, although the southwest chair was apparently preferred.

Food consumption in the ramada occurred in the east-south-eastern part (just southwest of the entrance). Food was placed on a wooden board instead of the folded cardboard-box "table" that had been used in the hogan; the board was kept next to the food cabinet when not in use. During meals, Chee sat on the eastern side of the wooden board, Bah on the west, and the other children at home on the north end (I sat on the south). Food preparation occurred between the food cabinet and stove.

With the exception of the chair in the southwestern quarter and Bah's goatskin bed near the west wall, the western half of the ramada was not extensively used. A metal single-bed frame covered with sheepskins was located immediately north of the exterior northwest corner of the ramada. It was used primarily by Chee and his youngest child, Tommy, to rest on during the day. Whereas during the spring, when they lived in the hogan, wood-chip area 2 was scarcely used by Bah (only once), during the summer wood-chip area 2 and ash area 2 were occasionally used, in addition to wood-chip area 1. The herd was kept in sheep corral 2 during the summer, instead of corral 1.

The basic types of activities performed at the camp were much the same in summer and winter. However, the presence of the children during the summer, home from boarding school, caused a greater number of activities to be performed. During the period between planting and harvesting fewer major economic tasks, such as shearing, were performed. Bah's main subsistence endeavor in summer was to weave a saddle blanket at storage area 3. In general, more time was spent outside during the summer than in spring, although a surprising number of activities were done in the ramada, including sleeping, talking, cooking, and eating.

Several factors influenced the location of an activity as outlined above. One was an individual's mood. This was particularly so in the case of Bah, who would eat by herself in the northern part of the hogan when upset; at such times the rest of the family ate, as usual, at the southwest "table." This occurred three or four times after Elsie left with the baby and went back to her home west of Tuba City. Twice, for no apparent reason, Elsie ate her meal sitting on her double bed.

Crowding also altered activity locations. When the younger children were home from school, for example, and Elsie and Teddy Big Mountain were visiting, both eating and sleeping locations were modified. In the spring, the ramada was occasionally used to sleep in when there was not enough room in the hogan, and the reverse was true in the summer. One spring weekend when the entire family was home, the individual sleeping positions in the hogan were shifted so that Sally and Tommy slept on Bah's goatskin bed, Willy slept on Gene's bed until Randy came in at 4:00 A.M. (Gene did not come home that night), Bah slept just west of Chee's sheepskin bed, and Chee slept on his bed in its usual position (I slept on my sheepskin bed, also in its usual location next to the double bed). That same night, Elsie, Teddy, and their baby slept on the double bed as usual. Crowding occasionally prevented everyone from eating at the southwest "table" at the same time. Consequently, either meals were eaten in shifts or people ate in other areas, such as on the double bed or in the northern half of the hogan.

Season affected not only the location of the activities, but also the activities themselves. During the spring months, for example, sheep were sheared in sheep corral 1; in the early summer, corn was planted in nearby plots. Because spring weather is unpredictable, Bah wove baskets, an activity that can be performed outside but can easily be transferred indoors should the weather change for the worse. In contrast, the large looms necessary for blanket weaving are not readily portable and tended to remain at one location—either indoors or outdoors—for the duration of a project. This lack of flexibility makes such activity susceptible to the weather. There is certainly less chance that a blanket will be ruined outdoors by bad weather during the dry early-to-mid-summer season than in the spring. As might have been predicted, most activities were performed inside when it was very cold. During the hot summers, activities were primarily conducted either inside the ramada or outdoors in the shade of a structure or tree at a storage area. However, though season and weather did alter the location of an activity area, *they did not affect the use of a locus* (whether it was sex-specific or monofunctional).

Several special activities were performed infrequently, but

Figure 23. Cleaning viscera at the butchering area, just northeast of the ramada.

at the same locus. For instance, butchering consistently occurred immediately northeast of the ramada. A rope with a pulley from which the carcass was hung was located outside on the northeast corner of the ramada wall and another was inside on the wall just north of the east-facing entrance. The viscera were cleaned inside the ramada when the weather was cold and outside at the butchering area when it was warm (fig. 23).

Sheep hides were tanned west and northwest of the hogan. The stakes used to stretch the skin were not left at the area after use, and the salt used to process the hides was eaten by the chickens. Consequently, little evidence was left at the hide-processing area from which an archaeologist could later infer that any activity had been performed there, much less that a sheepskin had been tanned. This was especially true at Navajo Mountain owing to the very sandy soil, in which postmolds would not be preserved.

Figure 24. Weaving a saddle blanket at storage area 3. The ramada is in the background, and the hogan is behind it.

The major criterion for the selection of an outdoor location at which to weave a basket was the availability of shade on hot sunny days, or of sunshine near dusk or on cool or partly cloudy days. For example, Bah wove a basket in the shade of the northeast wall of the hogan one warm afternoon but later moved to the still sunny southwest wall when the weather became chilly toward dusk. The few tools used in the manufacture of the artifact were never left in the area at which they had been used.

Chee smoothed the rawhide for his quirts at storage area 3. The file that he used for this purpose was kept there permanently. Dogs ate all the leather scraps he did not use, obliterating all evidence of the activity. When inside the hogan, Chee used tools from his box next to his bed to finish the quirt. Bah also used storage area 3, weaving a saddle blanket in the shade of a tree (fig. 24). Bah's oldest daughter, Betty, said that she occasionally used a small, unconventional metal loom that was kept year round at storage area 1, but I never observed Betty weaving.

The altered locations of activity areas in the hogan during Elsie's baby's First Laugh Ceremony are interesting. Several factors affected the typical spatial patterning, one being Chee's observance of the mother-in-law avoidance custom. Because his mother-in-law attended the ceremony in the hogan, Chee had to eat dinner outside, which he did next to the horse corral (Bah took a plate of food to him). Crowding also influenced the location of activity areas. As a result of the number of relatives present at the ceremony (a total of 18, primarily older women and children under 21 years of age), it was impossible for everyone to sit in the southwestern part of the hogan where food consumption usually took place. Consequently, people ate in all quadrants of the structure—but no one sat on the Euroamerican manufactured double bed. Food preparation for the ceremony took place in the northeastern portion of the hogan and at the split-oil-drum stove, as well as at the hearth located outside at ash area 1.

Comparisons

Every few days Bah would visit her mother's many legged-hogan located approximately 300 meters west of their camp (she went more frequently when upset). The interior spatial arrangement of objects in her mother's hogan was opposite to that in her own. Food, utensils, and a butane stove that apparently was not used were situated along the southwest wall. A Euroamerican manufactured double bed was next to the south wall in Bah's mother's hogan, trunks were near the west wall, and sheepskins were along the rest of the wall. A box of tools similar to Chee's was located near the northeast wall of the structure. The hogan appeared to be larger than Bah's and was noticeably less cluttered. A split-oil-drum stove with pots and pans on top was situated just east of the center; it was used for cooking.

In contrast, the tarpaper-and-plasterboard hogan of Bah's daughter, Elsie, and her husband, Teddy Big Mountain (which was located west of Tuba City) was, despite the addition of Euroamerican manufactured furniture, arranged similarly to

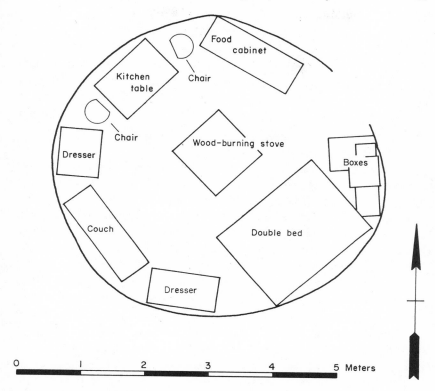

Figure 25. The Big Mountain hogan.

Bah's (fig. 25). The main exceptions were a couch situated along the west wall of Elsie's hogan, a Euroamerican manufactured double bed near the south wall, and a table with two chairs along the north wall. Substantial variation, then, exists in the arrangement of objects within hogans inhabited by members of a single extended family, and the location of activity areas varies as well. At Bah's and Elsie's hogan, objects associated with food preparation (food, utensils, and so forth) were stored along the northeast wall near where food is prepared. The opposite was true in Bah's mother's hogan.

Chapter 3

A DAY IN THE LIFE OF THE SEMITRADITIONAL
BITTER WATER HOUSEHOLD

Lisa and her husband, Johnny (fig. 26), got up around 5:30 A.M. to begin their summer day. They had slept in the hogan with the younger children, while the older children slept in the ramada. The commercial blankets they used to sleep on were returned to their storage area along the southwestern wall of the hogan (visible in fig. 30).

Breakfast was started by Lisa, who prepared the food in the hogan's southeastern quadrant and cooked on the wood-burning stove located in the center of the dwelling (fig. 27). Johnny brought wood in for the stove from wood-chip area 1 (fig. 28). He then swept the hogan and at about 6:00 A.M. tried to wake the older children sleeping in the ramada. They got up after some protests and washed their hands and faces in a plastic wash basin set in a small child's chair (visible in fig. 29) along the exterior northeast hogan wall. At approximately 6:30 A.M., everyone ate breakfast in the southeastern quadrant of the hogan, sitting on the floor around a piece of oilcloth upon which the food was placed. Breakfast consisted of fry bread, fried potatoes, and coffee. Nancy and Janet Bitter Water picked up the dirty dishes after breakfast and put the leftover food on the cabinet-table next to the southeast wall. The oilcloth that served as a table was folded and put on top of a cardboard box just south of the cabinet-table. Janet washed the dishes in a washtub on the stove and let them air dry on the cabinet-table along the southeast wall. Johnny sat on the double bed for a few minutes and then went out to the ramada, where he looked through and straightened the boxes along the western wall. Lisa nursed Jamie on the double bed while three-year-old Frank watched, lying on the floor in the northwestern part of the hogan. Joe left to visit friends.

Sammy and Alice, riding the same horse, took the herd out to graze about 9:30 A.M. Meanwhile, Laurie carried the child's chair over to the northwestern quadrant of the hogan, placed the plastic wash basin on it, and washed her hair. She then brushed her hair and played with it, alternating between sitting on the double bed and standing before the mirror hanging on the northeast wall near the entrance. Janet, sitting on the

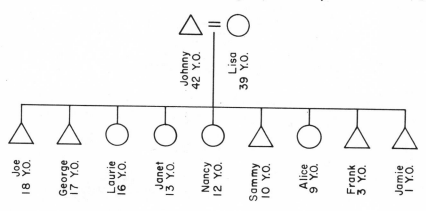

Figure 26. The composition of the Bitter Water household.

pile of blankets along the southwest hogan wall, mended a pair of slacks. Afterward she used the treadle sewing machine located next to the southern wall of the hogan to mend a blouse (visible in fig. 30).

Lisa and Nancy washed diapers in the washtub used earlier to wash the dishes. They worked inside the ramada just west of the entrance. Johnny later helped them hang the diapers on the clothesline that runs west-southwest of the hogan. Janet changed Jamie's diaper on the double bed in the ramada and wrapped him up again on the cradleboard. He was left on the bed to sleep. Crying for attention, Frank ran sobbing to Janet. She mixed canned milk with water in his bottle at the southeastern food cabinet-table and gave it to him in hopes of quieting his cries. Lisa and Johnny drove their truck to a friend's house to haul water for her (she does not own an automobile, and the communal well is about half a mile away). At home, Nancy, Laurie, and Janet all sat on the double bed in the hogan and talked and fixed each other's hair. Janet started lunch at the food cabinet-table around 11:30 A.M. Nancy hauled water from the storage tanks located east-northeast of the hogan and filled the coffee pot on the stove. She then brought in the wood she had chopped at wood-chip area 1 and rekindled the fire in the stove. Laurie swept the hogan and laid the oilcloth

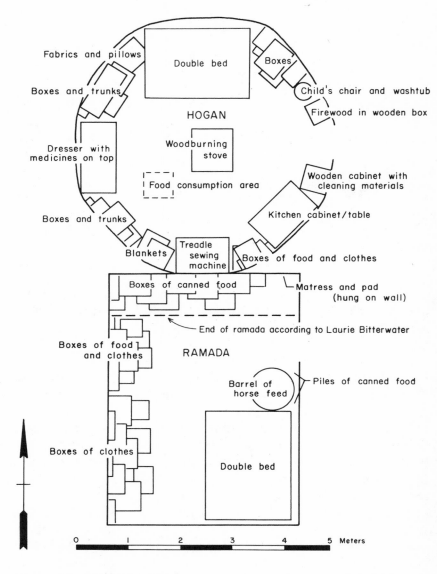

Figure 27. The Bitter Water summer camp hogan and ramada.

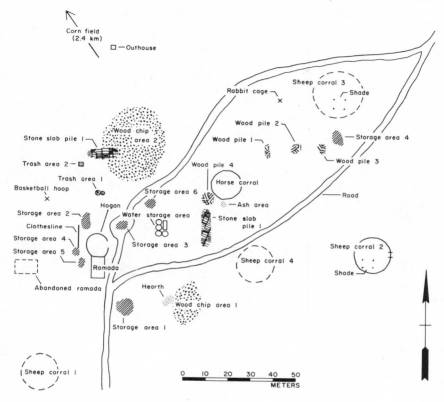

Figure 28. The Bitter Water summer camp.

down in the southwestern quadrant of the hogan. Sammy and Alice returned with the herd at about 12:30 P.M. and, after watering them at the storage tanks, penned them in sheep corral 2. Sammy tied the horse to the tree at storage area 1. He and Alice went into the hogan and sat on the double bed with Laurie, who was watching Janet prepare lunch.

Lunch was served in the southwestern quadrant of the hogan about 12:30 P.M., shortly after Lisa and Johnny returned. It consisted of fried potatoes, fry bread, and coffee. Janet and Nancy put the dirty dishes and leftover food on the cabinet-table. Johnny, sitting on the double bed, tried to repair an old tape recorder. He later took a nap at the same location. Frank

Figure 29. The Bitter Water ramada. Note the Euroamerican manufactured bed located inside the ramada and the small child's chair
just outside.

lay on the floor near the southwest wall. Lisa sat for a while
on the child's chair that had been moved to the western part
of the hogan. Later she went into the ramada and played with
Jamie on the double bed (bed visible in fig. 29). She then took
a nap in the hogan. Laurie, Janet, Nancy, Frank, and Sammy
all took naps on the double bed in the ramada. Joe returned
about half an hour later, and Lisa fixed him some food in the
southeastern quadrant of the hogan; he ate sitting on the double bed.

Sammy and Alice, told by Johnny to take the herd out at
approximately 4:30, did so on horseback. Everyone except
Johnny drove to the corn field northwest of camp. There they
planted corn, squash, and melons for about two hours. During
spring, they would have sheared sheep at the sheep corral.
Afterward, they went back to camp and Lisa spun wool with
a spindle and spindle whorl, usually kept hanging on the west
wall of the hogan. She sat on the child's chair near the entrance

Figure 30. The southern half of the Bitter Water hogan. The food cabinet-table is on the left, treadle sewing machine is center, and blanket storage area is on the right.

of the ramada in the shade of its wall. Janet changed Jamie's diaper on the double bed of the hogan. Meanwhile, Johnny repaired a tire at storage area 3. Joe took a nap on the double bed in the hogan and Laurie and Nancy looked at an old *Teen* magazine on the bed in the ramada (fig. 31).

Jimmy relit the stove at about 7:30, adding wood stored in the woodbox located next to the northeast wall. He told Nancy and Laurie to chop some more wood, which they did at wood-chip area 1. Nancy swept the hogan. Laurie threw the non-flammable garbage, such as tin cans, that had accumulated in the hogan during the past day or two into the barrels at trash area 1 while Janet walked around outside carrying Jamie, who had been crying. Sammy and Alice returned with the sheep about 7:30 P.M., and Nancy helped herd them into sheep corral 2, after the horse and the sheep had been given water at the storage tanks. The horse was penned in her corral. Sammy and Nancy took a bucket of the grain stored in the barrel near

Figure 31. The northwestern quadrant of the hogan. Note the stove, double bed, and storage along the west wall.

the entrance of the ramada to the horse corral and poured it in the upside-down car hood that served as a feed trough for the horses.

Laurie raked the area immediately in front (east) of the hogan, including the outdoor food-consumption locus. Johnny fried potatoes and tribal-issue canned beef on the stove in the hogan while Lisa made *náneeskaadí* (tortilla bread) at the hearth at ash area 1 (fig. 32). The oilcloth was placed outside on the ground just east of the hogan (southeast of the entrance). Dinner was eaten there about 8:00 P.M., after which Laurie, Nancy, and Janet carried the dishes and leftover food to the cabinet-table in the southeastern part of the hogan. The oilcloth was folded and returned to the box south of the food cabinet-table. Janet and Alice washed the dishes at the cabinet-table. Joe left to visit friends and did not return until the following day. Lisa, Frank, Jamie, and Johnny lay on a mattress outside next to the exterior northeast hogan wall and talked

Figure 32. Cooking at hearth at ash area 1. Wood-chip area 1 is in background. "Tortilla bread" (*náneskaadí*) is in a wash basin in the foreground.

until about 9:30 or 10:00 P.M. when they fell asleep. The other children all slept on the double bed along the east wall of the ramada. Johnny got up the next morning at around 5:30 to chop wood at wood-chip area 1; thus started another day.

Discussion

Most of the Bitter Water activities occurred in the hogan, the ramada, or at a storage area. Only two activities consistently took place at the same locus within the hogan: food preparation and dish washing always occurred in the southeastern quadrant and on the stove. Food consumption usually, but not always, took place in the southwestern quadrant of the hogan. The seating arrangement around the oilcloth upon which food was placed was generally consistent; in the hogan Lisa sat on the south end, Johnny and sometimes Laurie and/ or Nancy sat on the west side and the other children (and I) sat on the north end (the east side was too close to the stove to allow anyone to sit there). However, this arrangement was modified at times by several factors. Laurie occasionally ate on the north bed because she was crippled and it was sometimes difficult for her to get up and down. Crowding expanded the food consumption area to include the double bed. Since I lived with this household during the summer, the school-age children were home during my entire stay. Thus I observed the effects of crowding on several occasions. When everyone was in camp, meals were sometimes eaten in shifts, especially when food was consumed in the hogan, where space was more limited than outside. At other times, several individuals would eat in parts of the hogan other than the southwestern quadrant, the most common alternate location being the double bed.

An individual's mood occasionally caused an alteration in the location of activity areas. For example, Joe, who often was angry with a member of the family, frequently ate at the southeast cabinet-table with his back to the rest of the family, or ate inside when everyone else ate outside. One of the younger children sometimes would sleep in the hogan when angry with the other children, who were sleeping in the ramada.

At night, Johnny and Lisa slept on a mattress placed in the southwestern quadrant of the hogan, with blankets that were kept near the southwest wall during the day. Jamie, Frank, and occasionally Alice slept on a mattress placed at night on the floor in the northwestern part of the hogan. The double bed in the hogan was used more to sit on than for sleeping (fig. 31). The older children slept on the double bed in the ramada in the warm weather, and in the hogan when it was cold. Lisa, Johnny, and the younger children slept outside on a mattress next to the hogan's northeast wall when it was hot.

Other activities besides sleeping were performed both in and outside the hogan depending upon the weather. When it was hot, cooking occurred outside at the hearth located at ash area 1, although the stove inside the hogan usually was used in conjunction with the outdoor hearth. Meals were eaten outside as well as in the hogan; when it was warm, for example, dinner was served outside, usually southeast of the hogan's entrance. The seating arrangement around the oilcloth remained the same as in the hogan except that, since the east side was not obstructed, some of the children were able to sit there. Lunch and breakfast were always eaten inside, the former probably because of the lack of shade at lunchtime and the latter because of the early morning chill.

People washed their hands, face, and hair in a washbasin placed on a child's chair in either the northeastern quadrant of the hogan or just northeast of the hogan's exterior wall. Clothes were also washed in the northeastern quadrant of the hogan or near (just in or outside) the ramada's entrance. Wool was spun either in the northwestern part of the hogan or near the entrance of the ramada.

Butchering occurred at wood pile 4, which also served as a storage area (visible in fig. 8). A rope and pulley used to hang the carcass were permanently stored there, among other objects, including equestrian equipment. Viscera were cleaned and cooked at the hearth at ash area 1.

Several traditional cures were observed. One, which was successful, was designed to prevent their three cows from continually breaking out of the horse corral where they were being kept temporarily after having been brought up from Paiute Mesa, where they were normally left to wander free. It was felt that the cows kept escaping from the corral because someone had "witched them," necessitating special medicine to alleviate the problem. Lisa and Johnny boiled herbs in a metal pot on the stove in the hogan. According to Lisa and Johnny, the herbs produced a hot flush when they tasted them, which meant they were being blessed. A small fire was built near the south-southwest wall of the horse corral to burn the herbs so that the cows could breathe in the smoke. The sheep and horses were herded into a small circle near the fire so that they could also benefit from the positive effects of the medicine. Meanwhile, Lisa and Johnny sprinkled the boiled herb and water mixture on the animals.

On another occasion, a private ceremony was conducted at the camp in an attempt to cure Johnny's painfully swollen legs. A female singer was brought from a community some eighty miles away to conduct the ceremony, which was held inside the hogan. The singer sat with her young son near the southwest wall. Johnny sat next to her near the west-northwest wall, the older children all sat on the double bed (except Sammy and Alice who were tending the herd), and Lisa, the two youngest children, and Lucy Tall Man (Lisa's mother) sat near the south wall.

The singer first smoked a corn husk filled with an herb which she had lit with a corn cob. She then passed it to Johnny, who puffed on it for a while before passing it to the children. After each child had had a turn, they passed it to Lisa and Lucy, who each smoked it and passed it to the singer's son, who took a few puffs and returned it to the singer. According to the singer, smoking the herb would cause anything wished for to come true.

Johnny then drank about two-thirds of a mixture of herbs and water from a metal pan. The singer recited prayers while touching first Johnny's feet, then legs, hands, chest, and head. She used what appeared to be a quartz core tool of some type to cut one small incision on each of his fingers. They bled only a little. She examined the cuts closely and then gave Lucy a highly polished black hoe or wedge (it was difficult to see the artifact clearly) to hold for the duration of the ceremony. The singer held the quartz core tool and Johnny held a gray chertlike biface and a small leather pouch of corn pollen, while she recited a long series of prayers which Johnny repeated after her. According to an informant, the prayers were to the sun, moon, and earth to rid Johnny of the evil bothering him. After the prayers, Johnny put a little of the corn pollen on his tongue, sprinkled some in his hair, and tossed a little up in the air. The pouch was then passed in a clockwise direction around the hogan and everyone followed suit.

The pan with the remaining herbs and water mixture was taken outside, where the singer sprinkled it on the sheep, who had been herded south of the ramada by Sammy and Alice. At the same time, everyone put some of the mixture on their hands, face, neck, and hair. This was followed by a meal of fresh mutton (a sheep had been slaughtered earlier in the day for the ceremony), fry bread, and coffee. It was eaten in the southwestern portion of the hogan.

A few hours later, after Lisa and Jimmy drove the singer and her son back to their home, Nancy, Janet, Alice, and Sammy, following her instructions, moved the sheep corral from its location at corral 3 to corral 1 (fig. 28). It had to remain there for a minimum of four days, according to the singer's instructions.

The ceremony was not successful, so Lisa later tried another traditional ritual in an attempt to cure Johnny's swollen legs. She dug a pit approximately three meters southeast of the hogan's entrance (a little west of the outdoor food consumption area) and placed plants (sage, juniper, and an unidentified one) in the bottom of the pit. Rocks that had been heated at the hearth at ash area 1 were placed on top of the plants; over them were laid small sticks. The sticks were presumably to support Johnny's legs over the hot rocks. A blanket covered his legs and the pit. The attempt was also unsuccessful, as was his visit to a local health clinic.

Only a few activities were performed without being directly associated with either a structure or a storage area. One of these was food consumption, which, when it took place outdoors, occurred at a locus 6 to 10 meters east of the hogan's east wall. There were no activity areas that were sex specific and few that were monofunctional (the outhouse being an example of the latter).

Seasonal changes played an important role in the location of activities. The Bitter Water family lived in their winter camp until March, when they moved to their summer camp. Shearing was conducted in the spring at the summer camp but the activity did not take long to complete because of the small number of sheep that they owned (the majority of their herd consisted of goats).

Corn, squash, and melons were planted in the early summer at both their corn fields, one of which was located along a small stream in a tributary of Paiute Canyon, the other northwest of their summer camp. Harvesting took place during the late summer and early fall. Another seasonal factor affecting activity area location was the weather; as discussed above, particular activities were performed outdoors when it was warm but not hot.

Although I did not observe the Bitter Water household at their winter camp, I did visit the camp with a family member. I mapped the camp, and we discussed the identification of particular features and locations of specific activities (fig. 33).

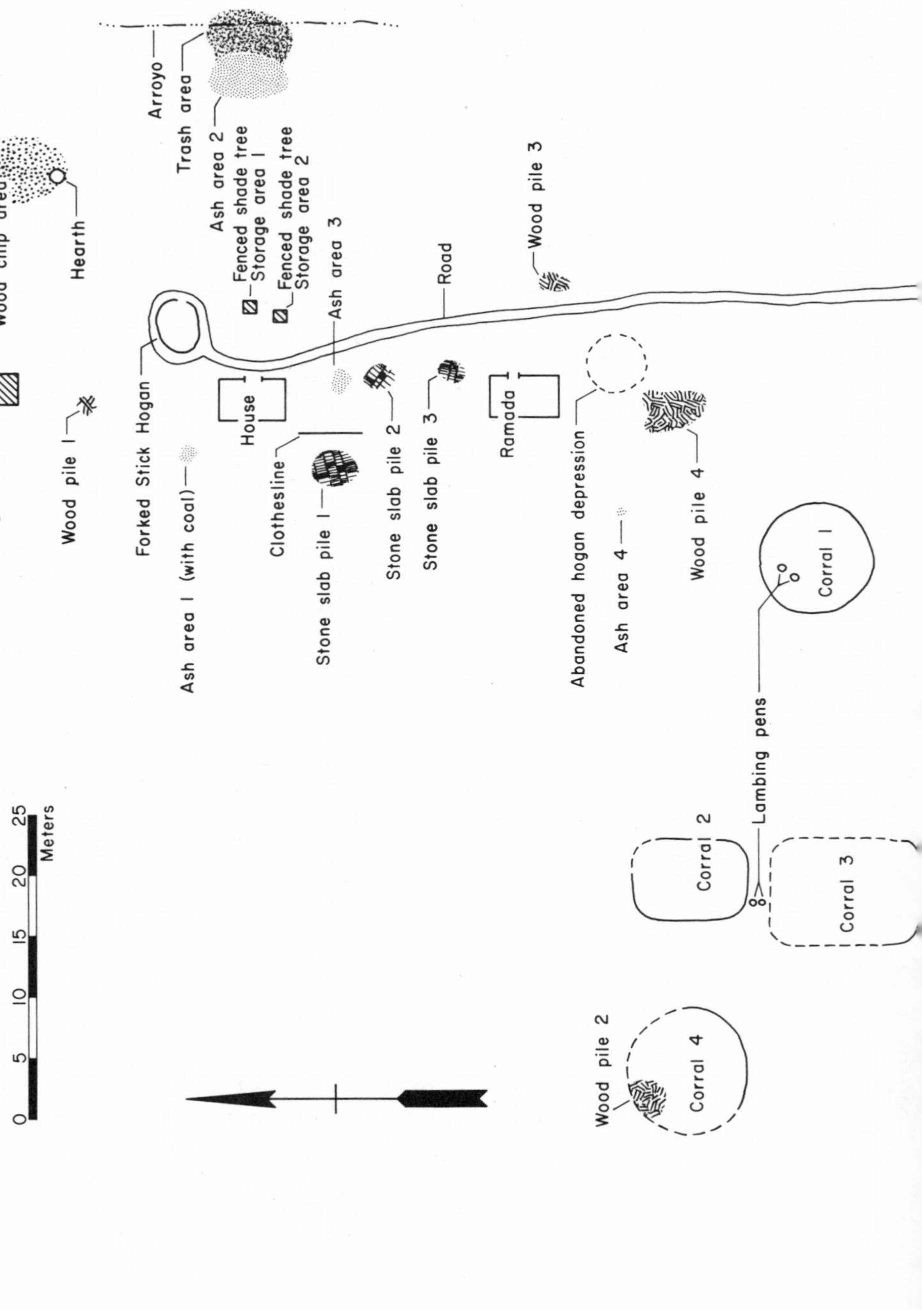

Figure 33. The Bitter Water winter camp.

Their winter camp house was a rectangular one-room stone dwelling with two windows. A forked-stick hogan located east of the house was currently used only for storage but had been their summer dwelling before they built their present summer camp three years ago. A circular depression located south of the house had been, according to Laurie, a wood-and-earth hogan which they had dismantled and set up at another camp three or four years before. All that was left of the hogan was a one-meter-deep circular depression with an opening to the east. It contained shredded bark, small pieces of wood, a few stones, one tin can, and small unidentifiable bone fragments on the surface. South-southwest of the house were four corrals of varying sizes, shapes, and states of preservation, most having a large section of their wall missing. Only corral 1 was completely intact. All that remained of corral 4 was the support posts. A large trash area east of the house was, in part, washing down the bank of an arroyo. The trash area primarily consisted of soda-pop, juice, coffee, and oil cans, two cardboard boxes, flashlight-size batteries, and a plastic flower pot.

In order to obtain an informant's view, I asked Laurie Bitter Water to draw a map of her family's winter camp (fig. 34). Notice how close together she placed everything and that she did not include two of the more dilapidated corrals located a distance from the house. Ash area 1, wood-chip area 1, and trash area 1 were omitted from the map. I asked Laurie to delineate the usual butchering area and the locations at which they cooked and ate when outdoors. The latter two activities were probably conducted more often inside the house because of the weather, but she indicated that when they were outside, they cooked at the hearth at ash area 1 and ate east of the house in an area similar to that where they ate when outside at their summer camp.

Earlier, I had asked Laurie to draw two maps of her family's summer camp. The first one (fig. 35) was drawn from memory, the second (fig. 36) while looking around the camp. Note that the shade (ramada) was drawn larger than the hogan on the first map but corrected to its proper size in proportion to the hogan on the second map. One explanation might be that the ramada was used more by the children than by their parents and, therefore, was conceptually more important to Laurie.

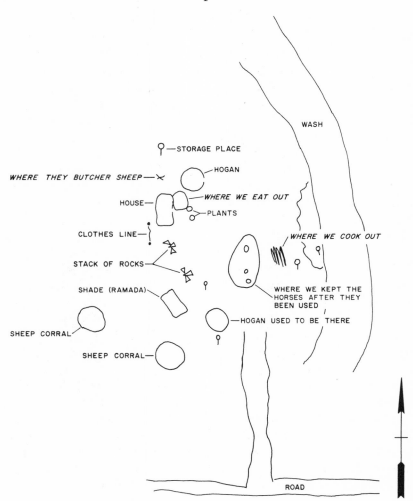

Figure 34. The Bitter Water winter camp drawn by Laurie Bitter Water while walking around the camp. Italicized designations were added at the author's request.

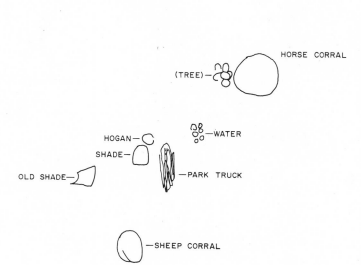

Figure 35. The Bitter Water summer camp drawn from memory by Laurie Bitter Water.

She and the other children usually slept and occasionally played there. However, Laurie and the other children also participated in numerous activities which took place in the hogan, such as cooking, eating, and washing. Consequently, it is difficult to ascertain the reason for the size discrepancy between the ramada and hogan on her first map. The maps were drawn while sheep corral 1 was still in use, which explains the absence of sheep corral 2 (the corral was moved because of its offensive odor when the wind blew). Laurie did not draw any of the storage areas or wood piles on her first map; this is perhaps not surprising, since there were few activities which she performed at them. Nevertheless, no activities were currently conducted at the old ramada, which was included on the maps, albeit at one time it had been used by Laurie and her family. Although anthropologists probably would consider the ramada as having extended to the south wall of the hogan

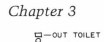

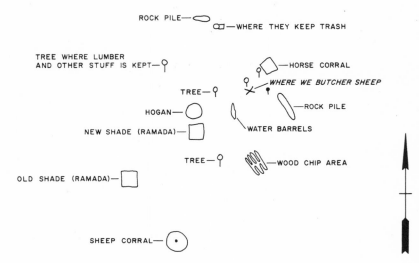

Figure 36. The Bitter Water summer camp drawn by Laurie Bitter Water while walking around the camp. Italicized designations were added at the author's request.

which it physically abutted, Laurie stated that it ended at a point that was, when measured, 0.99 meter south of the hogan. This would leave a gap of almost one meter between the two structures which she depicted on her maps.

Comparisons

The one substantial difference in the use of space between the Bitter Water and Many Sheep households was that the Bitter Water hogan was not used differentially on the basis of sex. The location of particular activities also differed between the two households. For example, food preparation and storage occurred in the northeastern quadrant of the Many Sheep hogan and in the southeastern quadrant of the Bitter Water dwelling. Also, butchering occurred at different loci at the two camps, and unlike the Bitter Water family, the Many Sheep household never washed, ate, or slept (except for brief naps) outdoors.

The fact that the Bitter Water family lived in different seasonal camps whereas the Many Sheep household occupied their camp year-round was another difference between the two. In addition, the Bitter Water family utilized their summer-camp ramada primarily as the children's sleeping area and for storage, whereas the Many Sheep household used theirs to live in during the summer, as well as for storage during the winter.

The Bitter Water family, like the Many Sheep family, performed few activities that were not associated with a structure or storage area. Nor were there sex-specific activity areas or many monofunctional ones. The primary monofunctional area was the Bitter Water outhouse (the Many Sheep camp did not have an outhouse but used the nearby arroyo). Both families ate in the southwestern portion of their hogan. As was true at the Many Sheep camp, activity-area locations were altered when an individual was emotionally upset.

The spatial arrangement of objects in Lisa's traditional maternal aunt's hogan (the Yazzie household; see fig. 37) located west of Kaibito, was more similar to the traditional Many Sheep hogan than to the semitraditional Bitter Water one. Nevertheless, this does not appear to be necessarily related to the degree the household departed from the traditional culture, since the spatial arrangement of objects in Bah Many Sheep's traditional mother's hogan differed from that in Bah's. In fact, food-preparation items at Bah's mother's hogan were in the same quadrant as they were in the Bitter Water hogan.

Maxine Begay, Lisa Bitter Water's semi-nontraditional sister, lived at Shonto boarding school in a rectangular three bedroom house. Lisa's semi-nontraditional mother inhabited a Bureau of Indian Affairs–built hogan, complete with electricity and indoor plumbing, located at the Navajo Mountain boarding school. Both semi-nontraditional households are described in a following section.

Lisa's semitraditional sister, Edith Begay, and her family lived in a rectangular cement one-room house and a wooden ramada with associated features during the summer (fig. 38). Their winter camp consisted of a hogan and associated features. All the cooking at the summer camp was conducted on the split-oil-drum stove located in the ramada (fig. 39). Most food preparation and consumption occurred at the picnic table

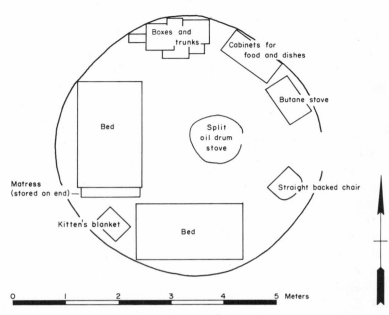

Figure 37. The Yazzie hogan.

near the southeast wall. Dishes were washed on the small night-stand table located near the northeast wall of the ramada. Nancy Begay and her blind paternal grandmother, Sally, who was visiting for the summer, slept on the beds in the house (fig. 40), while Diana, Edith, and Billy slept in the ramada. The other children slept either in the house or with their paternal grandfather in his rectangular one-room stone house located southwest of the Begay house (fig. 38).

A ceremony had been performed a few months before my visit in an attempt to cure their herd from the effects of having been "witched" (the sheep were urinating blood). The ceremony, which was successful, prohibited the slaughtering of any of the herd for four months, and this resulted in many meatless meals (usually potatoes, fry bread, and coffee). Mutton was only occasionally bought at the Navajo Mountain trading post to supplement the diet. The number of bones that was discarded was, therefore, dramatically reduced during the

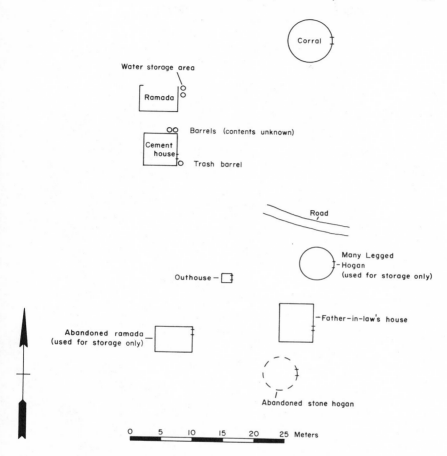

Figure 38. Edith Begay's summer camp.

four months following the ceremony. According to Nancy Begay, six sheep had bloated and died the year before, afer eating
a small poisonous plant. This was a relatively common occurrence; it happened every year, though not usually to quite
as many animals. Because the meat was not fit for human
consumption, they had cut open the carcasses and allowed
the dogs to eat them. The dogs had scattered the bones
throughout the area where the corral had been (the corral was
moved after the incident).

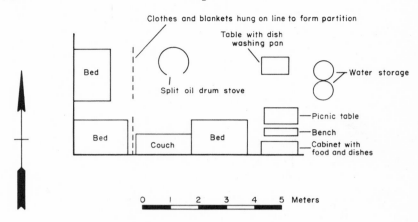

Figure 39. Edith Begay's summer camp ramada.

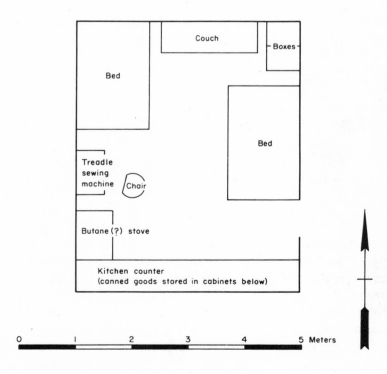

Figure 40. Edith Begay's summer camp house.

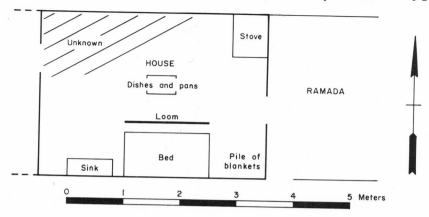

Figure 41. The Red Cliff house and ramada.

The semitraditional Red Cliff household occupied a multiroom rectangular house. However, the door to the second room was always shut, giving the impression that the house was a one-room dwelling. The location of activity areas, during my several brief observations, appeared to be similar to that noted in hogans. Though a butane stove was located next to the east wall of the house, the location and placement of the pots and pans in the house tended to approximate the locus at which they would be expected if the dwelling had been a hogan with a wood-burning stove (fig. 41).

In contrast to the other houses or hogans observed, this one had a loom set up inside the house, near the Euroamerican manufactured double bed which was along the south wall. During my visits, the daughter of the house usually sat on the bed weaving, while the female head of the household, a very old woman, always sat on a pile of blankets on the floor in the southeast corner of the house.

A DAY IN THE LIFE OF THE SEMI-NONTRADITIONAL MAXINE BEGAY HOUSEHOLD

Maxine Begay got up at 6:30 A.M. and swept the living-room floor of her rectangular multiroom tract house. Her husband,

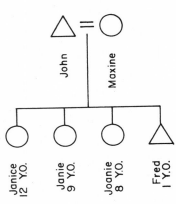

Figure 42. Composition of the Maxine Begay household.

John (fig. 42), slept all morning in bedroom 1 because of his late-night job shift, which was from 6:00 P.M. to 2:00 A.M. Her daughters, Janice and Jamie, put the mattress on which they had slept in the living room, along the north wall of bedroom 2, which served as its storage area during the day (fig. 43). Maxine and her mother, Lucy Tall Man, who was visiting for a few days, sat at the table in the dining area and talked. The children turned on the television set and watched cartoons in the living room. Still seated at the table, Lucy watched television while Maxine washed the dishes from the day before in the kitchen sink. Then Maxine and Lucy drank coffee at the table and the children ate popsicles in the living room, where they continued to watch television for about half an hour. Afterward, they went outside to play on the front lawn (south of the house) and on the west end, where there was some shade from the already hot sun.

Later, Maxine, Lucy, and the children drove to the nearby Shonto trading post, where they bought snack food for lunch and washed clothes at the laundromat; by the time they returned home, John had awakened and left. Maxine hung clothes on the clothesline in the back yard. The children turned on the television, but instead of watching it, they went outside to play in the front yard. Lucy used a sewing machine on the kitchen table to mend a blouse. She put the sewing machine

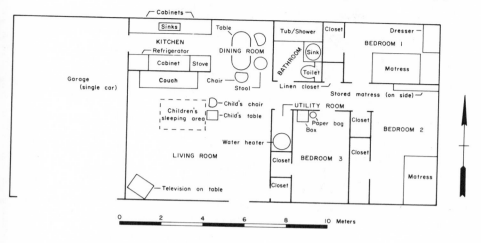

Figure 43. Maxine Begay's house.

away at its storage area in a closet after she had finished and turned the chair at the southern end of the table around so that she could watch television. Maxine watered the front lawn with a hose, and then joined Lucy at the table, where they talked while watching television. The younger children came in and watched televison while seated on the living-room couch. At the table, Janice fixed a bottle of canned milk for Fred, who had been crying. He took it into the living room and joined the children on the couch.

At approximately 7:45 P.M. John returned with a watermelon, which he placed on the table. He then went to bedroom 1, where he remained for half an hour until he left for work. Maxine and Lucy cut up and ate the watermelon at the kitchen table, and the children ate some in the living room in front of the television set.

Maxine went into the kitchen and prepared dinner at the south counter. She cooked on the stove. Janice peeled potatoes at the south counter in the kitchen, and then swept the living room and dining area. Maxine mixed bread dough in a bowl on the table in the dining room so she could talk to Lucy while she worked. She served dinner at the table about 9:30 P.M.; it consisted of fry bread and mutton stew (the meat had been purchased at the trading post). Maxine and Lucy ate at the southern end of the table so they could continue to watch television. The children also ate at the table but had to stand because of the lack of chairs. Aferward they pulled the mattress from bedroom 2, put it in their sleeping area in the living room, and lay on it to watch television.

John came back around 10:00 P.M. and ate dinner sitting at the table while talking to Maxine. Lucy had moved to the couch to make room for him at the table. He left shortly thereafter and Maxine joined Lucy on the living-room couch. The younger children moved several small toy chairs into the living room and briefly sat on them, before once more lying down on the mattress. The television set was turned off around 11:30 P.M. and everyone went to sleep—the children on the mattress in the living room, Lucy on the couch, and Maxine and Fred in bedroom 1. John returned early in the morning and went to sleep in bedroom 1. About 8:30 A.M. Maxine got up and swept the area around the dining room table. A new day had begun.

Discussion

I was with Lucy Tall Man, Maxine's mother, during much of the time I observed the Begay household. Hence most of the days I spent with them were atypical, since Lucy did not normally live with them. However, many activities regularly took place at the same loci the few times I visited without Lucy, indicating that much of what I observed was in fact typical. For example, the children still slept in their sleeping area in the living room on a mattress which was stored during the day in bedroom 2. John, Maxine, and Fred slept in bedroom 1, and bedrooms 2 and 3 remained unoccupied.

Television viewing was the dominant evening and night activity. Adults usually watched from the couch or, less frequently, from the table. Children sat either on the mattress or on the living-room floor and only occasionally on the couch.

John was seldom at home, except for meals and to sleep, but it must be noted that I did not stay with them during one of his days off (Sunday and Monday). In addition, the presence of his mother-in-law may have made him uncomfortable so that he was deliberately absent more than usual when she was visiting.

Usually food was consumed at the table, although people occasionally ate in the living room while watching television. Owing to the limited number of chairs, the children had to stand up when eating at the table. Food preparation occurred both in the kitchen, where the stove, refrigerator, and sink were located and utensils and food were stored, and at the table in the dining room.

The children primarily played in the living room and outside in the front yard. They once played with Maxine in bedroom 2. Other than that one brief incident, and once when Maxine sent Joanie to the room as punishment, bedroom 2 was not used, except for storage. Bedroom 3, where there was little furniture, was not used at all. When asked why bedroom 3 was never utilized, Maxine replied that it was "scary because there are no curtains at the window and people can come and look in." This would, however, not explain why bedroom 2 was never used: bedroom 2 had homemade curtains (made from pillow cases) at the windows, even though it also was only rarely used.

My visits to the Begay household spanned a total of eight separate days, from late spring to late summer, and included four overnight visits. The only seasonal change I noted in activity areas was in their location. Maxine and the children moved to Shonto in the late spring to join John, who lived there year round. During the academic year she and the younger children lived in the Bureau of Indian Affairs–built hogan on the Navajo Mountain school premises where she worked as an aide.

Activity areas at the Begay household were not sex specific. A few, however, were monofunctional: the kitchen, which was used for food preparation and the cleaning of utensils, and the bathroom, which was used for a specific set of activities. It is noteworthy that sleeping regularly occurred in the living room, despite the fact that both bedrooms 2 and 3, one of which contained a mattress bed, were vacant. Meals were eaten, with only one exception, at the table in the dining room, where other activities also occurred (talking, making bread, sewing, and others). This does not include snacks, which the children ate in the living room or outside. When eating, Maxine and John sat on the east side of the table and the children (and I) stood on the west side of the table. Lucy, when she visited, sat on the east side.

Comparisons

Maxine's mother, Lucy Tall Man, was classified as semi-nontraditional despite the fact that she lived in a Bureau of Indian Affairs–built hogan. The hogan was located on the grounds of the Navajo Mountain Boarding School, where she was employed as a cook. The large stone hogan had both indoor plumbing and electricity, as well as Euroamerican manufactured furniture.

Lucy usually rose early (around 5:30 A.M.) and went to bed early. She always slept on the bed along the northwest wall (fig. 44). She also sat on the bed during the day while performing a variety of activities, including mending, talking, and reading letters (fig. 45). Food was prepared at the counter along the west wall near the refrigerator and on the stove. Food was consumed at the table, with only one exception discussed below. The table was also used for sewing, talking, and writing letters, as well as for other miscellaneous activities. Lucy usually sat at the west side of the table. The couch was rarely used; I observed her sitting there only twice, briefly, while she was doing hand sewing. When the Bitter Water family occasionally visited to use her bathtub, they usually sat on the couch or at the kitchen table. The bunk beds were also used by the children.

The kitchen sink was used for a variety of activities, such as brushing teeth and washing hair, clothes, and dishes. The southwestern quadrant of the hogan was seldom used, except for storage (clothes, blankets, cloth) and for sewing on the treadle sewing machine. The center closet contained Lucy's clothes and shoes.

Activity areas inside the hogan were not sex specific or monofunctional, with the exception of the bathroom. As was observed at the other households, activity area locations were altered by an individual's moods. Lucy would sit on her bed, at the table staring forward, or would wander aimlessly around

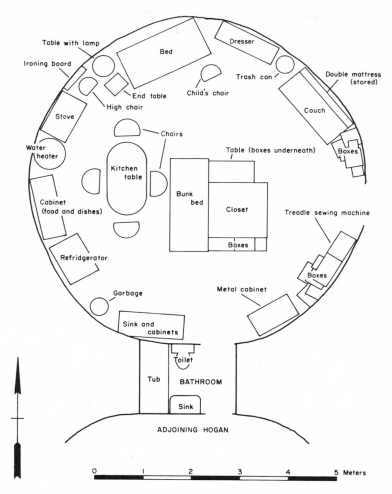

Figure 44. Lucy Tall Man's Bureau of Indian Affairs–built hogan.

the hogan when upset or depressed. She once ate dinner while walking around inside, too despondent to sit at the table.

The semi-nontraditional Christy Horseman household (fig. 46) lived at the same camp as Christy's sisters and parents. Their interesting dwelling consisted of a cement hogan with a one-room rectangular house built onto it (fig. 47). Christy slept with Joey, her adopted son, on the Euroamerican-style

Figure 45. The northwest quadrant of Lucy Tall Man's Bureau of Indian Affairs–built hogan.

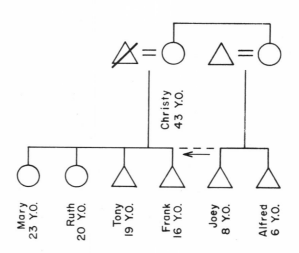

Figure 46. The composition of the Horseman household.

Figure 47. The front of the Horseman house/hogan.

double bed along the west wall of the hogan (fig. 48). Ruth slept on the Euroamerican-style bed along the north hogan wall, and Mary slept on the one along the south wall. The older boys slept on the couch, which pulled out to make a double bed and was located next to the southern wall of the house.

Food was prepared and cooked on the stove near the west wall of the house, and was eaten, in most cases, at the table next to the north wall. Exceptions did occur. Joey usually ate on the floor near the couch, whether or not there was room at the table. Illness was a temporary individual condition which, like personal moods, affected the typical location of activity areas. For example, Christy ate on her bed in the hogan when she was too ill to come to the table.

During the day, Joey and his cousin Alfred played on the couch for hours at a time. Ruth occasionally wove a black-

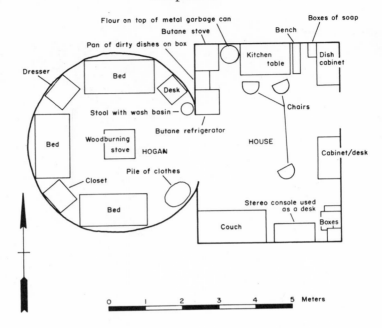

Figure 48. The Horseman house/hogan.

and-white checkberboard coiled basket sitting on the eastern chair near the table in the house. She stated that her mother wove baskets at storage area 1 (fig. 49), where her basketry material was stored, but I never observed this. The dogs were fed at the same storage area; a food pan was kept there for them. Ruth's loom, with a partially completed blanket on it, was set up in the ramada.

Although a few differences existed in the use of space among various Navajo families, these differences were not as consistent or as substantial as those occurring in the Euroamericans' use of space. In other words, intragroup spatial patterning differences were not as pronounced as those between groups. In fact, the greatest variation in Navajo activity areas was in their location, not their use.

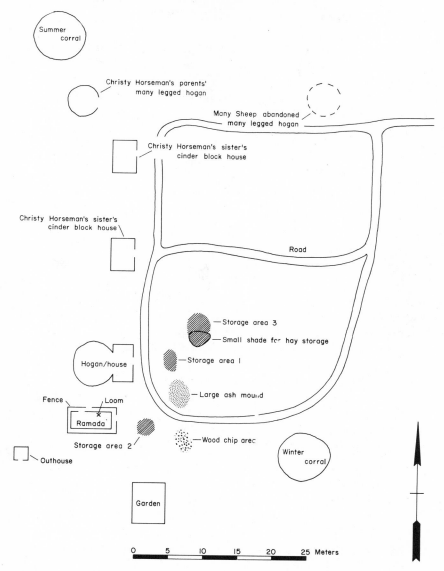

Figure 49. The Horseman camp.

Euroamerican Spatial Patterning

Euroamerican spatial patterning was consistent, cross-cutting both socioeconomic classes and types of residence (urban versus rural). The contrast between Euroamerican use of space and that of the Navajo discussed above was striking. See Chapter 2 for a general description of each of the following households.

A DAY IN THE LIFE OF THE RURAL, UPPER-LOWER-CLASS
SMITH HOUSEHOLD

Tim (fig. 50), the male head of the household, woke up at 7:00 A.M. He tried to wake the children but they ignored him until 7:30, when they reluctantly got up. The family members dressed in their respective bedrooms (fig. 51) and washed in the bathroom. Lillian prepared breakfast on the stove in the kitchen after washing the dishes left in the kitchen sink from the day before. Everyone ate eggs, bacon, and biscuits at the kitchen table, after which Tim left for work.

Mel watered and fed the hogs after breakfast (see fig. 52). The younger children took the school bus that came by the house at 8:00 A.M. and the older ones, Linda and Mel, left for school in Linda's car at 8:30. Lillian took a two-hour nap in bedroom 1 after the children left. She turned on the television set when she got up and went out to water and feed the numerous animals (see fig. 12), finishing the tasks around noon. Linda returned from school at about the same time (she was going only part-time since she was a high-school senior). She helped Lillian prepare lunch on the stove and at the table in the kitchen. It consisted of steak, pea salad, and fried potatoes.

Lillian ate at the kitchen table while Linda ate at the couch in the living room in order to watch the soap operas on television. When they finished eating, they stacked the dishes in the kitchen sink and put the leftover food in the refrigerator.

Linda left for work about 2:30 P.M. Lillian folded the clothes, which she had taken off the clothesline the day before, on the coffee table in the living room so that she could watch television at the same time. She put a load of dirty clothes in the washing machine located in the utility room and then re-

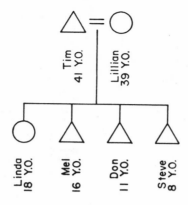

Figure 50. The composition of the Smith household.

sumed watching television. The school bus brought the other children home at 3:30. They came in the house and watched television. Don briefly looked at his English book in the living room, before he too devoted his entire attention to the television program. A little later, Lillian went out to feed and water the animals, helped by Tim when he returned from work.

About 5:30, each child fixed himself a peanut-butter-and-jam sandwich and a glass of milk at the kitchen table; they ate these in the living room while watching television. Lillian and Tim came in a little later and ate sandwiches at the kitchen table. They talked at the table until around 8:00 P.M., at which time they went into the living room to watch television. At approximately 11:00 P.M., Lillian and Tim went to sleep in bedroom 1. The boys, one by one, went into bedroom 3 to go to sleep. Linda returned from work at midnight. She watched television for half an hour before turning the set off and going to sleep in bedroom 2. Tim began a new day at 7:00 .A.M. when he got up and tried to awaken the children.

Discussion

Clearly, watching television was the Smiths' dominant activity during both the day and the evening. They ate food, folded clothes, did homework, read magazines, and so on, in the living room in order to watch television at the same time.

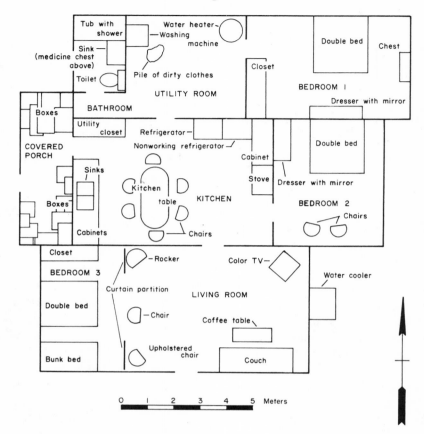

Figure 51. The Smith house.

Breakfast was usually eaten by the whole family at the kitchen table, since there was little that interested them on television at that hour. Lunch and dinner, however, were eaten by the children in front of the television. Tim and Lillian usually ate at the kitchen table before joining the children in the living room. The television set was turned on in the morning and left on all day and night, whether or not anyone was watching and until the last person went to bed.

Tim's position at the kitchen table remained the same regardless of the number of people present; he always sat at the

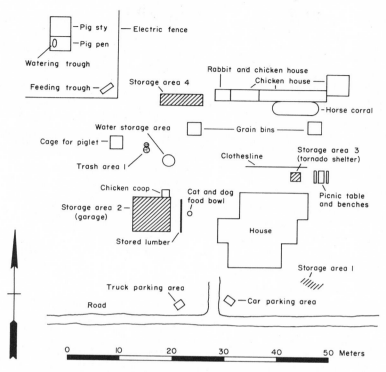

Figure 52. The Smith residence.

"head" of the table. This was the east end of the table until, when Lillian washed the floor, the table was turned sideways. It remained in the new position for the remainder of my stay. Even after the table had been moved, Tim still sat at the same end, which was now the north end. This indicates that it was not direction that determined Tim's position at the table, but his authority position in relation to the rest of the family. The table was used primarily as a food consumption locus, although occasionally, just before or after a meal, two or more family members would sit there and talk (usually Tim and Lillian). Tim sat at his usual north end even when just talking.

Both sex specific and monofunctional activity areas were observed at the Smith house. The bathroom, kitchen (except for the table), utility room, and bedrooms were monofunctional in that only a specific set of functionally related activities took place there. The bedrooms were also sex specific, with the exception of bedroom 1, which Tim and Lillian shared. All three boys slept in one bedroom, whereas Linda, the only girl, had her own room. The utility room was also both monofunctional, as it was used only to wash clothes, and sex specific, since the activity of washing clothes was a female one.

Weekends differed from weekdays in several respects, the most notable being that Tim and the children were home all day. Lillian, however, worked the afternoon and evening shift at the county hospital on weekends. With the exception of Steve, who got up early Saturday mornings to watch cartoons on television, everyone slept late, usually until 10:00 or 10:30 A.M. Lillian would then fix brunch in the kitchen, and everyone ate at the kitchen table. Afterward, the whole family did chores outdoors, taking care of their many animals. The children spent most of the day watching television, interspersed with some playing outdoors (usually only for a few minutes at a time). Tim drove Lillian to work around 2:30 P.M. and frequently then spent several hours in town. Weekend evenings, like other evenings, were devoted to television watching.

Because I lived with the Smith household only during the fall (September), I was not able to observe possible seasonal changes in the use or location of activity areas. However, I do not think there were many seasonal differences because, although the September days were pleasantly warm, television kept the family indoors. In fact, beyond tending to the animals, the Smiths spent very little time outside their house.

Comparisons

The rural, lower-class Jones household used space quite similarly to the Smith family—they also had both monofunctional and sex-specific activity areas. Bedrooms (fig. 53) were monofunctional and, with the exception of the parents' room, sex specific. The kitchen was used primarily for the preparation and consumption of food, and, except for the table, was sex specific (only females worked in it). The bathroom also was monofunctional.

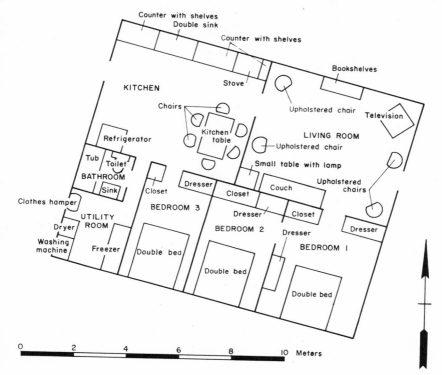

Figure 53. The Jones house.

The Joneses performed the same activities in their living room as did the Smith family (watching television, talking, doing homework, reading, eating). The dominant day- and nighttime activity at both households was watching television.

A DAY IN THE LIFE OF THE URBAN, UPPER-MIDDLE-CLASS JOHNSON HOUSEHOLD

Dale (fig. 54) woke up at 6:30 A.M. After helping his children, Bob and Jenny, reach the boxes of cold cereal and get the milk for their breakfast at the dinette table, he went downstairs to bathroom 2 (fig. 55) to shower and shave.

Linda got up a little later and washed in bathroom 1 upstairs (fig. 56). She put some additional boxes of cold cereal on the

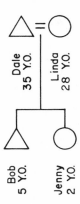

Figure 54. The composition of the Johnson household.

dinette table and fixed coffee in the electric coffee machine located on the south kitchen counter. Dale and Linda ate breakfast at the dinette table. Dale left for work at 7:30 A.M. The children, at Linda's request, went downstairs and watched television in the living room. Later, Bob got dressed in bedroom 3. Linda stacked the breakfast dishes in the dishwasher located in the kitchen, and then got dressed in bedroom 1. She dressed Jenny in bedroom 2. The children then played quietly with toys in front of the television (still on), while Linda swept both bedrooms and made the beds. She then went downstairs and wrote a letter at the desk in the living room. About 10:00 A.M. she went upstairs to continue to clean the house. The phone rang and she talked sitting on the kitchen couch, to a local friend for about half an hour. Afterward, she went downstairs, sat on the couch so she could watch television with Bob and Jenny, and folded laundry that had been washed the day before.

When she had finished, Linda picked things up in the living room for a few minutes and around 11:30 went upstairs to prepare lunch in the kitchen. Dale came home about 12:10 P.M. Everyone ate soup and sandwiches at the dinette table (fig. 57).

Dale left for work at approximately 12:50. Linda cleared the table and stacked the dishes in the dishwasher, while the chil-

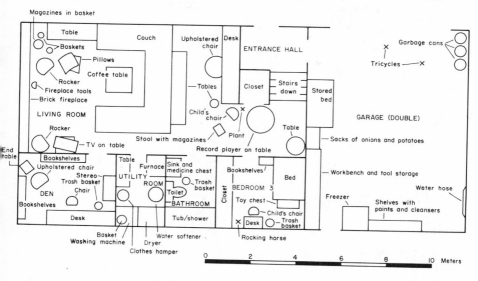

Figure 55. The bottom level of the Johnson house.

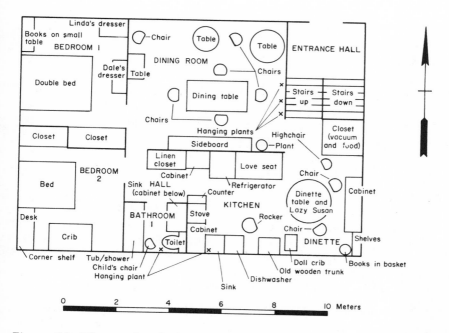

Figure 56. The top level of the Johnson house.

Figure 57. Lunch at the kitchen table at the Johnson house.

dren played briefly upstairs. Everyone then went into bedroom 1 where they took a two-hour nap. They were awakened by the mailman at 3:10, after which they went downstairs to watch television. A little later Linda brought down some cookies, fruit, and glasses of milk from the kitchen, and they all ate in front of the television set. At 4:00 P.M. Linda went up to the kitchen and began preparing dinner. Meanwhile, Bob and Jenny played with toys in front of the television set. An hour later Linda again went downstairs and watched television with the children (fig. 58).

Dale returned home at 6:00 P.M., and shortly thereafter Linda served dinner at the dinette table. It consisted of fried chicken, mashed potatoes, peas, biscuits, pudding for dessert, and milk. The children and Dale went downstairs to the living room to watch television after dinner, while Linda cleared the table, loaded the dishes into the dishwasher, set it, and cleaned up the kitchen area. She then joined the others downstairs and they all watched television for the rest of the evening. About 10:00 P.M. Dale and Linda carried the sleeping children to

Figure 58. Watching television in the Johnson living room.

bedroom 2 and then went to sleep in bedroom 1. Around 6:30 A.M. the children woke Dale, who got up and put the milk and boxes of cold cereal on the dinette table for them. A new day had begun.

Discussion

Television not only reduced the variety of activities the Johnsons performed but also the diversity of loci at which they occurred, since the set was located in the living room and most activities revolved around it. Television viewing was the dominant evening activity, even when friends visited, in which case conversation usually alternated with television watching. The television was watched sporadically by Linda and the children throughout the day and continuously by the entire family on weekends (especially during football season). Snacks and occasionally dinners were eaten in the living room so that the family could watch television.

The children rarely played outside during my stay, even though the weather was sunny although a little cool. Instead, they spent most of their time either playing in front of or watching the television. The television was turned on around 7:00 A.M. by the children and off about 10:00 or 10:30 P.M. by Dale or Linda when they went to bed.

There were both monofunctional and sex-specific activity areas at the Johnson house. Monofunctional areas were bathrooms, the utility room, bedrooms (although occasionally the children's bedtime stories were read to them there), the kitchen, dinette table, and dining room. Although an occasional exception occurred, the activities performed at the above locations were remarkably consistent. The Johnson household had more sex specific activity areas than any other household observed. The kitchen was primarily used by Linda, the den by Dale, the upstairs bathroom in the mornings by Linda, the downstairs one by Dale, and the utility room, which contained the washing machine and dryer, by Linda. The downstairs bathroom contained only Dale's toilet articles, whereas Linda's were stored in the upstairs one. However, both bathrooms were used by either sex during the day. The kitchen and the utility area were both monofunctional and, with only an occasional exception, sex specific. Although Bob had his own bedroom downstairs (bedroom 3), he was reluctant to sleep there because it was a distance from his parents' room upstairs. Nevertheless, the bedroom was referred to as "Bob's room," his clothes and toys were stored in it, and Linda, who was pregnant and planned to put the new baby in the room with Jenny, was trying to force Bob to sleep in bedroom 3 (a very different reaction from what would occur among the Navajos or Spanish-Americans). Linda labeled bedroom 2 "the girls' room" (she was assuming the baby would be female) and bedroom 3 "Bob's room" on a map of the house she had drawn at my request (fig. 59). However, they were looking for another house with more bedrooms so that each child could have its own.

Even some of the artifacts and storage areas were sex specific. Linda and Dale had separate closets and individual dressers in bedroom 1, as well as their own desks, Linda's in the living room and Dale's in his den. Each desk contained only Dale's or Linda's paraphernalia.

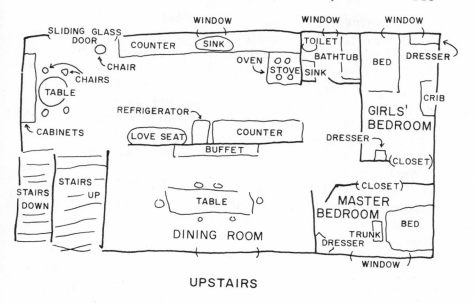

UPSTAIRS

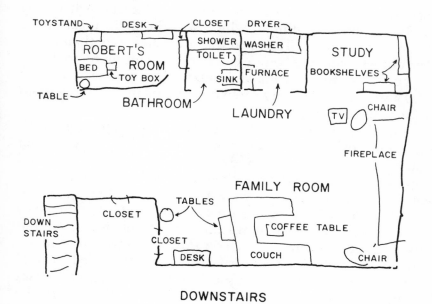

DOWNSTAIRS

Figure 59. The Johnson house drawn from memory by Linda Johnson.

The seating arrangement at both kitchen and dining-room tables was rigidly adhered to. Dale always sat on the north end of both the dinette and dining-room tables. Jenny sat on the northwest side of the round dinette table and on the east side of the rectangular dining-room table. Bob sat on the east side of the dinette table and the west side of the dining-room table. Linda sat on the west side of the dinette table and south side of the dining-room table. The dining-room table was usually used only for Sunday dinner, or when there were guests.

Weekends differed from weekdays in that Dale was home all day. The children slept until around 7:30 A.M. and woke their parents up by 8:00. Breakfast was served by Linda about half an hour later and usually consisted of bacon, eggs, biscuits, and coffee or milk. Dale spent Saturdays working around the house (painting, repairing things, adding weather stripping, yard work, and the like), and Sundays watching sports on television. Linda, besides preparing a large breakfast, spent Saturdays much the same way she did weekdays. Sundays were somewhat different in that she would fix a brunch around 9:00 A.M. and then dinner, which was the main meal of the day, around 2:00 P.M. The meal was more elaborate than weekday dinners and was often eaten at the dining-room table. Supper, consisting of soup and sandwiches, was served about 7:00 P.M. and was usually eaten downstairs in the living room in front of the television.

In an attempt to obtain an understanding of an informant's perception of space, I asked Linda to draw two maps of her house—one from memory and the other while looking around (figs. 59 and 60). Most of the differences between her drawings and mine (figs. 55 and 56) were a result of her having moved the furniture around before I drew mine and after she drew hers. Both of Linda's drawings exhibited much detail, and relatively little was left out even on the map drawn from memory. A comparison of her two drawings revealed several interesting things. Note that she drew only the two bookcases in Dale's den on her first map and included the rest of the furniture on her second after she actually looked at the room. An explanation for the discrepancy could be that the den was considered her husband's domain and, since she rarely went

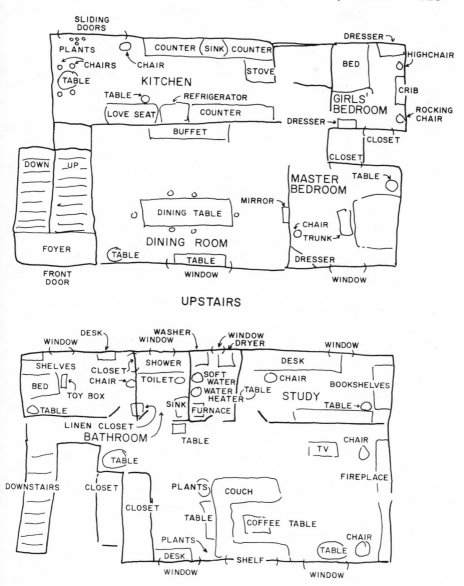

Figure 60. The Johnson house drawn by Linda Johnson while looking at the various rooms.

in there except to clean or answer the extension telephone, she was unfamiliar and/or unconcerned with the spatial arrangement of objects in the room. She was in bedroom 3 as frequently as in the den but remembered the location of furniture there more accurately. This may have been because the room belonged to her son, so that she considered it more a part of her domain than was Dale's room, just as she was only moderately interested in most aspects of Dale's job ("that is Dale's work and, therefore not, except in a general sense, my concern" kind of thinking), whereas she was very interested in every aspect of her son's endeavors.

Another interesting feature of the second map was the fact that Linda wrote on it, at my request, the location(s) at which meals were usually consumed. She said that breakfast, lunch, and dinner were all eaten at the dinette table, the only exception being that dinner was served three times a week at the dining-room table. My observations were different—the family ate at the dining table one breakfast (a Saturday and my last day with them), one noon meal (when a friend from Denver visited), and two dinners (one was a midafternoon meal on Sunday, and the other was a fairly formal Saturday dinner which was also my farewell dinner). Otherwise, only one Sunday dinner was eaten at the dining-room table. Linda also neglected to mention that some meals (two dinners during my stay) were eaten downstairs in the living room in front of the television.

Although the possibility exists that I witnessed atypical behavior the entire time I lived with the Johnsons, and that they normally do not eat in the living room and do eat dinner three times a week at the dining-room table, all indications suggest otherwise. In fact, Linda stated on another occasion that they ate dinner downstairs in front of the television three times a week. It must be remembered that three is a special number among Euroamericans, often used to denote an approximation. Nevertheless, on her second map Linda did not mention ever eating downstairs. The discrepancy is probably due to the difference between real and ideal behavior. Even though food is often eaten in front of the television set, the ideal food-consumption locus for Euroamericans is the dining room, and Linda's statement was probably an attempt to conform to this ideal.

Since I lived with the Johnson family only during the winter (November), I did not observe any seasonal changes in their use of activity areas or in the location of such areas. However, even on relatively warm and sunny days, the family members usually stayed indoors.

Comparisons

The Johnson family used space in a manner similar to the rural Euroamericans observed in that many of their activity areas were monofunctional and sex specific. Some of the similarities include the fact that watching television was the dominant day and night activity and was conducted in the living room, that the bedrooms, utility rooms, kitchens, and bathrooms were monofunctional, that relatively little time was spent out-of-doors, and that there were numerous sex specific activity areas. Despite differences in socioeconomic class, season of observation, and residence location (rural versus urban), the Euroamerican spatial patterning was homogeneous.

Spanish-American Spatial Patterning

The Spanish-Americans' spatial patterning differed from that of both the Navajos and Euroamericans. Chapter 2 contains descriptions of each Spanish-American household observed.

A DAY IN THE LIFE OF THE RURAL, UPPER-LOWER-CLASS MARTÍNEZ HOUSEHOLD

The alarm rang at 6:00 A.M. waking Félix, the male head of the household (fig. 61). It was only at his continual insistence that the children finally got up an hour later. They all washed in the bathroom, dressed in their respective bedrooms, and combed their hair in front of the mirror in bedroom 2 (fig. 62). Rosa fixed herself a cup of coffee in the kitchen and drank it at the kitchen table. No one else had anything for breakfast.

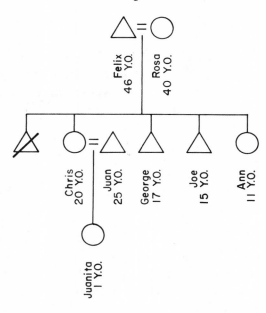

Figure 61. The composition of the Martínez household.

The school bus came by for Ann at 7:30 A.M. The others all left for work or school by 8:00.

As they frequently did, Chris and her baby, Juanita, had spent the night at her maternal grandmother's house less than a mile away. They returned home at 10:00 A.M., and Chris immediately turned on the television set. She spent the rest of the morning alternating between cleaning the living room and sitting and watching television. She picked things up off the floor and put the mattress, which Ann and Joe had slept on the previous night, in its usual daytime storage area on top of the bed in bedroom 2. Juanita slept most of the morning on the couch. Around noon Chris prepared a lunch of tomato soup in the kitchen; she and and Juanita ate it at the kitchen table. The dishes were left on the table, and the leftover soup on the stove. They returned to the living room after lunch to resume watching television. Juanita sat quietly on the floor playing with a couch pillow.

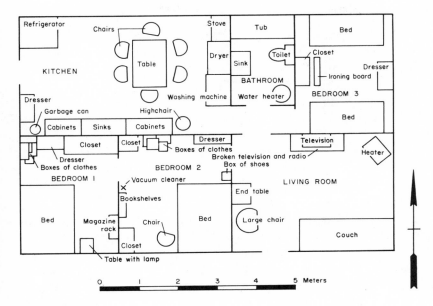

Figure 62. The Martínez house.

George, the oldest son, came home from school at 1:30 P.M. (he left school early in the afternoon because he was a high school senior). At the kitchen stove he heated a sloppy joe meat mixture left over from the night before and ate it in the living room. Chris and Juanita took a 15-minute nap in bedroom 1, after which Chris washed the dirty dishes in the kitchen sink. Then she joined George and Juanita watching television in the living room. The younger children, Ann and Joe, came home from school around 4 P.M. They both went into the kitchen and fixed themselves a sandwich at the table. The snack was eaten in front of the television set in the living room. About half an hour later, Ann started her homework on the living room couch. She later went into the bedroom to finish her arithmetic homework. George and Joe played basketball outdoors at their cousin's house next door.

Félix and Rosa returned from work about 5:30 P.M. Rosa put bologna, store-bought bread, and home-made tortillas on the kitchen table, where the family made their own sandwiches. Rosa, Chris, Juanita, and Félix ate at the table in the kitchen, and the others ate in the living room in order to watch television. After dinner, Rosa cleared the table and washed the dishes in the kitchen sink. She then joined the rest of the family watching television in the living room until 11:00 P.M., at which time the television set was turned off, and everyone went to sleep—Chris and Juanita in bedroom 1, Rosa and Félix in bedroom 2, and George, Ann, and Joe in the living room. At 6:00 A.M. the alarm went off, beginning another day.

Discussion

As was true at the Euroamerican homes, television was the single major factor influencing activities and their locations, but *not* the use of activity areas. Because of the nature of television viewing, the predominance of this activity reduced the variety of both the activities performed and their locations. Food was eaten in the living room so that the television could be watched at the same time. The only other food-consumption locus was the kitchen table, and it was more often used as a food-consumption area by the older family members (Félix, Rosa, and Chris) than by the younger ones, who preferred to watch television while they ate.

The only monofunctional activity areas at the Martínez house were the bathroom and bedrooms, the latter being used, with only a few exceptions, for sleeping and dressing. However, sleeping also occurred on a regular basis in the living room, which presented another interesting example of the discrepancy between real and ideal behavior. The ideal, according to both Félix and Rosa, was that the boys slept in their own room (bedroom 3), the girls slept in bedroom 1, while they slept in bedroom 2. This plan was rarely if ever adhered to. The kitchen was not monofunctional, for it accommodated such activities as washing laundry, in addition to the usual ones of cooking and eating.

The use of activity areas, as described above, remained essentially the same on weekends. Félix and George worked on Saturdays, so that the entire family was home during the day only on Sundays. The television set was usually on all day whether or not anyone was watching. On weekends Rosa performed time-consuming tasks that she had not been able to do during the week, such as washing clothes or making tortillas. Chris often kept Rosa company while she worked, and Ann divided her time between them and the boys, who usually alternated watching sporting events on television with working on a truck's engine outside.

Because I lived with the Martínez family only during the fall (end of October and early November), I was not able to observe possible seasonal variations in their use or location of activity areas. Although the weather was warm (no sweaters or coats needed when outdoors), surprisingly few activities occurred outside, as a result of the lure of the television. However, the Martínezes spent more time outdoors than did the Euroamerican families.

Comparisons

Differences in the use of space were more pronounced among the Spanish-Americans, Euroamericans, and Navajos than within each group. The conventions of Spanish-American spatial patterning appeared to crosscut socioeconomic class differences, as was the case with the Euroamericans. The discrepancy between the uses of space by the Martínez and Smith families, who belong to the same socioeconomic class but to different ethnic groups, further supports this contention.

A DAY IN THE LIFE OF THE RURAL, LOWER-LOWER-CLASS
GARCÍA HOUSEHOLD

Juan (fig. 63) rekindled the fire in the wood heaters located in the living room/kitchen and bedroom 2 at 6:30 A.M. The rest of the family woke up around 7:30. They each used the chamber pot located next to the southeast bed in bedroom 2 and dressed in both bedrooms 1 and 2. Juan sat on the couch in the living room and drank a cup of coffee he had made in the electric coffee pot that was permanently kept on the table (fig. 64). The children used the mirror on the kitchen wall to comb their hair; they washed in a pan placed on the dresser below it. The special education bus came by at 7:30 for Rosa, Juan's mentally retarded daughter, and the public school bus picked up the other children (except Anita and Martha) at 7:45

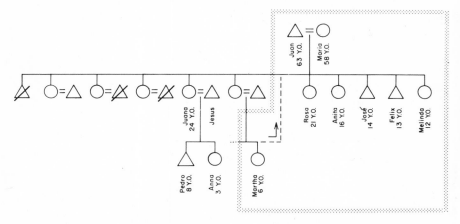

Figure 63. The composition of the García household.

A.M. Martha occasionally attended a Head Start preschool;
Anita, who spent most of the morning sleeping, had dropped
out of her sophomore year of high school.

María made everyone's bed but Anita's. She then placed a
pot of beans and tripe on the wood-burning stove in the kitchen.
Juan cooked breakfast for everyone except María, who cooked
her eggs herself on the stove in the kitchen. They both ate
breakfast, which consisted of eggs, bacon, sausage, toast, and
coffee, at the dining room/kitchen table. Afterward, Juan sat
momentarily on the couch before going outside to haul water
from the well located south of the house and wood from the
wood-chip area (fig. 65). He resumed his position on the couch,
where he remained, idle, the rest of the morning. María cleared
the table of dirty dishes and leftover food, putting the food in
the refrigerator or kitchen cabinet, depending on its perisha-
bility, and the dishes in a large pot of water on the stove. She
then swept the living room and bedrooms 1 and 2. Martha
woke up, and María dressed her and combed her hair in the
living room. Anita got up and dressed in bedroom 2 at 10:30.
Martha colored in her coloring book at the table until lunch
time. María continued to clean the house.

The women fixed hot dogs in the kitchen for lunch and ate
them at the living room/kitchen table; Juan did not eat. María

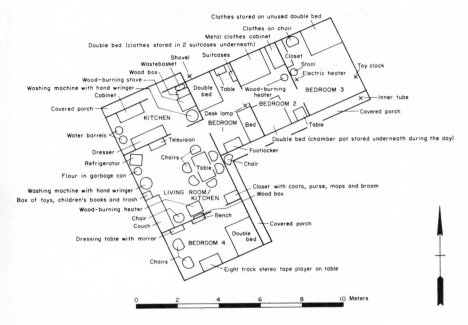

Figure 64. The García house.

cleared the dishes and leftover food off the table and put them in their appropriate locations. Anita and Martha played with pieces of clay at the table, while Juan continued to sit on the couch and María straightened up the bedrooms. The other children returned from school about 3:00 P.M. Melinda fixed herself an ice-cream cone at the living room/kitchen table and ate it on the couch, momentarily vacated by Juan, who had gone outside. Anita lay down on the couch for a few minutes until Juan returned. Juan sat on the couch for the rest of the afternoon. Melinda and Félix played cards at the table while the rest of the children watched. Rosa stood near the table much of the afternoon, silently watching the various activities being conducted. (Rosa usually sat by herself in bedroom 2 when she was not in the living room/kitchen.) About 4:00, the children went into bedroom 2, where they sat on the beds and talked, wrestled, and fought.

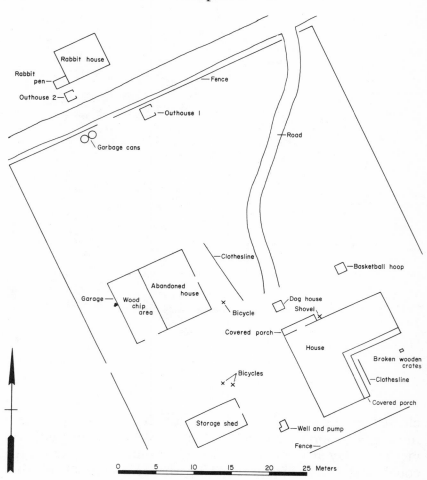

Figure 65. The García residence.

María started cooking dinner in the kitchen about 4:30 P.M. (fig. 66). Anita made a tossed salad at the living room/kitchen table. Dinner, which consisted of hamburger meat, beans and tripe, store-bought bread, and salad, was eaten at the table at about 5:30. Afterward, Melinda cleared the table and put the leftover food in the refrigerator or kitchen cabinet and the dirty dishes in the pot with the dishes from previous meals.

Figure 66. The wood-burning stove located in the García kitchen.

She washed them in the pot on the kitchen stove. María swept the kitchen floor at about 6:50 and then mopped the living room/kitchen floor. A friend of José's came over at 7:00, and the two stood talking next to the kitchen dresser. An hour later, all the boys went outside and played. Meanwhile, Melinda washed her hair in a basin placed on a chair between the heater and closet in the living room/kitchen. María and Martha ate an orange at the table. Anita's girlfriend stopped by about that time, and they talked for approximately 15 minutes near the dresser in the kitchen (fig. 67) before going outside. Anita returned a few minutes later and played cards with Melinda at the table. Martha, followed by María, washed her hair at the same location as Melinda had.

Anita made a sandwich at 7:25 and ate it at the table where Melinda brushed, blow dried, and curled her hair. At 8:10 Melinda again played cards with Anita, who had been playing by herself while Rosa watched. Martha colored in her coloring book for a brief moment and then watched Anita and Melinda

Figure 67. Looking into the García kitchen from the living room/ kitchen. The table is on the extreme right, the door to bedroom 2 behind it, and the television on the left.

play cards. Juan, still sitting on the couch, sewed together the end of a pillow case that he had stuffed with wool. The boys came in about 8:30, and they and Melinda ate a piece of store-bought cake at the table. María again swept the kitchen and bedroom floors. José and Anita then played cards at the table while the other children watched. Melinda later went into bedroom 1, where, seated on the double bed, she mended a blouse. Afterward, she rejoined the others watching José and Anita play cards. Juan went to bed first about 9:30, followed by Melinda, Martha, María, the boys, and last by Anita, who finally went to bed around midnight. Juan, María, and Martha slept on the double bed and José on the single bed in bedroom 1. The other children slept in bedroom 2. Juan woke up at 6:00 the next morning and added wood to the wood heaters in the living room/kitchen and bedroom 2. Another day had arrived.

Discussion

The television set was broken when I first arrived at the García household, but José managed to repair it. Because of their remote location and the fact that the set was not hooked up to a cable, the television received only an educational channel that came in poorly at best. Even so, once the set was functional, television viewing became the dominant evening activity. At that point, the types of activities and the locations at which they were performed became noticeably less varied.

Although most food consumption occurred at the living room/kitchen table, it occasionally also took place on the couch (mostly snacks) and once in bedroom 2 (ice-cream cones eaten by the children). The seating arrangement at the table during breakfast remained consistent—Juan sat on the west end of the table near the kitchen and María on the south side. No pattern was detected at dinner, with the exception that Juan always sat on the west end of the table.

Their sleeping arrangements were interesting in that all eight family members slept in two of the four bedrooms, leaving the other two unoccupied, even though both rooms contained beds. According to María, the reason that bedrooms 3 and 4 were not used was economic—they were too difficult and expensive to heat. However, they probably would have been no more difficult to heat than bedroom 1 and, as is often the case, they would have experienced financial hardship only in relation to their priorities since they had sufficient money to purchase such items as candy, soda pop, a hair dryer, and the like. The sleeping arrangement was shifted to accommodate me, so that Melinda and I slept on the double bed in bedroom 2, while Martha and María slept with Félix in bedroom 1. Juan slept on the couch in the living room/kitchen my first night there, but because he had been uncomfortable, he moved into bedroom 4 the second night.

I was unable to note any seasonal changes since I lived with the Garcías only during the winter (February). However, the children spent more time outdoors than did the Euroamericans, but less than the Navajos. They may have spent more time outside than usual because their television set was broken for most of my stay with them. The time spent inside markedly increased once it had been fixed.

The effects of individual moods on the use and location of activity areas was clearly evident from the observation of this family. Constant bickering among the children often resulted in one child going into a bedroom to sulk. Martha once refused to eat dinner, and stood by the heater in the living room/ kitchen while the rest of the family ate at the table.

The outhouses and wood-chopping area in the garage west of the house were monofunctional areas, as was the kitchen, which, with the exception of the southwestern quadrant, was used for preparing food. There were no sex-specific activity areas.

I did not observe the household on a weekend. However, both parents were home during the week since neither worked. In addition, several children usually stayed home from school. Consequently, the discrepancy between weekends and week-days probably was not as great as among the other households observed.

I asked Anita, Melinda, and Félix to draw the location of rooms in their house. Their interesting maps (figs. 68, 69, and 70) were drawn from a different perspective than the other informants' in that they showed the house in profile. Although, according to one clinical psychologist (Sedlacek 1979: personal communication), this is not an unusual response, it did differ from those elicited from the Navajos and Euroamericans who had been given the same instructions. The Spanish-American children's drawings did, however, conform basically to the house exterior (see fig. 15), albeit out of proportion. All three children, including Anita, who had once told me that it was her room, neglected to draw bedroom 3. This might be a result of the fact that it was used only for storage and the children were seldom in there; consequently the room was relatively unimportant and not included in the maps drawn from memory. Bedroom 4 may have been included on their maps because Juan was sleeping there during my visit; thus it was visibly in use during the time they were drawing.

Comparisons

I visited the house of María's brother (Virgil Sánchez) for approximately two hours. Everyone sat and talked in the living room/bedroom of the two-room house (fig. 71). Food was pre-

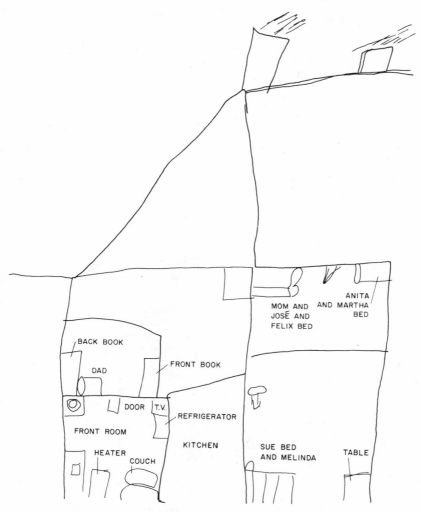

Figure 68. The García house drawn from memory by Melinda García. The name "Sue" in the bedroom on the right refers to the author.

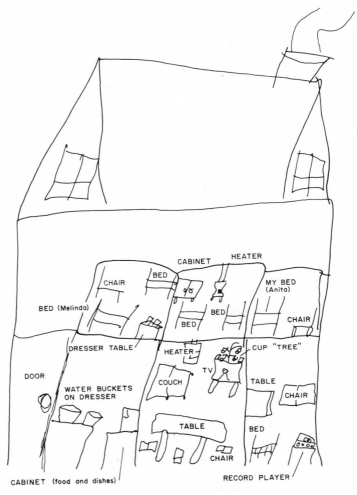

Figure 69. The García house drawn from memory by Anita García.

pared in the kitchen, although the refrigerator was located in the living room. Since my stay was so short, I was able to observe little beyond the fact that no part of the living room/bedroom seemed to be monofunctional or sex specific—both sexes ate snacks, drank wine, and talked there. Virgil Sánchez apparently slept in the room on the only bed in the house.

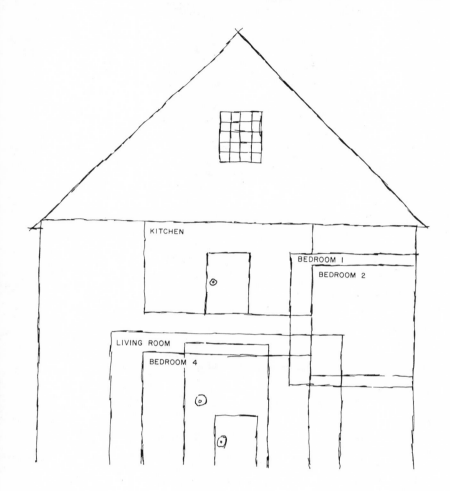

Figure 70. The García house drawn from memory by Félix García.

The García and Martínez households were more similar to one another in their use of space than to either the Euroamerican or the Navajo households. The Spanish-American families both had few monofunctional activity areas—more than the Navajos but fewer than the Euroamericans—and no sex-specific activity areas. The two households had furnished bed-

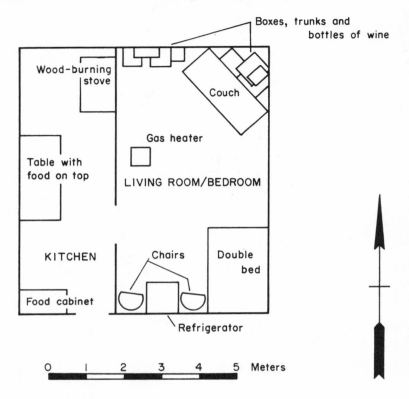

Figure 71. The Sánchez house.

rooms that were usually not used except for storage; instead, everyone slept in two bedrooms. An analysis of the similarities of the spatial patterning between the Spanish-American families is presented in Chapter 6 where such patterning is contrasted with that of the Euroamericans and the Navajos.

Summary

My ethnographic research indicates that the assumptions many archaeologists employ concerning the use of activity areas are based on their own culture's spatial patterning. Such assumptions reflect a suble ethnocentric bias in that they presume that all people use space in the same way—the way the Euroamerican anthropologist uses it. Unlike the Euroamericans, Navajos do not have sex-specific or monofunctional activity areas, the only exception being within the hogan, which is differentially used by the traditional Navajos on the basis of sex. In general, males tend to stay in the southern half of the dwelling and women in the northern half, although exceptions do occur, especially among the women and younger children. The most dramatic example of this sexual division of the hogan that I observed was in the behavior of the male head of the traditional household, who almost never ventured beyond his southeastern area. He not only slept and ate there, but also manufactured and repaired objects at his southeast sheepskin bed.

The location of activity areas within the hogan as I observed them is also quite rigid. Food preparation always occurred in the north, and usually specifically in the northeastern quadrant of the hogan. Food consumption took place in the southwestern quadrant. Activity areas, however, were multipurpose.

In contrast, both sexes in the traditional family performed activities at the same locus either outside the hogan or inside the ramada; in addition, activity areas were not monofunctional. Most activities that occurred outside were performed at a storage area, and activities such as scraping rawhide strips and weaving blankets were performed by different sexes at the same area. Butchering occurred next to the ramada at the traditional camp, but, depending on the weather, the viscera were cleaned either inside the ramada or outside at the butchering area.

The other, less traditional Navajo families used space in the same way, but with one exception—none of the activity areas, including those inside the hogan, were either sex specific or monofunctional. (A possible explanation for this discrepancy between the use of the hogan by traditional and semitraditional families is presented in Chapter 6.) The Navajos, with only this exception, did not have sex-specific or monofunctional activity areas. This was true of all nine families observed, who ranged from traditional to semi-nontraditional. In other words, despite the Euroamerican manufactured furnishings and rectangular tract multibedroom houses, the use of space by semitraditional and semi-nontraditional Navajos was more like that of traditional Navajos than like that of Euroamericans.

In an attempt to maintain consistency, I observed Spanish-American and Euroamerican families living in similar rectangular houses with three bedrooms, Euroamerican manufactured furniture, and a television set located in the living room. One Navajo family also occupied a similar structure. Only one Spanish-American family deviated from this pattern—the García house contained four bedrooms.

Although differences did exist, the Spanish-American use of space was more similar to the Euroamerican than to the Navajo usage. This was especially evident in the number of monofunctional activity areas: Spanish-Americans had more such loci than the Navajos, but fewer than the Euroamericans. The exception was that the Spanish-Americans did not have sex-specific activity areas.

It was interesting that the Euroamericans consistently had more sex-specific and monofunctional activity areas than did the Spanish-Americans or Navajos. This was true regardless of socioeconomic class, residence location (rural versus urban), or season of observation. The use of sex-specific and monofunctional activity areas was most pronounced among the urban Euroamericans. Most food consumption, for example, occurred at the kitchen or dinette table. This area, used only for eating, is a good example of a monofunctional activity area. The dining room, too, was monofunctional; only eating took place there. There were many other such areas at the urban Johnson house. Sex-specific activity areas were also numerous in the urban Euroamerican house. The kitchen, for example, was sex specific as well as monofunctional—it was primarily used by females to prepare food. The den was used by males; the children had separate bedrooms according to sex. Even the bathrooms were sex specific in the morning, although not during the rest of the day.

Television played a major role in the activities performed, not only at the urban Euroamerican household, but at every house that had electricity—including Spanish-American and Navajo homes. The influence of television affected the location and diversity of the activities performed, but not the use of activity areas. Navajo and Spanish-American families with television used space similarly to those in their group who did not have a television set.

4

Archaeological Site Descriptions

> It is assumed that some behavioral elements of sociocultural systems have material correlates; if they are incorporated in the archaeological record, such residues may be used to develop inferences about the behaviors with which they were associated. (Kramer 1979:1)

I investigated five archaeological sites in an attempt to locate activity areas and to test the assumptions being evaluated. In this chapter I describe the sites and the artifacts, bones, and botanical remains recovered from them. I shall analyze the activity areas in chapter 5.

The historic Navajo sites I excavated are located southwest of Farmington, New Mexico, on Block II of the Navajo Indian Irrigation Project land (fig. 72). The elevation of the sites varies from 1,702 to 1,768 meters above sea level. A mosaic of hummocks, deflated areas, sand dunes, and patches of flat terrain characterizes the physiography of the sites, some of which are located on or surrounded by cliffs and all of which have been affected by small arroyos, road disturbances, or both. The closest major water system to the sites is the San Juan River. Grasses and threadleaf snakeweed (*Gutierrezia microcephala*) are the dominant vegetation; other flora noted include Mormon tea (*Ephedra viridis*), rabbit brush (*Chrysothamnus nauseosus*), narrowleaf yucca (*Yucca angustissima*), and tumbleweed (*Salsola kali*).

The sites consist of hogans with associated features, among them wood-chip areas, ash areas, corrals, and masonry ovens. Hogan architecture varies from cribbed-log to many-legged to stone-wall. The dates of the sites, according to artifact analysis (Kent 1980a, 1980b, 1980c, 1980d, 1980e), range from A.D. 1890 to 1970.

The excavation strategy had to be modified at some sites.

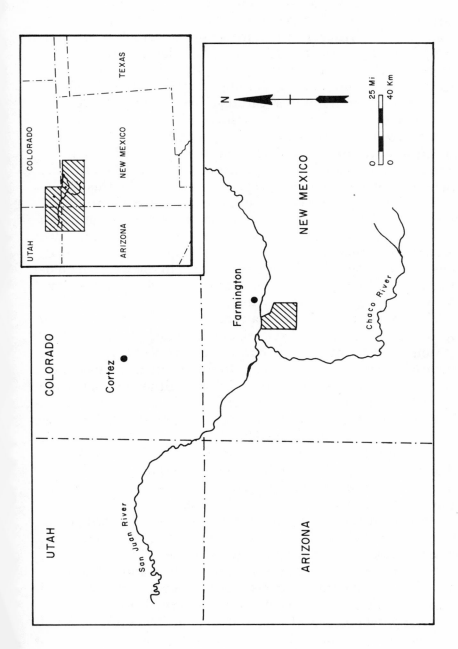

Figure 72. Locations of the archaeological sites investigated.

For example, I wanted to obtain exact proveniences for all artifacts and faunal remains located in a feature; but time constraints, a critical factor in most contract archaeology projects, did not permit this. At some of the largest sites, and in those cases where recording of exact provenience was not possible, objects were noted according to their vertical level and to the feature or (if not in a feature) to the 20-by-20-meter grid square with which they were associated.

All sites were first surveyed, boundaries were defined, artifacts and features flagged, and datum established (see fig. 3). Features and isolated surface artifacts were plotted on the site map by a plane table and alidade. Unfortunately, this procedure could not be used at two sites because of time limitations. Instead, isolated surface artifact locations were established from the closest feature at Site 2-C6-18 and were recorded according to their 20 by 20 meter grid square at Site 2-1-03. Only artifacts and faunal remains located in the western quarter of Site 2-1-03 were mapped with the alidade, and this quarter was used as a control for the rest of the site.

The surface and subsurface artifacts and faunal remains were recorded, described, and selectively collected. Because of the extremely large number of bulky artifacts at most sites (565 tin cans alone at Site 2-1-03!), duplicate artifacts and undiagnostic fragments were not collected, although they were recorded and described in the field.

There was time to excavate only within the defined features. All features were investigated by at least one 1-×-1-meter test pit, and in some cases as many as five or more test pits were excavated, depending on what was uncovered. Every hogan was completely excavated with the exception of three that were only tested at Site 2-54-28, and one at Site 2-1-03.

Horizontal and vertical proveniences of artifacts and faunal remains located on the surface and on the subsurface floor(s) of every hogan were obtained at each site. Proveniences recorded at the other features at Sites 2-54-28 and 2-1-03 consisted of noting the arbitrary vertical level and horizontal quadrant in which an object was found. Exact horizontal and vertical proveniences were recorded for artifacts from a small sample of every major type of feature (e.g., ash area, corral, etc.) from both sites. This was done in order to compare the data with those obtained from features where exact provenience was not measured. However, there was not enough time allocated for the investigation of Site 2-C6-18 to obtain exact provenience for any artifacts or bones, except those uncovered on the floor of its sweat house and only hogan. At Site 2-1-01, no features were associated with the one hogan that constituted the site.

Excavation was accomplished by troweling and skim shoveling. All hogan floors were troweled. Backdirt was screened when time permitted and/or when conditions necessitated the process.

Individual Site Descriptions

Although the sites were all historic Navajo occupations located in Block II, much variation existed in the hogan types and in the numbers and kinds of associated features (table 4). These differences may, in part, reflect the date of occupation, length of habitation, and/or individual preference. Below is a summary of the interpretation of the five sites; for a more complete description of each see Kent 1980a–e.

SITE 2-1-01

Site 2-1-01 consisted of a twentieth-century Navajo hogan that had been briefly occupied and burned (fig. 73). According to a local informant, it may have been a base camp prior to abandonment. Because of the lack of diagnostic artifacts and datable materials, it is not possible to postulate a more specific date than the twentieth century. The paucity of surface artifacts and the absence of corrals, wood-chip, and ash areas indicate a short site occupation. The hogan's floor was difficult to locate. Even though no other data were recovered to confirm this idea, I would venture to guess that the state of the floor resulted from a short occupation during which too few people were present to pack the soil down.

Although the possibility of an accidental fire cannot be overlooked, the deliberate burning of a hogan in which a death has occurred is a well-known Navajo practice, and there were

Table 4. Features located at five Navajo sites

Site Number	Postulated Date of Occupation	Features Present
2-1-01	20th century	1 burned many-legged hogan
2-1-03	A.D. 1917–55	4 stone-wall hogans 9 ash areas 7 wood-chip areas 4 corrals 1 masonry oven 4 artifact clusters
2-54-28	A.D. 1890–1930	4 stone-wall hogans 6 ash areas 4 wood-chip areas 1 masonry oven 2 rock and rock/log concentrations
2-C6-14	A.D. 1950–70	1 cribbed-log hogan 1 sweat house 1 isolated hearth 1 artifact cluster
2-C6-18	A.D. 1907–20	1 burned stone-wall hogan 2 ash areas 2 wood-chip areas over old corrals; one with adjacent hearth 2 masonry ovens 1 rock alignment

indications that this had, in fact, happened. For example, the normal abandonment processes, wherein the portable, still-functional objects are removed from a dwelling, apparently did not occur in the hogan. Using ethnographic analogy, I suggest that the artifacts located on the floor (teapot, coffee cup, spoon, bowl, saucer, plate, and lard bucket) represent the assemblage that would have been in the same location over a hearth during habitation. The charred remains of the dwelling, the artifact assemblage, and the spatial distribution of objects on the floor all indicate that a death had occurred at the site and that the hogan was subsequently burned.

The presence of Navajo Painted sherds near the hogan's entrance may lend support to the above hypothesis, for the majority of Navajo Painted pots were used in ceremonial contexts (Brugge 1963). The Navajo Painted vessel could have

SITE DATUM 23 m

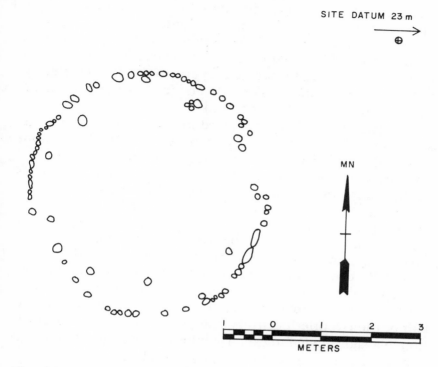

Figure 73. Map of Site 2-1-01.

been connected, then, with an unsuccessful curing ceremony. It has also been reported in the literature that one or more pots were customarily broken in a hogan where a death had occurred (Tschopik 1941; Leighton and Kluckhohn 1948). The hogan at Site 2-1-01 apparently had been abandoned and deliberately set on fire because a death had occurred in it. This implies that the occupants still adhered to traditional Navajo religious tenets. The distribution of charcoal in the test pits excavated outside the hogan suggests that the wind direction at the time of the fire was from the southwest, as it is today.

SITE 2-1-03

Site 2-1-03 was an extremely large, temporally multicomponent Navajo habitation with 30 separate features, including

4 stone-wall hogans with associated wood-chip and ash areas and 4 corrals (fig. 74). Over 2,310 recorded artifacts, 313 identifiable faunal remains, and numerous botanical remains were scattered over 128,800 square meters. The remains of material culture ranged from teapots to car parts to perfume-bottle fragments. Tin cans and glass bottle and jar fragments were the most common artifacts recovered.

The date of the site, as reflected in the artifact assemblage, was circa A.D. 1917 to 1955. Three to four separate occupations occurred, most of which, if not all, were during the fall and possibly winter seasons. This conclusion is based on analysis of the faunal and botanical remains and the presence of coal at the site. It is conceivable that two of the dwellings were occupied contemporaneously. The datable artifacts suggest that there was a five-year hiatus between the abandonment of the first hogan and the beginning of the second occupation (Kent 1980b). We can infer that the inhabitants of the various hogans were probably related and from the same extended family, since it has been reported in the literature that during the first half of the twentieth century, the proposed period of occupation, Navajos tended to exercise inherited use-ownership land rights, wherein a particular family would use a specific area generation after generation (Kluckhohn and Leighton 1962:106; Downs 1972:43–44).

The number and diversity of Euroamerican goods present might indicate the relative economic status of the site's households because it implies an ability to purchase the objects. The items included car parts, wood-burning stove(s), Euroamerican manufactured toys, perfume bottles, and other luxury goods, many of which suggest that at least some of the site's occupants were relatively wealthy according to Euroamerican standards. However, it must be kept in mind that values and priorities vary among cultures, especially concerning the use of money. Among the Navajos, wealth is traditionally defined by the size of one's sheep herd and by the number of horses and pieces of jewelry owned. That 92.83 percent of the faunal remains identified were those of sheep may suggest wealth according to these traditional Navajo standards—that is, if such a proportion indicates that their herd was large enough to make it unnecessary for them to purchase meat. However,

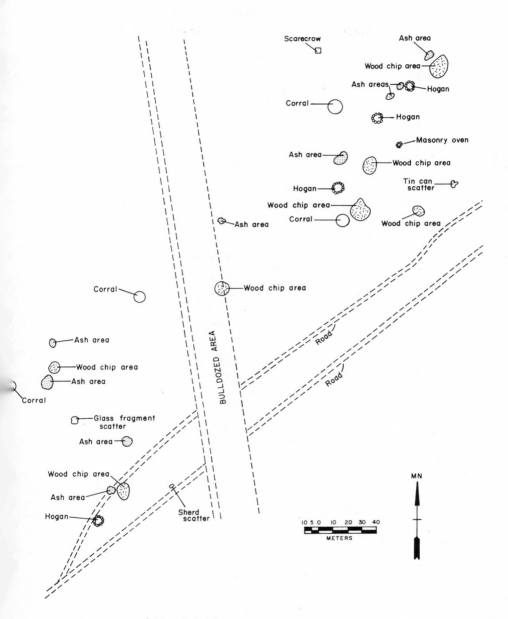

Figure 74. Map of Site 2-1-03.

the fact that most Navajos prefer mutton to beef must be taken into account; given the choice between purchasing beef and mutton, they will usually choose mutton.

It is difficult to determine the occupants' degree of departure from traditional culture solely from the material culture; inferences based upon a fragmentary archaeological assemblage do not always provide an accurate picture of the intangible parts of the inhabitants' lives. The proportion of Euroamerican products to aboriginally manufactured ones might reflect affluence or proximity to a store, rather than an intentional departure from traditional culture. One might expect the presence of a large number of Euroamerican-produced goods because of the relatively recent date of the site. The particular types of Euroamerican goods recovered are of interest, however, for they indicate that at least some of the occupants may have been semitraditional rather than traditional (Kent in press). For example, the ash area contained a ballpoint pen, the presence of which could imply that someone at the site was literate, which might indicate nontraditional schooling—although other explanations are also possible. In addition, a folding chair and bed springs were recorded at the site, which could suggest some culture change, since most traditional families even today sit and sleep directly on the floor. The eight different types of medicinal containers identified indicate that nontraditional Euroamerican medicine was at least occasionally used (Kent 1980b). Nevertheless, medicine is an area where many traditional Navajos are pragmatic and willing to try anything that might work, which often results in the use of a combination of aboriginal and Euroamerican remedies. The presence of one or more wood-burning stoves at the site (rather than the split-oil-drum stove) and two perfume bottles indicates either departure from traditional culture or affluence (or both). The flashlight parts and batteries found could also be an indication either of departure from traditional culture or of wealth; they would have been more expensive to operate than the more traditional kerosene lanterns that were also found. The traditional family I stayed with at Navajo Mountain did not use flashlights or even want them, although they had the money to purchase them. The large number of storebought toys (a tricycle, toy airplane, marbles, and others) might further suggest either culture change or affluence. The presence of two sardine cans at the site may reflect the rejection of some aboriginal customs. The consumption of sardines would have been a violation of the traditional Navajo taboo against eating fish (Kluckhohn and Leighton 1962:201). The presence of car parts and oil cans suggests ownership of an automobile, which probably enhanced the mobility of the occupants and allowed access to nearby Euroamerican centers such as Farmington, New Mexico (approximately twenty miles away), and to people with different customs and ways of thinking.

Religion is also difficult to assess solely from the archaeological assemblage. That a sandstone rock with an incised cross was used to form the wall of a masonry oven may connote some of the occupants' disrespect or disregard for a symbol of Christianity. However, it is also conceivable that the cross was not associated with Christianity, or that the cross was deliberately used to bring good luck. Although it is difficult to evaluate the significance of the cross, its presence, coupled with the following information, may suggest that some of the inhabitants no longer adhered to their traditional religion. The location of pottery in ash areas could also indicate a possible departure from traditional belief systems. According to Brugge, a trait associated with the Blessingway was "the practice of disposing of broken pottery vessels under a bush or ledge away from the dwelling rather than in the ash heap" (Brugge 1963:220). At Site 2-1-03, except for the fragments from one Navajo Painted vessel, more sherds were recovered in ash areas than in any other types of features or as isolated artifacts.

Few of the artifacts found reflected traditional Navajo culture. There was some evidence of jewelry manufacture in the form of turquoise, glass beads, and the like. Today, however, jewelry is often made in the absence of any other marketable skills or available jobs, and is thus one of the few possible sources of income, meager as that usually is, for an individual or family (as was the case with Elsie and Teddy Big Mountain; see chapters 2 and 3).

Taken individually, none of the above artifacts denotes change from traditional Navajo customs and belief systems; together, however, they suggest that Site 2-1-03 was occupied by at least

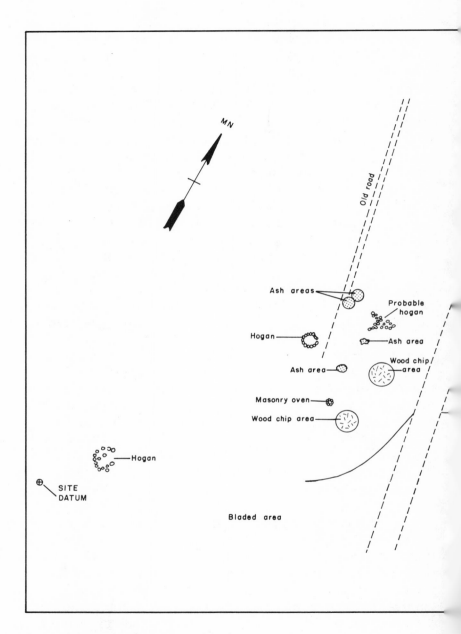

Figure 75. Map of Site 2-54-28.

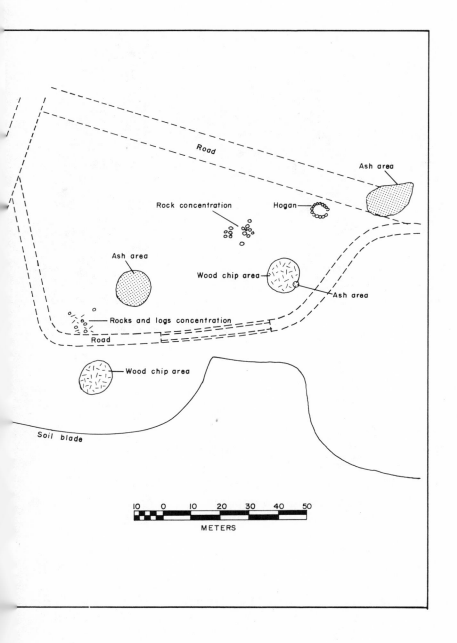

Road

Ash area

Rock concentration

Hogan

Ash area

Wood chip area

Ash area

Rocks and logs concentration

Road

Wood chip area

Soil blade

```
10    0    10   20   30   40   50
                METERS
```

Figure 76. Ash area with coal located at Site 2-54-28.

one, if not more, semitraditional households (see Kent in press for a more complete discussion).

SITE 2-54-28

Site 2-54-28 was a multicomponent, four-stone-wall-hogan Navajo camp that had been occupied between circa A.D. 1890 and 1930. Ash and wood-chip areas and a masonry oven were near the hogans (fig. 75). The site contained some of the earliest datable artifacts found at Block II Navajo sites, among them a piece of black glass, Arbuckle Brothers coffee can lids, and a 1927 New Mexico license plate (Kent 1980c). Various other objects found included an imported porcelain doll, tin cans, probable blue-jeans buttons, and glass bottle and jar fragments. Both cow and sheep bones were recovered from the site.

The presence of coal at an ash area could suggest that the site had been used during the winter season (fig. 76). Because

Figure 77. Partially standing stone wall hogan located at Site 2-54-28.

of the traditional use-area inheritance rights recognized by most Navajos (Kluckhohn and Leighton 1962:106; Downs 1972:43–44), it is likely that the hogans (fig. 77) were occupied by related families who were probably from the same extended family. It was extremely unusual that no associated corrals were found on such a large site, but it is conceivable that they were originally located in what are now plowed agricultural fields to the south of the site. Approximately 2.5–3 meters of barbed wire was found. This isolated artifact could have been part of a corral fence, but there was no dung associated with it.

The inhabitants' economic status, based on Euroamerican standards of wealth, was apparently high compared to that of other Navajos of the same time period. Despite the fact that this was a relatively early site, artifacts, such as car parts, stove pieces, and meat tins, were present; these items, with the cow bones that were also found, might suggest that one if not more of the households was semitraditional.

Unfortunately, there were not enough appropriate data at the site to permit inferences about the religion of the occupants. Nor were enough data recovered to ascertain whether or not the occupants had had large herds of horses and sheep—the traditional Navajo index of wealth. The presence of cow bones could imply either that their herd was small enough that the inhabitants' protein intake had to be supplemented with beef or that the occupants were relatively affluent (if it denotes that they were able to afford the meat). The buying of beef could also have been the result of other factors, such as a temporary ceremonial prohibition against slaughtering animals from their herd, which would have necessitated the occasional purchase of meat.

Site 2-C6-14

Site 2-C6-14 was a briefly occupied single-component Navajo habitation (fig. 78). The only structures at the site were a cribbed-log hogan and, in a secluded spot nearby, a partially standing sweat house (fig. 79). They are presumed to have been used contemporaneously by either a nuclear or an extended family, although no data were recovered to confirm this. No corrals, ash areas, or wood-chip areas were found (see table 4). The artifacts, which included a plastic Avon shampoo container, oil cans, a pickle jar, a washtub, and a plastic baby doll, suggest an A.D. 1960s occupation (Kent 1980g).

The sweat house was anomalous in one respect: the interior fire-reddened rock pile was situated near the southern wall rather than the more usual northern wall, traditionally chosen in order to obstruct the movement of colds and coughs, which were thought to originate in the north (Franciscan Fathers 1910:341). The sweat house was actually of a traditional construction in all but this one feature, which could be accounted for either by nonbelief in or by ignorance of the necessity of a northern positioning of the rocks. Brugge (1956) noted that the orientation and placement of rocks were reversed in sweat houses used for war and hunting parties, but he also wrote that the traditional orientation was not adhered to in some nonconventional Navajo sweat houses.

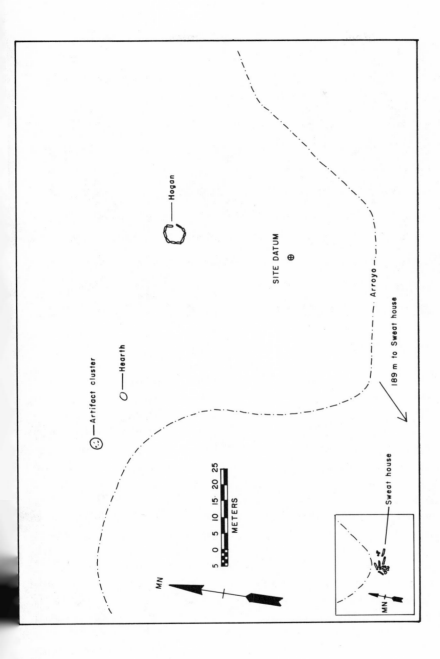

Figure 78. Map of Site 2-C6-14.

Figure 79. A partially standing sweat house at Site 2-C6-14.

It is interesting that no corrals were found; they may have been located on top of the mesa in what are now plowed agricultural fields. Nor were any wood-chip or ash areas located at the site. Only two features were found in addition to the hogan and sweat house, and they were difficult to interpret. One was an isolated cluster of objects that was in the process of washing down one of the lower drainages from the surrounding sandstone cliffs. Objects were not found on the mesa immediately above the drainage, but excavation near the top of the drainage revealed a few small chunks and flakes of charcoal. The charcoal and other objects (cloth fragment, Navajo-ware sherd, tin can, animal bones, and lithic flakes) may have been associated with a nearby hearth (located approximately fourteen meters to the east). The relationship, if any, between the two features remains unknown. The hearth was surrounded on three sides by a natural outcrop of fire-reddened sandstone. Its artifact inventory was similar to that found at the artifact cluster, with the addition of two tin-can rattles and porcelain and glass fragments. The only deer bone recovered from the site (and the only one from any of the

Block II sites investigated) was excavated in a test pit just west of the hearth. The visible butchering marks indicated that the bone's meat had been used for food. The radius-ulna fragment might have been a gift from a relative and not necessarily procured near the site or even by the occupants. The affiliation between the hearth and the hogan is unclear. Navajos often eat and/or cook outside during the hot weather, and this could explain the presence of the hearth. However, it is equally possible that the feature represented a temporary campsite used either before or after the rest of the site had been occupied.

Though the presence of a sweat house may imply that the inhabitants were traditional, this is by no means certain; there were not enough data at the site from which to draw any firm conclusions. It also was not possible to ascertain the economic status or religious affiliation of the occupants.

SITE 2-C6-18

Site 2-C6-18 was a single component Navajo camp consisting of a burned stone-wall hogan and associated features, such as wood-chip and ash areas and masonry ovens (fig. 80). Sheep dung found on the surface of and below the two wood-chip areas probably indicates that both had been the sites of corrals prior to their use as wood-chopping areas (fig. 81). Frequently, only fecal material marks the location of abandoned corrals since fence posts are usually dug up to be used elsewhere and postmolds are not preserved in the sandy soil. Artifacts found included tin cans, Mentholatum jar fragments, enamelware bowls, tin-can rattles, and a spoon.

The hogan was probably occupied during the fall between A.D. 1907 and 1920 by a nuclear or limited extended family (Kent 1980e). According to a local informant, the hogan had been deliberately burned as a result of a death that occurred in the dwelling. If this was the case, it is interesting that excavation revealed that virtually everything had been removed from the hogan, presumably prior to the fire, for such removal would have been contrary to traditional Navajo religious practices. Typically, a hogan is abandoned and burned after a death occurs in it with nothing removed from the dwelling except when, in some instances, the corpse is taken out

Figure 80. The artifacts located on the floor of the burned stone wall hogan at Site 2-C6-18.

for burial. If the fire was accidental, however, objects could have been removed from the hogan without infringing upon any religious tenets. An alternative possibility is that the occupants, cognizant of the impending death, removed most of their possessions while they were still able to do so without violating any religious dogma. The presence (in a wood-chip area) of a piece of glass flaked in the shape of a cross could suggest that the inhabitants (or one of them) had become at least nominal Christians, whose new beliefs would have been in conflict with traditional ones. Such a possibility is pure conjecture. It is also possible that the worked glass fragment simply represented someone's recreational activities.

The relatively large percentage of cow bones identified (20 percent of the faunal assemblage) suggests that beef was consumed more frequently at Site 2-C6-18 than at the other sites investigated. The fact that only five different cow skeletal parts were present could be explained in various ways: (1) the cow may have been slaughtered at the site, and most of its meat and bones given to relatives, (2) the beef may have been

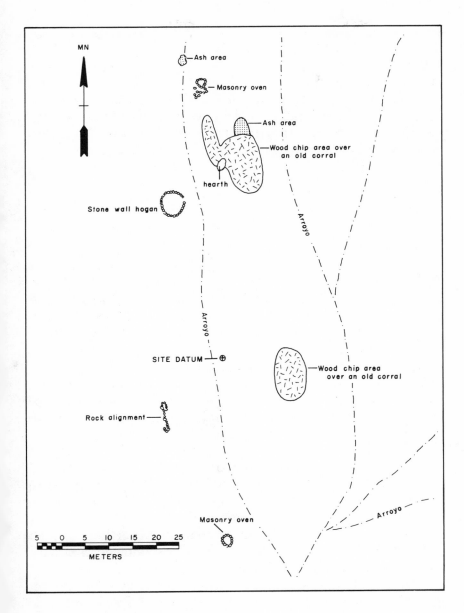

Figure 81. Map of Site 2-C6-18.

given to the occupants by relatives or purchased at a trading
post or store, or (3) the inhabitants could have abandoned the
site shortly after butchering the animal, taking the majority
of the meat (and bones) with them.

Unfortunately, there were not enough of the appropriate
kinds of data at the site to allow me to assess the occupants'
degree of departure, if any, from traditional culture. There also
was not sufficient information found for me to determine the
financial status of the inhabitants.

Material Culture, Faunal Remains, and Botanical Remains

THE ARTIFACT ASSEMBLAGE

The artifact inventory from the sites consisted of a diverse
assortment of objects. Euroamerican-produced goods far out-
numbered aboriginal ones. In fact, no native manufactured
objects were found at Site 2-C6-18, although a few objects had
apparently been modified for indigenous purposes (e.g., tin-
can rattles). The large diversity of the historic artifacts was
surpassed only by their number. A total of 2,249 were recorded
at Site 2-1-03 alone and there simply was not enough time to
note the others located at the site.

Euroamerican Manufactured Artifacts

The Euroamerican manufactured artifacts were assigned to
functional categories since one of the assumptions being evaluated in this study is concerned with the number of monofunctional activities performed at an area. Nevertheless, such
a classification contains inherent problems when dealing with
the often fragmentary nature of an archaeological assemblage,
and these difficulties are magnified with the attempt to categorize artifacts used by a different culture. The recycling and/
or reuse of artifacts is a common practice among most groups,
but usually is extremely difficult to detect in an archaeological
context (Schiffer 1976). However, occasionally artifacts have
been sufficiently modified so as to make it possible to discern
their second function—examples are tin-can rattles, an ena-

melware plate with a bullet hole, and modified files and ax-heads. In spite of the possibility for error in assigning artifacts to functional categories, such a classification is, nevertheless, a useful device in organizing the historic data from the sites. It is entirely possible that the users of the objects would have placed the artifacts in different categories from those I selected. My categorization is only a suggestion based on a review of the literature and on ethnographic and archaeological fieldwork.

Subsistence. Subsistence was one of the largest categories of the functional classification (table 5). It included juice, coffee, syrup, chili, evaporated milk, spice, meat, and possible vegetable and/or fruit tin cans. Some of the contents from the baking powder and lard cans probably had been used in the ubiquitous fry bread or the Navajo-style tortilla (*nánees-kaadí*)—one of which is usually an integral part of every meal. Alcoholic beverage containers, especially wine bottles, were common at Site 2-1-03 but were absent at the other sites. Soda-pop bottles were found at all sites except 2-1-01.

Artifacts used in food preparation and/or consumption included metal dippers or ladles, spoons, cast-iron-stove parts, milk glass, spoons, enamelware pots, pans, cups, teapots, and coffee pots. Also present were stoneware, porcelain, and iron-stone plates, cups, and saucers.

Personal Adornment and Clothing. The more spectacular kinds of artifacts in this category included an assortment of jewelry from Site 2-1-03, which ranged from a turquoise pendant or earring to brown plastic bracelets to numerous glass, plastic, and turquoise beads. A shampoo container, combs, a mirror fragment, and perfume bottles were the only objects found that may have been used for personal hygiene.

Evidence of clothing was scarce and was extrapolated from the zippers, small scraps of cloth, and plastic and mother-of-pearl buttons recovered. Most of the metal snaps, rivets, and metal buttons collected were probably from blue jeans. Soles, heels, nails, eyelets, and other shoe and boot parts constituted the most frequent type of artifacts ascribed to the personal adornment and clothing category. Possible lenses from sun-glasses were recovered at two sites (2-1-03 and 2-54-28).

Toys. Euroamerican manufactured toys were identified at

Table 5. Distribution of artifacts by individual site feature type and functional category

| | Artifact Functional Categories | | | | | | |
Site Feature Type	Subsistence	Personal Adornment and Clothing	Toys	Medicinal Supplies	Transportation	Animal Husbandry	Miscellaneous
Site 2-1-01							
Isolate	2	— —	— —	— —	— —	— —	2
Hogan	9	— —	— —	— —	— —	— —	12
Site 2-1-03							
Isolate	273	79	5	4	14	8	88
Hogan	22	30	1	4	2	— —	44
Ash area	82	64	9	16	7	1	103
Wood-chip area	16	8	4	5	1	— —	7
Corral	21	4	— —	— —	1	2	15
Other	51	— —	1	— —	— —	1	— —
Site 2-54-28							
Isolate	29	11	3	9	1	— —	17
Hogan	20	5	1	2	— —	— —	18
Ash area	6	7	4	4	— —	— —	5
Wood-chip area	1	10	1	— —	— —	— —	6
Other	2	— —	2	1	— —	— —	7
Site 2-C6-14							
Isolate	17	1	1	— —	6	2	4
Hogan	— —	— —	— —	— —	1	— —	2
Other	5	2	— —	— —	— —	1	1
Site 2-C6-18							
Isolate	15	2	— —	3	2	1	10
Hogan	3	1	— —	— —	1	— —	1
Ash area	4	2	— —	1	2	— —	5
Wood-chip area	5	— —	— —	— —	— —	— —	4
Other	— —	— —	— —	— —	— —	— —	3

Sites 2-C6-14, 2-54-28, and 2-1-03. Dolls (one porcelain and the other plastic) were found at the former two sites, and a wide variety of toys were located at the latter. These included a toy airplane, truck, station wagon, pistol, glass marbles, and tricycle fragments.

Medicinal Supplies. Mentholatum jar fragments were the most frequent artifacts assigned to this category. Other medicine that had been used included Moroline, Alka-Seltzer, and Sloan's Liniment. Also present were aspirin containers, Vick's

VapoRub jars, and a nose- or eye-drop bottle complete with lid and eyedropper.

Transportation. Equestrian equipment was located at all sites except 2-1-01. It included harness buckles and other fragments, cinch buckles, horseshoes, a stirrup, snaffle and other bits, and bridle fragments. The presence of automobiles was documented by car fragments, such as a tailpipe, a car or truck front fender, a 1927 New Mexico license plate (fig. 82), and a cable connector. A gallon gas can and numerous oil cans might also indicate the use of a car at the sites, although it is conceivable that they could have been used for purposes other than to service an automobile.

Animal Husbandry. Most of the artifacts assigned to this category were tin-can rattles or noisemakers with wire handles and, occasionally, with rocks inside. They are commonly used in herding. Sheep shears were located at Site 2-1-03 (fig. 83). Cans that had contained black paint were recovered from Sites 2-1-03 and 2-C6-14. Their contents could have been used to brand the herd, a relatively common practice on some parts of the reservation.

Miscellaneous. Numerous artifacts that did not fit into any of the above categories were assigned to the miscellaneous ones. These included tin cans that had contained tobacco, kerosene lamp parts, bed springs, nuts, bolts, washers, nails, battery carbon rods, wire, rattail files, flashlight parts, and Clorox bottle fragments and caps. Other objects placed in this potpourri category were ballpoint pen parts, a screwdriver, a two-jar trap, staples, bullet shells, metal washtubs, pocket-watch fragments, metal trunk parts, and pails. Charred fabric, probably the remnant of a cotton quilt, was uncovered at Site 2-1-01. Glass scrapers were recovered from Sites 2-1-03, 2-54-28, and 2-C6-18. Worked (unifacially retouched) glass flakes, possibly utilized (evidenced by uniform microflake removal and possible edge-wear damage) glass flakes, and unmodified glass flakes were scattered near a hogan at Site 2-54-28 and may represent a glass-tool-manufacturing locus. Similar glass tools have been observed in use ethnographically, and have been noted at other Navajo sites (Ward, Abbink, and Stein 1977:274). The glass artifacts might have been used in a cere-

Figure 82. An example of the transportation artifact category. A 1927 New Mexico license plate in situ at Site 2-54-28.

monial context, or have had mundane functions (e.g., scraping hides), or been merely the results of recreational activities.

Indeterminate Contents and Functions. This category contained artifacts with contents and/or functions that I could not determine: They included sheet metal, chunks of raw turquoise, unidentifiable pieces of rubber, plastic, and leather, metal hooks, fragments of cast iron, unidentifiable metal objects, tin cans with indeterminate original contents, glass fragments, metal rods and pipes, strips of copper and/or brass, and pieces of plywood.

Lithic Artifacts

Unmodified lithic flakes were located at all the sites except 2-54-28. Cores, one-hand manos, ax/adze/mauls, a hammerstone, and a whetstone were also recovered. Most, although not necessarily all, of the lithic artifacts probably had been transported by the occupants from nearby prehistoric sites.

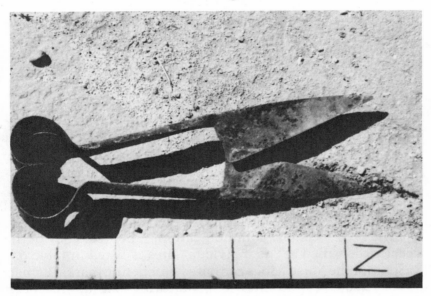

Figure 83. An example of the animal husbandry artifact category. Sheep shears in situ at Site 2-1-03.

The relative paucity of the lithic artifacts and debitage and the well-known Navajo practice of picking up lithics from prehistoric sites negates the possibility that they were from an earlier occupation located beneath the historic one. They could have been used for ceremonial purposes or for mundane functions such as scraping hides and processing vegetal materials, or they could have been picked up and kept merely as curiosities.

Aboriginal Ceramics

Navajo Utility sherds were collected from Sites 2-1-03 and possibly 2-C6-14 (the surface of the only piece recovered from 2-C6-14 was too eroded for a positive identification). Navajo Painted pottery was found at Sites 2-1-01 and 2-1-03. A historic red slipped ware, probably of Acoma-Laguna-Zuni origin, and historic Tewa pots were both located at Site 2-1-03 (Kent 1980b). The pots may have been used in ceremonial contexts, for mundane functions, or kept for aesthetic reasons. The pottery dates from circa A.D. 1700 to the present.

FAUNAL REMAINS

The bones from Sites 2-1-03 and 2-54-28 were numerous and included almost every part of the skeleton. Although not as prevalent, faunal remains were also present at Sites 2-C6-14 and 2-C6-18. None were found at Site 2-1-01. Sheep (*Ovis aries*) was the most common species identified, followed in descending order by horse (*Equus* cf. *caballus*), cow (*Bos* sp.), jackrabbit (*Lepus* cf. *californicus*), kit fox (*Vulpes* cf. *macrotis*) deer (*Odocoileus* sp.), and prairie dog (*Cynomys* cf. *gunnisoni*; Lyman 1978: personal communication). The frequency of the species identified at the individual sites is listed in table 6.

Some of the horse bones exhibited butchering marks (Lyman 1978: personal communication), indicating that they had been used for food. However, the specific remains recovered of the jackrabbit and prairie dog (usually the cranium or mandible), and their locations at the sites (often the fill of the hogans), lead to the conclusion that they were intrusive and not a food resource, although Navajos do on occasion use them for food.

BOTANICAL REMAINS

The majority of botanical remains identified were of edible cultigens and included apricot pits (*Prunus armeniaca*), peach stones (*Prunus persica*), squash rind (*Cucurbita pepo*), watermelon seeds (*Citrullus vulgaris*), and corn kernels and cobs (*Zea mays*; R. Ford 1980:1281–85). Other plant food remains recovered were pinyon nut shells (*Pinus edulis*) and pigweed seeds (*Amaranthus* sp.). Floral remains that were identified in the samples from various features but probably not utilized as a food resource were ricegrass (*Oryzopsis hymenoides*), prickly pear cactus (*Opuntia* sp.), bristlegrass (*Setaria viridis*), and juniper (*Juniperus monosperma*; R. Ford 1980:1281–85). These plants were growing in the immediate site areas during excavation and their remains probably blew or washed into the features or were carried there unintentionally by either humans or animals. The vast majority of the charcoal iden-

Table 6. Frequency of bones by species

Species	Site 2-1-01		Site 2-1-03		Site 2-54-28		Site 2-C6-14		Site 2-C6-18	
	N	%	N	%	N	%	N	%	N	%
Sheep (*Ovis aries*)	— —	— —	220	70	68	66.02	6	22	25	49.02
Horse (*Equus* cf. *caballus*)	— —	— —	9	3	11	10.68	— —	— —	1	1.96
Cow (*Bos* sp.)	— —	— —	1	1	7	6.80	— —	— —	7	13.73
Jackrabbit (*Lepus* cf. *californicus*	— —	— —	— —	— —	4	3.88	4	14	— —	— —
Kit fox (*Vulpes* cf. *macrotis*)	— —	— —	1	1	— —	— —	— —	— —	— —	— —
Deer (*Odocoileus* sp.)	— —	— —	— —	— —	— —	— —	1	4	— —	— —
Prairie dog (*Cynomys* cf. *gunnisoni*	— —	— —	— —	— —	— —	— —	2	7	— —	— —
Indeterminate rodent	— —	— —	— —	— —	— —	— —	3	11	— —	— —
Indeterminate or unidentified	— —	— —	82	26	13	12.62	12	43	18	35.29
Total	0	0	313	101	103	100	28	101	51	100

tified at the five sites was juniper, followed in descending order by pinyon, cottonwood (*Populus* sp.), and willow (*Salix* sp.; Ford 1980:1290–93). Since neither cottonwood nor willow is native to the site areas, they must have been brought in from elsewhere.

The five sites varied in the types of hogan present, the numbers and kinds of features found, and the quantities of artifacts and faunal and botanical remains recovered. The consistent factor was that all contained a majority of Euroamerican artifacts. The spatial distribution of both the artifacts and faunal remains at these twentieth-century sites is discussed in the following chapter.

5

The Testing of a Hypothesis

Studies of the contemporary use of space by living people can contribute not only to an understanding of their way of life and to the possible improvement of their living conditions through appropriate planning and design, but also to our interpretation of the archaeological record. Such studies can help us identify, make explicit, and examine our assumptions and perhaps recast them as testable hypotheses. They can shed light on just how the archaeological record is formed, that is, what kinds of remains certain activities leave, how these remains are patterned and what accounts for this patterning. (Portnoy 1981:213)

This chapter is concerned with evaluating the first hypothesis presented in chapter 2—that the content and spatial patterning of artifact and faunal remain assemblages define activity areas. Corollaries of this hypothesis are (1) that artifacts and faunal remains were abandoned at the locus at which they were used, and (2) that the refuse abandoned at an activity area permits inferences regarding the area's function or functions.

If the hypothesis is valid, flaking debris at a locus would indicate that flint knapping had been performed there, and cut and splintered bone would suggest butchering. Assumed to be valid by many archaeologists, this hypothesis is at the base of every assumption concerning the delineation of activity areas. The following discussion is an attempt to test the validity of the hypothesis through an examination of the spatial distribution of artifacts and faunal remains located at the archaeological and ethnographic sites investigated. It is also an attempt to understand the spatial distributions I observed.

The Problem

Most archaeologists have some ideas concerning when artifacts will be deposited at the area of their use (for instance, when they are accidentally dropped and unintentionally abandoned). Perhaps more important to archaeologists, but less understood, are the questions of why and under what conditions objects are disposed of away from the locus at which they have been used.

By determining what factors influence the deposition of artifacts, we can attempt to assess the hypothesis that objects are deposited where used. Further, we can come closer to understanding the conditions behind the patterns we observe in the archaeological record. The first step in the analysis of disposal patterns is to ascertain the artifact distributions at the sites excavated in order to detect possible patterning. Then we can attempt to interpret these distributions and the factors affecting them.

Artifact Distributions

Artifacts from five sites located on Block II of the Navajo Indian Irrigation Project were assigned to categories as described in the previous chapter. All sites were from roughly the same period of time, but they varied in size and duration of occupation and ran the gamut from one hogan with associated features to as many as four hogans with numerous features (table 4).

Site 2-1-03 contained more artifacts than the other four sites, and this may have skewed the following statistics somewhat. All of the cultural material recovered from corrals was located at Site 2-1-03. The remains of probable corrals beneath the two wood-chip areas at Site 2-C6-18 yielded no artifacts.

The locations of the artifacts that had been assigned to functional categories were then plotted within the five sites, except for certain feature types, such as masonry ovens, that were not included due to the paucity of their associated cultural material; artifact clusters were also omitted because of their rarity. Moreover, the huge number of glass fragments encountered, which may represent only a small number of shattered bottles, precluded collecting anything but large fragments and bases.

The chi-square test was calculated in an attempt to examine the null hypothesis that no relationship exists between feature types (locations) and artifact functional categories. The chi-square test is a parametric measure of the strength of association between two expressions of frequencies of observed phenomena. The application of the test is stated as a hypothesis that there is no association between the expressions of frequencies of the two populations. An acceptance of the hypothesis is based on the probability that the two expressions of frequencies are independent.

A significant (*P* less than .05) chi-square would have indicated that the two categories were not independent. The test statistic was significant at the .01 alpha level. This allowed the rejection of the null hypothesis (that no relationship exists between feature type and artifact functional categories). The artifact functional catetory proportions were different for each feature type.

However, an alternate method of examining the data was necessitated by the low number of artifacts in certain categories. This fact resulted in 11 cells with an expected frequency (*fe*) below 5 (see appendix 1 for calculations). More than one expected frequency under 5 with five or more categories violates the basic assumptions of the test. Therefore, another procedure was necessary to determine which of the proportions were significantly different.

A .95 confidence interval (assuming a significance level of $\alpha = .05$) was found for each proportion by computing:

$$\hat{p} \pm z_0 \sqrt{\frac{\hat{p}(1 - \hat{p})}{n}} \, ,$$

in which $z_0 =$ upper $\alpha/2$ point of the standard normal distribution (1.96 in the example, appendix 1); $\hat{p} =$ the sample proportion (.640 in the example); and $n =$ the sample size (525 in the example).

In comparing any two proportions, if the confidence intervals overlap, the conclusion is that the proportions are not significantly different. If the two confidence intervals do not overlap, the conclusion is that proportions are significantly different at the .05 significance level or better.

In the example in appendix 1, the confidence interval for the isolated subsistence-oriented artifacts ($.599 < p < .681$)

does not overlap with the confidence interval of the hogan subsistence-oriented artifacts ($.078 < p < .129$). In other words, the two proportions are significantly different. The confidence intervals indicate that significantly more subsistence-oriented artifacts were recovered as isolated occurrences than were recovered from the hogans. The other confidence intervals are listed in the tables in appendixes 2 and 3.

If the artifact functional categories were randomly distributed, they would each be proportionately equally represented at the individual feature types. However, if different percentages of the various artifact functional categories are located at particular features, possible activity areas may be suggested. For example, if a relatively large percentage of the subsistence-oriented artifact category—which consists of such objects as food and beverage containers, pots, pans, and cups (see chapter 4) —is associated with hogans, one may hypothesize the presence of food preparation/consumption activity areas. In the following description of artifact distributions, the terms *overrepresented* and *underrepresented* are relative terms indicating that the artifacts are more or less common than what would be expected if the distribution were random.

DESCRIPTION

It is evident from appendix 2 that subsistence-oriented artifacts were most often found as isolated occurrences and were overrepresented compared to what would occur with a random distribution. The subsistence-oriented artifacts were underrepresented in hogans (which contained the next largest number of these artifacts). The subsistence-oriented-artifact frequencies at the 13 wood-chip areas and 6 corrals can be accounted for by random distribution (see appendix 2).

Personal adornment and clothing artifacts were most commonly located in the 17 ash areas, where they were slightly overrepresented, and as isolated occurrences, where they were underrepresented. Both the 11 hogans and 13 wood-chip areas had substantially fewer personal adornment and clothing artifacts than were found in ash areas or as isolated occurrences. The number of artifacts here can be accounted for by random distribution. The corrals contained the smallest number of these artifacts, and their presence was probably due to random distribution.

Toys were not numerous at any of the sites. Most of those found were recovered from ash areas or as isolates. However, because of the small number of toys located at the sites, no conclusion can be formulated concerning their distribution, since it could be accounted for by chance.

Medicinally related artifacts were most abundant at ash areas, with a higher frequency than would be expected as a result of random distribution. Somewhat fewer were found as isolates, with lower frequencies than expected. About the same number were found in hogans, where their frequency can be accounted for by random distribution. The number of medicinal artifacts was even smaller in wood-chip areas, and their frequency was that expected in a random distribution. None were found in corrals, which is below the expected proportion.

Transportation-oriented artifacts were most frequently found in ash areas and as isolated artifacts, as could be expected from a random distribution. The transportation artifacts found in ash areas, like those found in hogans, wood-chip areas, and corrals, could simply have been the result of a random distribution. Artifacts associated with animal husbandry, scarce at all sites, were most prevalent as isolated occurrences; however, owing to their small numbers, no conclusion can be drawn from their distribution.

I also analyzed the percentage of artifacts in each of the functional categories at the individual features, and as isolated artifacts. Among isolated artifacts, the subsistence category was by far the largest and contained more than that expected from a random distribution (see appendix 3).

Miscellaneous, although underrepresented, constituted the next largest category, but overlapped with personal adornment and clothing. The latter category was slightly underrepresented and was followed in frequency by transportation, which contained an expected number of isolated artifacts. The toys, medicinal, and animal husbandry categories appeared in similar percentages, which were substantially lower than those for the other categories. The medicinal supplies category was underrepresented, while the other two functional categories could both be accounted for by a random distribution of artifacts. Hogans, on the other hand, contained more artifacts assigned to the miscellaneous category than to any other, and such artifacts were more common than could be accounted for by a random distribution. The subsistence and personal adornment and clothing categories constituted smaller portions of the hogan artifact inventory, followed by the transportation, medicinal, and toy categories. All categories except toys, which were slightly underrepresented, could be accounted for by random distributions. No animal-husbandry-oriented artifacts were found at wood-chip areas, a representation less than that expected from a random distribution. This was not unlike the distribution of the various categories of artifacts at the corrals. Subsistence, miscellaneous, and personal adornment and clothing artifacts were, in descending order of frequency, most commonly found at corrals, followed by animal husbandry and transportation artifacts. No toys or medicinal artifacts were located at corrals. The personal adornment and clothing, toys, and medicinal supplies categories were underrepresented at corrals, whereas the animal husbandry category was overrepresented, and the rest were what would be expected according to a random distribution of artifacts.

HYPOTHESIS TESTING

The above data do not consistently validate the hypothesis being tested—that activity areas can be discerned from the content and patterning of artifact and faunal remain assemblages—or its corollaries, (1) that artifacts and faunal remains were abandoned at the locus at which they were used, and (2) that the refuse abandoned at an activity area permits inferences regarding the area's function(s).

If the distribution of artifacts at the sites is the result of primary refuse deposition and the hypothesis is valid, we would expect artifacts to be found where they were known to have been used. Therefore subsistence-oriented artifacts, for example, should have been most prevalent in the hogan, where, within the proposed dates of the archaeological sites' occupations (as well as at present), most food preparation and consumption occurred. Contrary to what would be expected according to the above hypothesis, most subsistence-oriented artifacts were found as isolated occurrences, and the second largest concentration was found in ash areas. The distribution of these artifacts, then, is an example of secondary refuse deposition (Schiffer 1972:161, 1976:67–69).

Archaeologists, however, are not usually so naïve as to rely solely upon artifact clusters or architectural remains if other evidence is present. For example, microbotanical or phosphate analyses may delineate food-processing and/or -preparation areas, wood chips can denote a wood-chopping area, stone alignments and burned soil can distinguish hearths from ash areas, and dung, soil discoloration, postmolds, and vegetational changes often mark the location of a former corral. Nonetheless, with the passage of time (and depending on postdepositional factors such as climate, soil acidity, and so on), such nonartifactual indicators become increasingly scarce, forcing archaeologists to rely more on artifacts for their activity area interpretations.

At Site 2-1-01, artifacts had been abandoned inside the hogan at the probable locus at which they had been used. The dwelling apparently was a *chindii* hogan in which a death had occurred and which the occupants had subsequently deliberately burned, abandoning most of the artifacts in situ (see chapter 4). Consequently, Site 2-1-01 represents a special situation. In most cases, however, artifacts were not found at the areas in which they probably had been used, but instead were at the locus at which they had been secondarily deposited. Most archaeologists are aware that objects are sometimes left at the area where they were used and sometimes not (when they are curated, for example; see Binford 1976). Several factors affected artifact disposal at the sites I investigated, influencing whether or not objects were left where used.

In the case of the archaeological sites investigated, it is my opinion that the distribution of artifacts was affected by the presence of large quantities of Euroamerican manufactured goods. I maintain that this factor made it impossible to test my hypothesis accurately.

Mass-produced products and a market economy have had a profound effect on the discard practices of different peoples around the world. The ramifications of mass production and the effects of a market economy are important for ethnoarchaeologists (as well as other anthropologists) who attempt to formulate or test hypotheses based on observations of the use and disposal of nonaboriginal material culture, which are then applied to the archaeological record. For instance, Longacre (1974) addressed this subject when he conducted a study of the inheritance of ceramic design motifs by the Kalinga, who make pottery for their own use, in order to contrast it with Stanislawski's (1969, 1973, 1974, 1978) continuing research among the Hopi and Hopi-Tewa, who today make pottery largely for sale to tourists. An example of the need for such research arises in Murray's examination of the Human Relations Area Files (composed primarily of descriptions of post-European/Euroamerican contact groups) seeking information on discard behavior. She concluded that "both sedentary and migratory populations discard materials outside their use locations and that only some migratory peoples discard material elements at their use location" (P. Murray 1980:490). However, my data suggest that the adoption of European/ Euroamerican material culture (which has occurred to some degree in most twentieth-century groups described in ethnographies) has resulted in modifications of the prehistoric spatial distribution of artifacts. In fact, several anthropologists (e.g., Binford 1978a; O'Connell 1979; South 1979) have noted the effect of object size on the disposal of artifacts. Large, bulky materials are ordinarily dumped away from the area where they are used. Any society that produces or obtains large quantities of bulky goods is likely to discard materials away from activity areas. This evidence makes such studies as P. Murray's (1980) unreliable for certain types of activity area analyses (specifically for determining whether or not objects are customarily abandoned at the area where they were used).

Of relevance to the present study is the fact that Euroamerican-produced goods were far more prevalent at the archaeological sites than those of native manufacture; at one site, these goods were present to the exclusion of the latter. This was also true at the ethnographic sites I observed. Mass-produced goods are relatively inexpensive in terms of the time expended for their procurement, fairly accessible at nearby trading posts (although usually in a limited selection), and abundant, with bulky, durable by-products, such as tin cans and glass containers.

The adoption of Euroamerican material culture has probably resulted in some modification of the distribution of artifacts simply because of the resulting copious quantities of mass-produced objects present at a site. For example, the number of tin cans recorded from Site 2-1-03 alone was staggering, and the site was only partially investigated. Another consideration is the durability of certain objects, such as metal pots, pans, knives, axes, and so on, in contrast to vessels and tools traditionally made of clay or stone. The metal artifacts are not as likely to break and do not need replacement as often as their native-made counterparts. A cast-iron pot, for example, does not often break, and, if it does, it does not crumble into as many pieces as would a clay vessel. In addition, some pieces of a broken clay pot probably would be intentionally or accidentally left at the location where the vessel broke, whereas an unusable cast-iron pot could be easily tossed away from the activity area, leaving no sherds behind. Because objects made from friable materials tend to leave more pieces at the locus at which they were broken, archaeologists can not only determine the artifacts' presence, but may also be able to infer the function(s) of the area.

The sheer numbers of mass-produced objects, such as tin cans, at the twentieth-century sites investigated, would have necessitated some modification of traditional refuse patterns. Lithic detritus and ceramic sherds at an activity area can be walked upon with only minimal difficulty, some being trampled into the ground (cf. Gifford 1978:81–83), whereas the refuse from large numbers of Euroamerican-produced goods would create problems. For example, if allowed to pile up, tin cans will eventually cover the locus at which they are used. Some form of disposal is required, unless the occupants are willing to perform activities at loci covered with several meters of tin cans, car parts, wash pans, containers of various types, pieces of metal pots and pans, and so on. This situation has been described by Schiffer, who writes that refuse disposal can be viewed "as the balancing of 2 major sets of variables. The particular solutions arrived at by site occupants for handling the by-products of activity performance will take into consideration the ease of moving the activity or activities versus the ease of moving the refuse" (Schiffer 1972:161). It is my contention that, regardless of aboriginal disposal methods, the presence of Euroamerican manufactured goods at the sites investigated necessitated one of three strategies: (1) discarding refuse at loci other than those where the objects had been used, (2) using less permanent sites, or (3) frequently shifting activity area locations within a site in order to prevent an enormous trash buildup at activity loci.

Some ways of dealing with bulky manufactured discarded items may not have differed from traditional patterns. The inhabitants could have tossed the refuse away from the activity area (creating isolated artifacts not associated with a particular feature). Another alternative would have been to deposit refuse at loci that were exclusive trash areas (common ethnographically), or to dump trash in preexisting areas such as ash or wood-chip areas (common archaeologically and ethnographically). An additional pattern, used more commonly today and near population centers and small communities, is the community trash dump. What the aboriginal mode of Navajo refuse disposal actually was is immaterial; the overall historic pattern would be the same—objects no longer in use would be disposed of away from the activity area. Consequently, most twentieth-century archaeological sites are not amenable to testing the hypothesis I tried to evaluate.

The necessity of moving discarded objects from their place of habitual use to a special disposal locus is not limited to historical sites inundated with Euroamerican mass-produced goods. In some prehistoric (e.g., Anasazi; Rohn 1977) and/or non-Western (Near East; Mellaart 1967) sites, trash areas were regularly used, owing to the occupants' sedentism and copious material culture. Such sites would best lend themselves to activity area analyses when the natural abandonment processes had been disrupted by a catastrophe or other unusual event (not an uncommon occurrence in the archaeological record). For example, when a disaster has caused the inhabitants literally to drop what they were doing, an archaeologist can clearly discern activity areas. At other sites, however, activity areas can usually still be discerned because of the friable nature of many of the artifacts—if broken, parts would probably have been accidentally or intentionally left at the area of their use.

Another consequence of the adoption of mass-produced material culture is the scarcity of artifact-manufacturing areas, which are often among the most visible areas at prehistoric sites. Particularly prominent are areas of lithic tool manufacture (see Flenniken 1980; Flenniken and Stanfill 1979; Goodyear 1974; Griffin 1974; Hester 1972; Schiffer 1976). I observed basket weaving and rawhide quirt manufacturing, activities that were performed at the same area (see chapter 3), but left little or no refuse and relied primarily on multipurpose tools that were curated rather than left at the activity locus. Consequently, virtually nothing remained of these activities to indicate to future archaeologists the presence of the manufacturing activity area. Stone tools, in contrast, are not only manufactured with specialized equipment, such as hammerstones, but also produce enough debitage to allow an archaeologist to ascertain that the activity did occur at a particular site.

Another factor influencing the deposition of objects and a possible cause of the difference in artifact distribution patterns between prehistoric and historic sites is the use of wagons and/or automobiles among groups who formerly did not possess any means to transport large quantities of goods. This is an influential factor that must be considered whenever using information about groups with the ability to transport a large number of objects as an aid in the interpretation of the archaeological artifact distributions left by people who did not possess any means of large-scale transportation.

Many of the artifact distribution patterns at historic sites, when compared to those at prehistoric sites, have been modified to some degree by the impact of Euroamerican mass-produced goods (and in other parts of the world by Western European manufactured goods). Such modification does not, in my opinion, necessarily extend to the patterned usage of activity areas (e.g., sex specific and/or monofunctional) discussed in the next chapter. I do believe, however, that the presence of large quantities of Euroamerican cultural material at both the historic archaeological and the ethnographic sites I investigated made it difficult to conduct an accurate test of the hypothesis being evaluated, that activity areas can be discerned from the content and patterning of artifact assemblages.

The elucidation of factors that influence the deposition of artifacts (e.g., the presence of mass-produced, durable, bulky objects), the absence of refuse (e.g., the use of ready-made items), and the relatively easy curation of artifacts (e.g., the availability of animal or machine transportation) will allow archaeologists to ascertain whether or not, as well as under what conditions, objects were left at the areas at which they were utilized. The distribution of faunal remains, however, is not necessarily affected by the same factors as the cultural material.

Faunal Remains Distribution

Meat has been a part of the Navajos' diet since prehistoric times. Although different species of animals have been introduced, bones are still the by-products of part of their diet. In fact, it has been suggested that the current method of cooking mutton is reminiscent of the way in which venison was prepared in prehistoric times (Kluckhohn and Leighton 1962:92). Whereas today sheep are kept near the camps and deer prehistorically were not, meat was not available every day at the households with which I lived any more than it probably had been aboriginally. The pieces of meat occasionally purchased from the trading post were cuts that also contained bones. While the actual species used and the butchering patterns may have been different prehistorically, it is certainly plausible that the spatial distribution of historic faunal remains, unlike the artifact distribution, resembles prehistoric patterns. The bones consequently provide one means to test my hypothesis, although the resultant conclusions must be restricted to the distribution of faunal remains. It should not be assumed that what is true for bones is also true for material culture distributions antedating the influx of Euroamerican mass-produced products, because bones and artifacts do not necessarily have the same distribution. However, some of the factors conditioning artifacts may also affect the distribution of faunal remains. For example, the presence of large quantities of big bones may affect disposal patterns (Binford 1978a), and the use of animal or machine transportation may influence decisions concerning moving large bones from the procurement area to a habitation site. Nevertheless, the distribution of faunal remains needs to be examined separately from that of the artifacts because different factors may be involved.

As was the case with the artifacts, more bones were recovered from Site 2-1-03 than from the other sites. No faunal remains were located at Site 2-1-01. See Kent 1980a, 1980b, 1980c, 1980d, and 1980e for detailed descriptions of the faunal remains from the individual archaeological sites.

DESCRIPTION

Most of the faunal remains probably used for food were located in ash areas (50.71%), followed by wood-chip areas (25.86%), as isolated occurrences (7.07%), in hogans (6.67%), and in corrals (1.21%). The chi-square statistical test was employed to determine significant associations between feature-type categories and (1) limbs and skull and (2) midsection skeletal parts. The bones had to be grouped into these two skeletal categories in order to be able to fulfill the chi-square assumption that all expected frequencies be equal to or greater than 5. Although the limitations of grouping the bones this way are obvious, the grouping was necessary as a result of the small sample size. The limb-bone category consisted of the humerus, ulna, radius, carpals, metacarpals, phalanges, femur, tibia, fibula, calcaneum, astragalus, naviculur cuboid, tarsals, and metatarsal. The skull (most pieces were fairly intact) and midsection category was composed of the cranium, hyoid, mandible, scapula, vertebrae, ribs, and pelvis. Although numerous fragments of tooth enamel and horn fragments were found, teeth and horns were not included in either category. Many unidentifiable shaft fragments and a few bones located in features not used in the chi-square test (e.g., artifact clusters, masonry ovens) also were not a part of the bone counts.

Several articulated bones were recovered. One was the hind leg of a horse found at a wood-chip area located at Site 2-1-03. It is conceivable that the horse had not been used for food and may even have died in between or after the site's occupations. There were not enough bones recovered from corrals to include them in the chi-square calculations.

The chi-square test revealed an association between skeletal section category and feature type that is significant (with three degrees of freedom at the .01 level; see appendix 2 for the computations).

HYPOTHESIS TESTING

If the first corollary of the hypothesis is valid, that faunal remains were left at the locus where they were butchered, cooked, or otherwise used, then the distribution of faunal remains indicates that meat was butchered and/or eaten primarily at ash areas where 50.71 percent of the bones were left. However, ash areas, it was shown in the preceding section, were trash areas, not activity areas. Thus, the question to pursue is, Were the bones deposited at ash areas because they also were considered to be refuse? Although this is certainly a logical explanation for the distribution of faunal remains, ethnographic observations revealed a completely different factor that affected their spatial positioning.

At every Navajo, Spanish-American, and Euroamerican residence with pets, dogs were more influential in the spatial distribution of faunal remains than were humans (Kent 1981). Bones were routinely and intentionally given to the dogs, who would then take them to various places (e.g., ash and woodchip areas in the case of the Navajos) in order to avoid competition with other animals. Some households had as many as 12 dogs. Even without competition from other animals, dogs at Spanish-American and Euroamerican houses usually hid bones under couches inside the house, or under trees outside, so they were still influential in the distribution of faunal remains.

Dogs were responsible for scattering the bones located at a sheep corral at Edith Begay's summer camp, for example. According to one informant, a number of sheep annually die from eating a small poisonous plant. Their carcasses are cut open at the corral and, because of the contamination of the meat, rendering it unfit for human consumption, the dogs are allowed to eat it. The dogs subsequently scatter the bones around the corral. Butchering routinely occurred next to the ramada at the Many Sheep camp. Nevertheless, no bones were left afterward to mark the location where the activity had occurred. Also, no bones were located at the butchering activity area at the Bitter Water camp.

In addition, observations disclosed the important role of dogs in obliterating the evidence of activity loci. For example, they ate all the rawhide scraps of Chee Many Sheep's quirts that had been left at the manufacturing locations. Consequently, nothing remained at the area to denote the particular activity that had occurred there.

Ethnographic observations indicated that the Navajo-owned dogs merely removed meat that the humans had left on the bones. They did not gnaw on or play with the bones for any length of time. In fact, only the Euroamerican and Spanish-American family pets chewed on a bone after the meat had been removed (Kent 1981). This may have been a consequence of the relative infrequency with which they were given bones.

A few of my colleagues suggested that just the removal of meat from a bone by a dog would produce gnawing marks sufficient for an archaeologist to detect later. Unfortunately, I was unable actually to collect and inspect the bones after the Navajo-owned dogs had removed the meat. To have done so would not only have jeopardized my position in the families as daughter and good friend, but could also have led to accusations that I was a witch. Unusual behavior, except from a stranger, is not often tolerated in most groups. Consequently, not having the ethnographic data, I conducted the following experiment in an attempt to test the hypothesis that a bone from which the meat had been removed by a dog would exhibit marks that an archaeologist could later discern.

THE BONE-GNAWING EXPERIMENT

Three dogs of varying sizes and breeds were chosen for the experiment (Kent 1981). Haida was a mature female Eskimo malamute who weighed about 45 pounds—larger than most of the dogs I had observed. BT was a medium male beagle-poodle mixture who weighed approximately 25 pounds, which was within the average size range of the dogs observed. Annie, the smallest dog used in the experiment, was a female terrier-poodle mixture who weighed 11 pounds, and was within the size range of the dogs I had observed.

In order to maintain as much control as possible, most of the bones I used in the experiment were left distal femurs from mature cattle. All the bones were cooked, and in an attempt to simulate common aboriginal cooking practices, half the bones were boiled, and the other half were broiled (thought to be analogous to roasting). Most of the meat was cut off the bone before it was given to the animals, since the bones received by the dogs I observed ethnographically had had most of the meat removed by humans.

A broiled bone followed by a boiled bone was given to Annie for 48 hours. A broiled bone followed by a boiled one was then given to Annie and Haida for separate 24-hour periods. Finally, broiled and later boiled bones were given to all three dogs only for the length of time required to remove the meat (approximately 15 minutes). This last step was later repeated by each dog.

The experiment yielded several interesting results. Dogs clearly had more difficulty in removing the meat from broiled bones than boiled ones. The articular surfaces of both the boiled and broiled bones that had been gnawed on for separate 24- and 48-hour periods contained much evidence of chewing, although the bones gnawed on for 24 hours had fewer marks on them (figs. 84, 85, 86).

However, the broiled and boiled bones that the same dogs chewed on only until the meat was removed *contained no evidence of gnawing* (fig. 87). Although three dogs is a small sample, the experiment did demonstrate that dogs *do not necessarily* leave marks on bones from which they have chewed meat. In other words, bones that have been spatially disturbed by dogs need not be scarred (Kent 1981). Although concerned only with the alteration of bones caused by larger carnivores than domesticated dogs (such as bears, wolves, hyenas, and large cats), Haynes noted that:

Modern carnivore gnawing does not always produce identifiable tooth marks on bones. In such cases (which are the rule at many

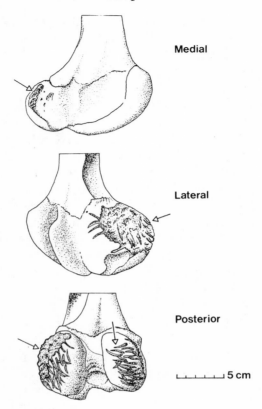

Medial

Lateral

Posterior

⌊ ⌊ ⌊ ⌊ ⌊ ⌊ ⌋ 5 cm

Figure 84. Broiled distal femur which had been gnawed on by Annie during a 48-hour period. Arrows point to areas of gnaw mark concentrations.

kill sites) overall modification of elements is often the only evidence of carnivore activity [this probably being more distinctive as a result of his observations of large carnivores rather than small carnivores like the domestic dog]. (Haynes 1980:343; emphasis added)

The reservation dogs that I observed were not solely dependent upon bones for their food. They were also given leftover fry bread (several days old) and other edible refuse. Consequently, although usually hungry, they certainly were not starving. The dogs I used in the experiment were probably better nourished than the reservation dogs; however, it is dif-

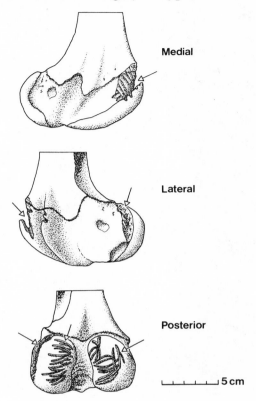

Figure 85. Boiled distal femur which had been gnawed on by Annie during a 48-hour period. Arrows point to areas of gnaw mark concentrations.

ficult to determine whether the difference between them was so significant as to bias the experiment. If the reservation dogs were inadequately fed, I suspect they would supplement their diet by hunting small animals so they would still not be starving. I hypothesize that the practice of giving dogs all the edible trash and bones (or their just taking it) occurred in the past, as well as today, among many different groups. Unfortunately, I know of no data with which to evaluate this hypothesis. In any case, I believe that the discrepancy between the dogs used in the experiment and the reservation dogs was

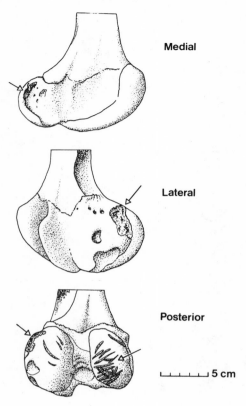

Medial

Lateral

Posterior

Figure 86. Boiled distal femur which had been gnawed on by Annie during a 24-hour period. Arrows point to areas of gnaw mark concentrations.

not significant enough to invalidate the conclusions derived from the experiment, or my contention that dogs appear to be, in many cases, the agents responsible for the spatial distribution of faunal remains.

There are, of course, exceptions; bones are sometimes obviously distributed by humans. Examples include an African group's deliberate segregation of the bones from different species (Hodder 1979), the patterning of bones inside a pithouse located near the Snake River in Washington (Lyman 1976), and an ash area which was the only Navajo component at an

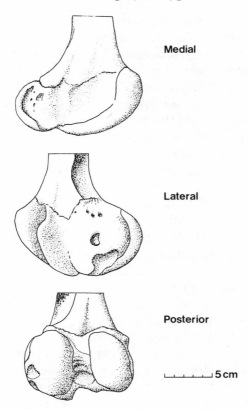

Medial

Lateral

Posterior

5 cm

Figure 87. Boiled distal femur which had been gnawed on by Annie until the meat was removed. There were no gnaw marks; this was also true of broiled bones gnawed on by Haida and BT until the meat was removed.

otherwise Anasazi site that contained all but one of the 237 bone fragments found at the entire site (Kent 1980f). Because of these and other exceptions, I do not advocate abandoning all spatial distributional studies of faunal remains. Instead I suggest that, unless a very specific pattern emerges from analysis, as was the case with the exceptions cited above, the spatial positioning of bones should in most cases be attributed to dog and/or other scavenger behavior rather than to human behavior (Kent 1981).

It has been documented in several publications that dogs have been influential in the frequency and attrition of specific skeletal parts found archaeologically. These include general studies of scavenger behavior (Binford 1981) and those conducted among the Navajos and Nunamiut Eskimos (Binford and Bertram 1977), the Hottentots (Brain 1969), the Bisa of Zambia (Crader 1974), and the Wachipaeri of Peru (Lyon 1970). My experiment further demonstrates the effects of activities performed by dogs, in this case the "creation" and obliteration of activity areas, that archaeologists need to take into consideration.

The implications of both my experiment and my ethnographic observations are of importance to archaeologists, for both sets of data indicate that the corollaries of the hypothesis being evaluated (that faunal remains were abandoned at the locus where they were used, and that enough refuse was abandoned at an activity area to permit inferences as to its functions) are not consistently valid. Therefore, the hypothesis that activity areas can be discerned from the content and spatial patterning of faunal remain assemblages is not supported in these instances and thus is shown to be an unreliable assumption for archaeologists to use in interpreting sites. Like most research, mine may raise more questions than it answers; nonetheless, it does indicate that archaeologists cannot merely *assume* that the faunal remains at a site are spatially undisturbed, even with the absence of gnawing marks on the bones. Instead, they must *demonstrate* that the faunal remains have not been spatially disturbed by dogs or other scavengers. In fact, all the evidence gathered from the Navajo, Spanish-American, and Euroamerican families observed with dogs suggests that archaeologists who analyze the spatial distribution of faunal remains are, in many cases, studying dog behavior rather than human behavior (Kent 1981).

6

A Model of the Interrelationship of Culture, Behavior, and Cultural Material

The known behavior of the whole and the known behavior of a minimum of known parts often makes possible the discovery of the values of the remaining parts as does the known sum of the angles of a triangle plus the known behavior of its six parts make possible evaluating the others. (Fuller 1970:66)

In the course of this book, I have tried to demonstrate that different groups use activity areas differently; the Euroamericans had more sex-specific and monofunctional activity areas than did the Spanish-Americans, who had more than the Navajos. The data indicate that activity area usage was a cultural phenomenon, as demonstrated by the fact that the use of activity areas was consistent throughout a single group and crosscut socioeconomic class, house type and size, and residence location. Navajos living in Euroamerican manufactured, three-bedroom tract houses used space more similarly to Navajos living in ramadas than to Euroamericans living in the same type and size of house. The use of space was more isomorphic among rural and urban Euroamericans from different socioeconomic classes than it was between rural Euroamericans and rural Spanish-Americans who were of the same socioeconomic class.

In my introductory chapter I briefly discussed a model that attempts to understand the similarities and differences I observed in activity area usage. Much of what follows is an effort to elaborate that model and although some of it may be speculation based on inference, speculation and inference are both necessary to the understanding and interpretation of descriptions collected by archaeologists and ethnographers. My discussion is an attempt to organize and understand the data I have presented in the preceding chapters.

185

The Model

The proposed model (fig. 1) illustrates how activity area usage, as part of behavior, is a reflection of the culture of a particular group. This type of model has been termed "interpretive" by Kaplan (1964:267), who wrote that such models have "long been important as devices by which a system can be shown to be consistent, or at any rate, as consistent as some other system which serves as an interpretation." The greatest merit of the interpretive model

is that it allows us to use what we know of one subject-matter to arrive at hypotheses concerning another subject-matter structurally similar to the first. The new area may provide an interpretive model for the old theory. . . . Interpretive models are thus peculiarly suited to interdisciplinary [and cross-cultural] approaches. . . . The hope is that ultimately two apparently distinct areas [or cultures] will be capable of being identified, or reduced to variants of a single underlying phenomenon. . . . An interpretive model also serves to show that a more general theory still applies to an earlier, restricted domain, by showing that the latter may be construed as a particular model for the former. In this way, the construction of models also serves the ends of scientific explanation. (Kaplan 1964:275)

The model consists of three levels of abstraction: (1) *culture,* a shared system of meanings and symbols (Dolgin, Kemnitzer, and Schneider 1977:33); (2) *behavior,* actions interpreted within a system of meaning, culture being that system of meaning; and (3) *cultural material,* the tangible products of behavior (including artifacts and, when appropriate, faunal and botanical remains).

These levels are interrelated and must be viewed together as parts of a whole. Culture is reflected in behavior as behavior is in cultural material and vice versa. Most anthropologists are not interested in behavior per se, but in cultural behavior. Examples of the former would be the physical acts of eating, eliminating waste, and sleeping, whereas cultural behavior would be what food was consumed, how, when and why. Therefore, the term *behavior* is used in the model to refer to actions interpreted within a system of meaning, culture being that system of meaning. Behavior is a reflection of culture and, in a gross sense, environment (which is perceived through a cultural filter), as is cultural material.

No level is independent, but each level can be artificially separated from the others for analytic purposes. In fact, the tendency to view each level as independent of the others has led to some of the fallacious assumptions currently employed by archaeologists. Examples are the activity-area-usage assumptions I have evaluated—that activity areas are usually sex specific and/or monofunctional. Such assumptions result from the tendency of archaeologists to view spatial behavior as independent of culture. In this case, it has led to the implicit acceptance of assumptions about the use of space that apparently are valid for Euroamericans, but not necessarily for other groups. As noted earlier, confusion between cultural material and behavior can be seen in statements to the effect that a certain type of pottery "expanded" into the San Juan Basin and that Type A projectile points became "restricted" to the High Plains (when, in fact, only people, as part of their behavior, can expand into or become restricted to an area). Although these statements rely on metaphors, the persistent use of metaphors or of any figurative language can lead to conceptual confusion, and these types of statements illustrate the potential for confusion between cultural material and behavior.

My data indicate that Euroamericans tend to use more separate monofunctional and sex-specific activity areas than do the other groups studied. If viewed on a continuum ranging from segmentation to unity, Euroamerican usage of activity areas would fall toward the segmentation end of the continuum. Navajos, in contrast to Euroamericans, tend to have multipurpose and non-sex-specific activity areas, which puts them, relative to Euroamericans, closer to the unity end of the continuum. Segmentation is the division of a systemic whole into a number of parts, the tendency toward differentiation. The opposite of segmentation is unity, which is a totality of related parts, or parts that make up a systemic whole. The continuum between the extremes of segmentation and unity is resident at the cultural level of the model, but is manifested in the two other levels, behavior and cultural material.

The use of the continuum clarifies the differences in activity area usage among the three groups examined by allowing us to contrast these groups. This is necessary since we are comparing elements that are never absolute. As a consequence, groups need to be compared to others and their locations along the continuum are relative; their positions can be viewed only in relation to each other. One group cannot be said to have an absolute amount of segmentation (or specialization, or emphasis on the differences between the sexes, and so on), only more or less than or the same as another group. The following discussion compares Navajos, Spanish-Americans, and Euroamericans to one another; the outcome might have been quite different if they had been compared to other groups. Navajos can be seen as less segmented only in comparison to Spanish-Americans and Euroamericans—not necessarily to Pygmies or to Bushmen. Navajos relative to these latter groups are actually more segmented. The utility of relative comparisons has been recognized by various anthropologists and sociologists (e.g., Redfield 1960; Tönnies 1887). Hsu notes:

Unless we can reduce all statements about human behavior to quantitative terms, our qualitative statements about human affairs must be comparative to have any meaning. There simply are no exact measurements that will enable us to see them in absolute terms. For example, how do we measure despotism? How do we measure sibling (or any other) rivalry? How many fights or quarrels or lawsuits must we see for a relationship to be termed rivalrous? And we have to remember that despotism and rivalry are relatively easier entities to gauge than others such as religiosity and prejudice.

Systematic comparison will enable us then to say, for example, that political oppression would seem greater in society X than in society Y because the incidence of escapism seems to be higher in the former than the latter, or that people A seem to be more prosperous than people B because the percentage of unemployment is lower in the former than the latter. (Hsu 1979:528)

I postulate that specialization (or segmentation) generates monofunctional activity areas. Monofunctional activity areas are loci where only activities functionally related to one another occur. Their use leads to the tendency to use functionally specific artifacts. Most people who manufacture their own tools know (consciously or unconsciously) that they could make either three separate tools or one tool that performs three separate functions. The amount of specialization, and ultimately of segmentation, that a group has will affect whether people conceive of one tool that performs several functions or several tools that perform one. Groups near the segmentation end of the continuum tend to use monofunctional tools and activity areas, whereas groups near the unity end of the continuum tend to use multipurpose tools and activity areas.

Segmentation is also reflected in groups' conceptions of the sexes and in the rigidity of the division of labor. Segmented groups emphasize the differences between the sexes, perceiving males and females as different beyond the basic biological differences recognized by all groups. Sexual divisions of labor are dependent upon the emphases placed on these sexual differences, which go beyond the universally recognized biological differences between the sexes. These are not the only manifestations of the segmentation-unity gradient, but they are the significant ones for the study of the usage of activity areas. Why some groups are closer to the segmentation end of the continuum than others is discussed at the end of the chapter, but I will first show how the model works, using ethnographic data to elucidate the interrelationships among culture, behavior, and cultural material.

CULTURE

The cultural level of the model can be used to compare Navajos, Euroamericans, and Spanish-Americans. In other words, their particular systems of meanings and symbols can be examined in relation to each other on a continuum between segmentation and unity.

Euroamericans believe that the differences between the sexes are substantial (Graebner 1975; Mead 1967). One of the results is that special deodorants, vitamins, and cold cereals are advertised as being specifically for use by one sex, because the sexes are thought to have different needs. Although many such specialized products and advertisements are merely gimmicks manufacturers use to increase their sales, they must have some market appeal based in the culture for such ideas to be acceptable to the public.

Euroamericans also have a comparatively differentiated division of labor. Additionally (although written from the woman's perspective, this statement is equally valid for men):

cultural definitions about women [and men] become so taken for granted that people confuse them with biological definitions, and can assume a woman is a female before she is a human being. Another example is the way cultural definitions of women and their roles lag behind changes in their activities. For instance, women are defined—and treated—as if they were full time mothers who stayed at home, as most women formerly did. Yet . . . most women today work outside the home. But so far, these facts have had little impact on the definitions of women being transmitted to the young. (Graebner 1975:29)

The emphasis placed on the differences between the sexes and on differentiation in the division of labor is less apparent in modern Spanish-American families than it was in the past when sexual roles contrasted strongly, as they still are among Mexicans and Mexican-Americans (see Bullock 1970:150; Grebler, Moore, and Guzman 1970:361–64). Various accounts

of a typical Mexican American family . . . perpetuate the model of an age- and sex-graded, multigenerational, authoritarian, patriarchal family. . . . Such descriptions may have been partially true some generations back. . . . At that time, their family structure reflected their Mexican heritage more closely than it does today. . . . Today, nuclear families are predominant; and female heads of households are prevalent in the barrios. (Stoddard 1973:100)

According to Kutsche and Van Ness (1981:35):

Within the [Spanish-American] household, domestic jobs are divided by sex and age in a marked but not rigid fashion. . . .

The division of labor is not absolute. If age and sex distribution in a family, or illness, or jobs away from home, make it inconvenient to go by custom, then anyone does anything without stigma. Many men and adolescent boys wash, cook, iron, and do other women's chores. Women construct buildings and bridges and do heavy farm work. . . . Swadesh . . . and Mead . . . describe the same flexibility.

In comparison to Euroamericans and Spanish-Americans, Navajos do not emphasize the differences between the sexes as much as do the other two groups. Males and females are not thought to be as different as they are in the other groups (table 7).

Because of the simplicity and homogeneity of traditional Navajo society, one can safely say that there is a consensus on the definition of roles, that expectations for proper role behavior are shared by the society as a whole. No role except the strictly biological male role is closed to women. . . . (Shepardson and Hammond 1970:66–67)

Navajos also have a weakly differentiated sexual division of labor (Downs 1972; Kluckhohn and Leighton 1962; Kluckhohn, Hill, and Kluckhohn 1971; Lamphere 1977). In my research, for instance, both males and females of all ages were consistently observed herding sheep. Either men or women would purchase groceries and other items at the local trading post. One sex did not dominate the performance of various chores like wood chopping, butchering, planting crops, and so on. This does not mean, however, that there is neither a division of labor nor a perceived difference between the sexes among the Navajos. For example, food preparation and child care were most frequently, *although by no means exclusively*, conducted by women. In general, Navajos emphasize the differences between the sexes substantially less than Euroamericans or Spanish-Americans and have a much less rigid division of labor.

Euroamericans, as a group, are specialized (i.e., have functionally specific and sexually specific occupations—male ferry operators and lumberjacks; female secretaries and nurses) and are hierarchical (i.e., have socioeconomic classes and political stratification). Examples of hierarchy are the lower, middle, and upper classes present in Euroamerican society and the numbered and graded positions present in federal, state, and county governments.

In contrast, among the Spanish-Americans, "Job specialization by occupation is very limited. . . . There are no . . . curers, midwives, therapeutic masseurs . . . who work at these trades enough to speak of [sic] even as a part-time specialty" (Kutsche

Table 7. Comparison of culture, behavior, and cultural material within the three groups investigated

Group	Emphasis on the Differences Between the Sexes	Division of Labor	Sex-Specific Activity Areas	Sex-Specific Artifact
Urban Euroamericans	much present	strongly present	many	many
Rural Euroamericans	much present	strongly present	many	many
Rural Spanish-Americans	much present	strong to moderately present	few to none	few to none
Semi-nontraditional Navajos	little present	weakly present	few to none	few to none
Semitraditional Navajos	little present	weakly present	few to none	few to none
Traditional Navajos	little present	weakly present	some	few to none

and Van Ness 1981:35). Spanish-Americans are also less hierarchical than the Euroamericans, although they are more so than the Navajos (see González 1969:75–80 for a description of Spanish-American social classes; also see table 8). Navajos have neither functionally specific nor sexually specific occupations, nor do they have classes or political hierarchies (see Kluckhohn and Leighton 1962, among others).

Traditional Navajo religion also is not markedly segmented, as is pointed out by D. Murray (1977:219):

The Navajo ceremonial system is treated as a whole which functions in different ways, the emphasis to depend on the circumstances. . . . A particular element appears as an independent unit of ceremony only for a specific emphasis or function, but it symbolically connotes all others in an interlocking fashion.

In contrast, most Euroamerican Christian sects (the number of separate varieties of Christianity in itself is an indication

Specialization	Hierarchies	Mono-functional Activity Areas	Mono-functional Artifacts	Frequency and Diversity of Artifacts
much present	strongly present	many	many	much
much present	strongly present	many	many	much
much to some present	strong to moderately present	some	some	some
little present	weakly present	some to few	some to few	some to little
little present	weakly present	few to none	few to none	little
little present	weakly present	few to none	few to none	little

of segmentation) contain hierarchical levels from good to evil—Jesus and God are above angels, who are above ministers/priests, who are above laymen who are believers, who are above those who do not believe, who are above the devil. It is important that a group's entire assemblage of traits be taken into account in order to determine its relative location on the segmentation-unity continuum. The Euroamericans, as reflected in their emphasis on the differences between the sexes, their differentiated division of labor, degree of specialization, and in the presence of hierarchies, are more segmented than the Spanish-Americans, who are more so than the Navajos (table 7).

There are other indicators of the three groups' positions along the continuum. For example, while Euroamericans tend to view the natural world as a sphere of conquest and Spanish-Americans see man as subjugated by nature, both view man and nature as a distinct dichotomy. However, the less seg-

Table 8. The relative location on the segmentation-unity continuum of various aspects of the three groups investigated

Aspects of Model	Segmentation ←	——(continuum)——	→Unity
Emphasis on the differences between the sexes	Urban Euroamericans Rural Euroamericans	Rural Spanish-Americans	Traditional Navajos Semitraditional Navajos Semi-nontraditional Navajos
Division of labor	Urban Euroamericans Rural Euroamericans	Rural Spanish-Americans	Traditional Navajos Semitraditional Navajos Semi-nontraditional Navajos
Sex-specific activity areas	Urban Euroamericans Rural Euroamericans	Traditional Navajos	Rural Spanish-Americans Semitraditional Navajos Semi-nontraditional Navajos
Sex-specific artifacts	Urban Euroamericans Rural Euroamericans		Rural Spanish-Americans Traditional Navajos Semitraditional Navajos Semi-nontraditional Navajos
Specialization	Urban Euroamericans Rural Euroamericans	Rural Spanish-Americans	Traditional Navajos Semitraditional Navajos Semi-nontraditional Navajos
Hierarchies	Urban Euroamericans Rural Euroamericans	Rural Spanish-Americans	Traditional Navajos Semitraditional Navajos Semi-nontraditional Navajos
Monofunctional activity areas	Urban Euroamericans Rural Euroamericans	Rural Spanish-Americans Semi-nontraditional Navajos	Traditional Navajos Semitraditional Navajos
Monofunctional artifacts	Urban Euroamericans Rural Euroamericans	Rural Spanish-Americans Semi-nontraditional Navajos	Traditional Navajos Semitraditional Navajos
Frequency and diversity of artifacts	Urban Euroamericans Rural Euroamericans	Rural Spanish-Americans Semi-nontraditional Navajos	Traditional Navajos Semitraditional Navajos

mented Navajos' conception differs: "If the conceptualization of the man-nature relationship is that of Harmony, there is no real separation of man, nature, and supernature. One is simply an extension of the other, and a conception of wholeness derives from their unity" (Kluckhohn and Strodtbeck 1961:13).

Another indication of their relative position on the continuum is provided by the Euroamerican and Navajo views of good and evil. Euroamericans often consider people and things as either good or bad (the two tend to be mutually exclusive categories). In contrast:

"Not definitely bad although not entirely good either" is a view reiterated time and again in the whole corpus of Navaho texts. . . . The Navaho conception is not Neutral towards *human nature*. It is definitely a mixture of Good and Evil, and this mixture is immutable (invariant). (Romney and Kluckhohn 1961:335; original emphasis)

Both my own evidence and the literature suggest that Euroamericans are highly segmented and that Spanish-Americans are less so, but are definitely more so than Navajos, who tend toward the unity end of the continuum. This is also reflected in the next level of abstraction, that of behavior.

BEHAVIOR

The emphasis placed on the differences between males and females and on a differentiated division of labor is reflected behaviorally in the prevalence of sex-specific activity areas, wherein loci tend to be used exclusively by one sex. Euroamericans, as might have been predicted from their highly segmented culture, have more sex-specific activity areas than do the other groups I observed. The Johnson family, for instance, segregated their two bathrooms by the sex of the principal user, who then stored his or her toilet articles there. This sex-specific use of bathrooms has been observed at other Euroamerican houses as well, but not in either Spanish-American or Navajo houses. The frequency of sex-specific activity areas at Spanish-American residences is minimal and is, in fact, similar to that found among the Navajos. This deviation from the expected pattern may be the effect of culture change, which is beyond the scope of this study. Navajos do not have sex-

specific activity areas other than those located inside the hogans of traditional households. This disparity can be attributed
to the sacred symbolic connotations of the hogan (discussed
in a following section). The frequency of sex-specific activity
areas, loci predominately used by one sex, is congruent in most
cases with the rigidity of each group's division of labor.

Increased segmentation, and concomitant specialization, is
reflected in the presence of monofunctional activity areas,
areas where only functionally related activities occur. Examples of Euroamerican monofunctional activity areas include
the kitchen, where only activities related to food preparation
occur, and the dining room, where only activities related to
food consumption are performed. In contrast, traditional and
semitraditional Navajos do not use function-specific areas. It
was not unusual, for example, to observe an area used by either
or both sexes for a variety of different activities. At different
times during one day Bah Many Sheep wove a blanket at the
same out-of-doors locus at which her husband, Chee, had earlier manufactured a leather quirt. At the semitraditional Bitter
Water camp, both men and women chopped wood at the wood-
chip area which also occasionally doubled as a cooking area.
Johnny Bitter Water roasted meat for lunch at the same wood-
chip area where, on different occasions, his wife Lisa, boiled
stew or made *náneeskaadí* ("tortilla" bread) at the hearth. In
this same household, men *and* women would sit on the Euroamerican manufactured bed in the northern part of their
tarpaper-and-plasterboard hogan to perform a variety of functionally unrelated activities, such as eating, repairing objects,
talking, and taking short naps. At the semi-nontraditional
Horseman family's cinder-block house/cement hogan, both
males and females ate meals either on or near the southern
couch or at the northern kitchen table, where different unrelated activities also occurred. The Euroamericans I observed
had noticeably more monofunctional activity areas than did
the Spanish-Americans, who had more than the Navajos (see
chapter 3).

The use of activity areas corresponds to the location of each
group along the segmentation-unity continuum. Other indicators of the groups' positions are also manifested in their

behavior. The Euroamerican breakfast, lunch, and dinner, for example, are conceptually different from those of the Navajo. Each meal consists of different foods (e.g., cereal or eggs for breakfast, sandwiches or soup for lunch, and meat, potatoes, and vegetables and/or salad for dinner). In addition Euroamericans tend to view certain types of food as sex specific in that they are most often associated with either males or females. For instance, in a recent satire entitled *Real Men Don't Eat Quiche: A Guide Book to All That Is Truly Masculine*, Feirstein (1982:73) wrote, "By now you're probably wondering: If a Real Man doesn't eat quiche, just what does his diet consist of? Essentially, Real Men are meat and potatoes eaters. Real Men eat beef." And, of course, "Real Women" eat quiche (Feirstein 1982:91).

Although ethnically specific foods like tortillas and posole are eaten, the Spanish-Americans also use different types of foods for different meals. This distinction is, except on rare occasions, nonexistent among the Navajos, who eat mutton or pinto beans or whatever three times a day. This is not a reflection of their financial situation; Navajos simply do not consider each meal as a separate entity requiring different foods—a less particularistic or segmented view than that present among the other groups.

The sleeping arrangements made when I lived with each group also differed significantly. At both the Spanish-American and Navajo households, I usually slept in a bed with at least one and often more children, although empty beds were available. In contrast, I always had my own bed at the Euroamerican homes, even if it meant displacing a child so I could have his/her double bed to myself. This may be a result of Euroamerican segmentation. Even when I was not present, Spanish-Americans and Navajos living in Euroamerican-style multiroom houses used only one or two bedrooms, although other rooms were available. The Spanish-American and Navajo orientation toward the family as a united whole, in contrast to the individualism characteristic of Euroamerican attitudes, whereby each person should have his/her own room and his/her own bed is possible, might explain this phenomenon.

CULTURAL MATERIAL

According to the model, a more segmented group with sex-specific and monofunctional activity areas will have more sex-specific monofunctional artifacts (and concomitantly, a higher frequency and more diverse types of artifacts) than a group located closer to the unity end of the continuum. In fact, the Euroamericans I observed did tend to have a greater diversity of artifacts than did the Spanish-Americans, who appeared to have more than the Navajos. The Navajos had more multi-functional and non-sex-specific objects.

Euroamericans had the most functionally specific artifacts, which was consistent with their position along the segmentation-unity continuum. In the Johnson kitchen alone, there were a Mr. Coffee machine, a dishwasher, salad forks and plates in addition to dinner forks and plates, steak knives, butter knives, paring knives, and serrated knives, juice, wine, whiskey, and general beverage glasses, and so on. In contrast, the Spanish-Americans and Navajos had fewer monofunctional artifacts. This was especially evident among the Navajos, who used oil drums both to store water and to cover the hogan hearth (used for cooking and as a source of heat). Unlike the Navajos, the Spanish-American García family had separate wood-burning stove and heaters, each of which was used only to cook or to heat the house. The Navajos also used the same knife in cooking, eating, and basketry manufacture and had one washbasin to wash dishes, people's hair, the baby's diapers, and anything else that needed washing.

Euroamericans had numerous monofunctional clothes—pajamas, robes, bathing suits, tennis dresses, running shoes, party clothes, work clothes, season-specific clothes, and so on. Although this trait was not as pronounced as among the Euroamericans, the Spanish-Americans also used different clothes for different activities, such as pajamas, party clothes, and so on. The Navajos, in comparison, all slept in the same clothes that they had worn that day and planned to wear the next. This was not a result of their economic status. They usually had one good set of clothing, somewhat newer than their everyday wear, reserved for special occasions. They did not use pajamas, season-specific clothes, bathing suits, and the like. This pattern is consistent with the model.

Euroamericans also had a higher frequency of sex-specific artifacts; for instance, the sex-specific desks and dressers at the Johnsons' house. Another example is the his-and-her hand towels some Euroamericans have. The almost total lack of sex-specific artifacts among the Spanish-Americans correlates with the dearth of sex-specific activity areas in Spanish-American houses. The Navajos also had few or no sex-specific artifacts, as has been discussed in the ethnographic literature:

Though one sex or the other dominated, use roles tended to be mixed. For example, women made and used pottery and most baskets; on occasion, however, these were used by male chanters. Men dressed in buckskin, but women made and used many articles manufactured from it, including ropes, saddles, moccasins, and skin bags. Men did not grind corn, but used the metate and mano to grind pigments for a sandpainting or bark for dyeing buckskin. The batten used by a woman in weaving might be borrowed by a man to smooth a sandpainting. [The latter two examples also indicate the prevalence of multipurpose tools.] In addition, *there was evidence that not only was the same type of tool used by men and women, but the same tool was transferred from one to another as needed.* (Kluckhohn, Hill, and Kluckhohn 1971:429; emphasis added)

Euroamerican culture, then, is more segmented than Spanish-American culture, which is substantially more so than Navajo culture, and table 8 summarizes this continuum. In all but two cases, the relative amount of segmentation is consistently reflected in each group's culture, behavior, and cultural material, all of which are actually intertwined with one another. The main exception, the traditional Navajo's sex specific activity areas within the hogan, is discussed in the following section.

The Traditional Hogan: Symbolism and Sacredness

The only sex-specific activity areas used by Navajos are in the hogan, where traditional Navajos segregate space into sex-specific areas. Chee Many Sheep, the male head of his household (chapter 3), used only the southeastern portion of his hogan, regardless of the activity being performed. Gene, the oldest son living at home, used primarily the southwestern quadrant. The women and younger children conducted most activities in the northern half of the hogan, although exceptions did occur—most notably in the case of food consumption, which took place in the southwestern quadrant. However, the same family did not have any sex-specific activity areas when living in the ramada or working out-of-doors. Other anthropologists have also noted the sexual division in the use of hogans (e.g., Brugge 1980; Kluckhohn and Leighton 1962; Lamphere 1977). Nevertheless, according to the model discussed above, the Navajos, because of their flexible division of labor and relative position on the continuum, should not have had more sex-specific activity areas in their dwellings than the other groups investigated. The fact that ramadas, which are occupied during a different season than are hogans, but where similar mundane activities are conducted, do not have sex-specific activity areas compounds the apparent enigma. However, this discrepancy can be understood from the standpoint of symbolism (Kent 1982b).

To the traditional Navajo, the hogan is conceptually different from the ramada, although identical activities of daily living occur in both. The hogan is perceived as a sacred dwelling; the ramada is not. The hogan is mentioned in important myths and ritual prayers (one of which is the Blessingway) and specific parts of ceremonies must be conducted only within a hogan. Consequently, there are instances where Navajos inhabit Euroamerican-style rectangular houses while maintaining a hogan for ceremonies (Haile 1954:11). I suggest that the circular hogan symbolizes the circular cosmos, whereas the rectangular ramada and the out-of-doors do not. The round, sacred hogan is divided into the same male and female areas as is the round, sacred cosmos. The male-female division of the cosmos is reflected in sex-specific activity areas inside the hogan. The division of hogan space by the sex of the user, then, *is not* a reflection of the Navajo's emphasis on the differences between the sexes or of their division of labor; instead, it is a reflection of the sacred, circular cosmos.

Because the ramada is not a sacred dwelling, Navajos do not

divide it into sex-specific areas. The use of space in the ramada and out-of-doors, where activity areas are not sex specific, is consistent with their relative lack of emphasis on the differences between the sexes and with their flexible division of labor. This all conforms to the Navajos' position along the segmentation-unity continuum. The use of space inside the hogan is affected during mundane day-to-day occupation, as well as during ceremonies, by the sacredness ascribed to the dwelling. In other words, the *division of hogan space on the basis of sex is not a result of the Navajos' division of labor or sex roles, but of the hogan's symbolism of the cosmos, which is similarly divided.*

Those Navajos who depart from traditional culture do not have sex-specific activity areas within their hogans or Euroamerican-style houses because of the weakened influence of the traditional religion. The hogan is no longer sacred to them, and a Euroamerican-style rectangular house never was. For example, a singer and the semitraditional Bitter Water family conducted a curing ceremony within their tarpaper-and-plasterboard hogan. Nevertheless, the Bitter Water family never observed sex-specific activity areas within the dwelling, and the seating arrangement during the ceremony itself was sacrilegious (males and females between the ages of 13 and 19 sat in the northern half, and the older female household members sat in the southern half of the hogan). The ceremony was probably held in the hogan only because they had been taught that that is where ceremonies should be held. Devoid of much of its original symbolism, the hogan was as secular to them as their Euroamerican-style winter house.

The Archaeological Realm of the Model

For reasons presented in chapter 5 (the astronomical increase in refuse as a result of the use of nonperishable, bulky, mass-produced Euroamerican goods) the excavated twentieth-century Navajo archaeological sites cannot be used to demonstrate the mechanics of the model in an archaeological context. Consequently, I can only discuss how the model would hypothetically operate. Since few precontact Navajo sites are available for study, I will use another Southwestern prehistoric group, the Mesa Verde Anasazi, to illustrate how the model would operate archaeologically.

The model can be used to test the hypothesis that population increases occurring during the Anasazi pithouse-to-pueblo shift, circa A.D. 600–900 (Hayes 1964; Rohn 1977; Swedlund and Sessions 1976; and others), required the adoption of a sociopolitical organizational strategy that was first relied upon during the Basketmaker II–III shift to sedentary village life. Population aggregations and sedentism required the development of increasingly specialized political and social organizations, since in the newly sedentary Basketmaker III village life aggregates of people were interacting with one another on a permanent basis. I hypothesize that most of these changes were in the direction of segmentation on the segmentation-unity continuum. Later, this strategy, the intensification of political and social specialization, had to be amplified in response to the continuing population increases and aggregations that occurred during the early Pueblo periods. The ramifications of change in the sociopolitical organization, according to the model of the interrelationship of culture, behavior, and cultural material, were substantial and far reaching.

Village leaders became necessary to make and/or implement community decisions on economic, political, social, and religious matters. Incipient social stratification and hierarchies developed, as did some level of political stratification since, except in band-level societies, most headmen have achieved status with recognized influence and some power. All of this concurs with Cordell's (1979), Steward's (1937), and Birkedal's (1976) contentions that Basketmaker III villages may have been organized on a band level, and Gillespie's (1976) suggestion that villages became lineage residence groups when the shift to aboveground structures occurred among some groups in the Southwest. The relationship between increasing population size and organizational complexity has also been noted by Hassan (1981:181–82), and by others.

According to the model, change toward an increasingly specialized social and political organization will be reflected in other changes in culture, such as a greater emphasis on the differences between the sexes and a more differentiated division of labor. These changes will also be reflected in behavior as an increase in the use of sex-specific and monofunctional activity areas. Cultural and behavioral change will be reflected in cultural material in the way people use their artifacts, in the form of an increase in sex-specific and monofunctional objects.

To research this hypothesis would require the excavation of several sites from the various Anasazi time periods in question. It would, in addition, present some interesting methodological challenges, although these could be overcome. For example, the present study has already demonstrated that activity areas are not cross-culturally sex specific or monofunctional, and that, consequently, one must demonstrate whether or not activity areas at a site were sex specific or monofunctional. Determining which sex used a tool can only be done by inference from ethnographic and ethnoarchaeological data, and determining the specific function(s) for which a tool was used or the exact activities performed at a site may not always be possible. As Plog (1974:162) has pointed out, however, the precise reconstruction of a function or an activity is not essential to many studies. More important to this research is the ability to determine whether a tool was multipurpose or monofunctional, whether or not different types of activities occurred at a locus, and if each sex used separate areas to perform his/her activities. In fact, there are indications that it is possible to ascertain whether lithic tools were multipurpose or monofunctional (see Keeley 1980; Nance 1971; Nelson 1981; and others). The ratio of monofunctional to multipurpose tools from each time period can be compared with that from the other time periods in order to detect possible changes in the ratio through time. The actual reconstruction of specific functions and activities may be interesting, but it is extremely difficult to determine and not really necessary in order to apply the proposed model. It is possible to apply the model by ascertaining whether or not artifacts were monofunctional and sex specific and inferring whether or not activity areas (including storage areas) also were (fig. 88).

Whereas in ethnographic situations one can observe the reflection of behavior and cultural material in culture, the nature of the archaeological record forces one to observe the

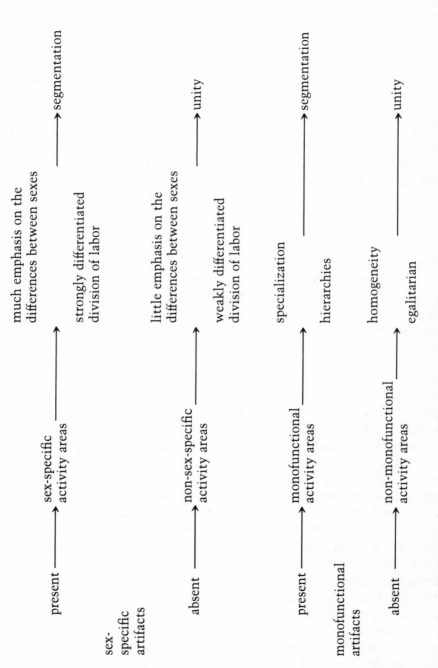

Figure 88. Idealized hypothetical example of the mechanics of the archaeological realm of the model.

reflection of culture in cultural material and behavior. If these three levels are as interrelated as the ethnographic data indicate, it should be possible to speculate about aspects of a group's culture by inferring parts of its behavior and determining its use of cultural material.

In sum, my model could be used to study culture change and its ramifications during the Mesa Verde Anasazi pithouse-to-pueblo transition in the Southwest. Plotting data on the segmentation-unity continuum would visually order the information to reflect change through time. In addition, the model could be used to investigate intergroup variation among contemporaneous Southwestern groups, such as the various Anasazi branches and/or the Sinagua and Mogollon. This would allow archaeologists to study the nature and magnitude of intergroup differences and to predict where other differences might be expected. The model of the interrelationship of culture, behavior, and cultural material facilitates the study of intersite variation on both a diachronic and synchronic level and thereby contributes to the understanding of culture change.

A General Principle Underlying the Continuum

The segmentation-unity continuum is merely a descriptive device that can be used for comparative purposes between groups, either through time or through space. It is nothing more than that. Nevertheless, one might ask why groups' cultures can be placed on this segmentation-unity continuum. I hypothesize that the continuum is a reflection of something else—a general principle, which is a continuation of the pattern elucidated in the model discussed earlier. The principle (or structure) is, I suggest, the relationship between compartmentalization and holism, and it permeates culture, behavior, and cultural material. The presence of such underlying principles is not a new concept to either cultural anthropology or archaeology (for the latter see Glassie 1975; Hodder 1982; and Leone 1982, among others).

As has been shown, groups with sex-specific and monofunctional activity areas tend to produce sex-specific and monofunctional cultural material. Aspects of their culture are consistent with their behavior and cultural material as well (i.e., in the above case, they exhibit much rather than little emphasis on the differences between the sexes, a differentiated division of labor, specialization, and so on). In other words, there are relationships within a group between the various aspects of each level of the model. These relationships can be formulated: sex-specific and monofunctional activity areas are to sex-specific and monofunctional cultural material as non-sex-specific and multipurpose activity areas are to non-sex-specific and multipurpose cultural material. A parallel relationship is: strict division of labor is to emphasis on the differences between the sexes as weak division of labor is to nonemphasis on the differences between the sexes. In addition, the above demonstrated that the presence of hierarchies are to the presence of specialization as the absence of hierarchies is to the absence of specialization. This is more succinctly expressed in table 7.

Hence, groups with monofunctional and sex-specific activity areas, according to the model, will tend to have some form of hierarchies, specialization, emphasis on the differences between the sexes, a relatively strong division of labor, and monofunctional and sex-specific cultural material. The converse is also true. The ethnographic data presented earlier illustrate these relationships (also see chapter 3).

It appears that groups who compartmentalize space into segments do the same with everything about them, from their technology to their conception of the sexes. In other words, they unconsciously conceive of their world as made up of parts (often obscurely related to wholes). An example is the person who sees him/herself as a separate individual first and part of a family second—a tendency of Euroamericans, for instance. In contrast, groups who do not divide space to the same extent (who maintain a more holistic perspective) also do not divide aspects of culture into segments, and they treat everything about them in the same way, from their use of artifacts to their division of labor. In other words, they conceive of their world as made up of wholes (often obscurely related to parts). Navajos, for example, conceive of themselves as part of a family first and as individuals second.

This pattern appears to be valid cross-culturally beyond the groups investigated, as evidenced by the ethnographic/ethnoarchaeological literature. For example, relative to the Navajos, Euroamericans, and Spanish-Americans, the !Kung Bushmen appear to be located closer to the unity end of the segmentation continuum. This can be consistently seen in the Bushmen's culture, behavior, and cultural material. The division between the sexes, beyond the basic biological differences recognized by all groups, is not as pronounced as among Navajos or Euroamericans. The !Kung have a division of labor between the sexes as do all groups known; however, it is less differentiated and is more flexible than that present among other groups.

Most members of the Harvard !Kung Bushman Study Project who have thought about the subject of !Kung women's status agree that !Kung society may be the least sexist of any we have experienced. This impression contradicts some popularly held stereotypes about relations between the sexes in hunting and gathering societies. Because sex is one of the few bases for the differentiation of social and economic roles in societies of this type, it has probably been attributed more weight than it deserves. The men are commonly depicted in rather romantic terms, striving with their brothers to bring home the precious meat while their women humbly provide the dull, tasteless vegetable food in the course of routine, tedious foraging. *Contrary evidence is now emerging from several researchers that men and women of band-level societies have many overlapping activities and spheres of influence. . . . The distinction between male and female roles is substantially less rigid than previously supposed. . . .* (Draper 1975:77; emphasis added)

The !Kung have virtually no political or social specialization or hierarchies. They have one of the least stratified political organizations known and are often classified as egalitarian, although informal leaders do exist. "Whatever their skills, !Kung leaders have no formal authority. They only persuade, but never enforce their will on others. Even the !Kung vocabulary of leadership is limited" (Lee 1979:343–44). In fact, a Bushman's answer to Lee's question of whether or not the !Kung have headmen was, " 'Of course we have headmen' he replied, to my surprise. 'In fact, we are all headmen,' he continued slyly, 'each one of us is headman over himself!' " (Lee 1979:348).

As might have been predicted by the model, Bushmen do not use sex-specific or monofunctional activity areas (Yellen 1977a:91, 195–97). The pattern outlined in the model also is consistent in the cultural material level—artifacts tend not to be monofunctional. "!Kung tools are few in number, light-weight, made from available materials, and *multipurpose*" (Lee 1979:119; emphasis added). According to Yellen (1982: personal communication), most objects are used by both sexes among the !Kung Bushmen, with only a few exceptions such as certain articles of clothing. Thus, the Bushmen culture, behavior, and cultural material do fit the pattern predicted by the model.

Another hunting and gathering group that uses fewer sex-specific or monofunctional objects than do the Navajo or the other study groups is the Batek De' Negritos of the Malay Peninsula (Endicott 1979). Although more data are necessary in order to substantiate this comparison, it appears that the Batek are less segmented or are closer to the unity end of the continuum than are the Bushmen.

Batek tools are made and repaired by both men and women. Specialized tools, primarily hunting equipment, tend to be made by men since they are the persons who use the equipment all the time. However, women know how to make darts and some can do basic blowpipe maintenance. Digging sticks are made by both men and women by cutting a sapling to the desired length and either carving one end to a point or lashing on a metal blade with rattan. (Endicott 1979:77; emphasis added)

Unfortunately we have no data on the Bateks' use of space. However, there are many examples from the culture level of the model to indicate that the pattern is internally consistent with the Batek. According to the model, the relative lack of sex-specific tools is a reflection of a relatively undifferentiated division of labor. Both men and women hunt (even with the blowpipe), fish, and gather. It is true that women do not hunt as much as do men; however, 74 percent of the food weight procured by males is vegetable and only 26 percent is meat (Endicott 1979:21–55).

Most of the activities of the Batek are performed by members of both sexes. In some food-getting activities one sex or the other dominates in frequency of performance of the activity and in yields. This statistical dominance is not matched by a cultural stereotyping of the particular activity as man's work or woman's work, however; both sexes are allowed to do the work. (Endicott 1979:92)

Concomitantly little emphasis is placed on the differences between the sexes:

> The Batek make little use of the sexual idiom in their view of the world. They do not classify the cosmic or natural worlds according to a male-female distinction. (Endicott 1979:15)

> The brevity of this chapter [titled "Batek Ideas About the Sexes"] is testimony to the small extent to which considerations of gender distinctions influence Batek cultural thought. (Endicott 1979:18)

Both men and women can become informal leaders, and although the Batek have no term for these leaders (because of their lack of political specialization and hierarchies), they usually are older, charismatic persons (Endicott 1979:104–5). Even on the basis of these somewhat limited data, it can be seen that Batek culture and cultural material, as was true with the Bushmen, Navajos, Euroamericans, and Spanish-Americans, are congruent with the proposed model.

The model appears to be internally consistent among a small but diverse sample of groups. Although more data are needed, it is postulated that the model is predictive for past, present, and future groups of people (although probably not applicable to any society earlier than *Homo sapiens*). If only the culture of a group is known, one ought to be able to predict their behavior and cultural material using the model. Conversely, the model should allow one to predict a group's culture by knowing its behavior and cultural material. The latter capability has important implications for archaeologists, who usually deal only with a group's behavior and cultural material. The development of such predictive models is one way to begin to actualize one of archaeology's most important goals: that of understanding the past. It is also particularly informative to try to understand the variables responsible for groups that do not fit the pattern predicted by the model.

Although more testing of the consistency of the model is still necessary, one or two exceptions do not invalidate it. In fact, such exceptions are valuable in delineating the factors involved in intergroup variability. For instance, the Australian Aborigines and Eskimos appear to contradict the model. Although it is completely beyond the scope of this chapter to examine these two groups in the depth necessary to understand their deviance from the patterning predicted by the model, a brief discussion is possible.

Three points may influence the Aborigines' aberrant patterning among their culture, behavior, and cultural material: (1) the quality of the research conducted among the Aborigines has been quite varied (Meggitt 1968); (2) the changes resulting from European influences have not been considered enough when describing supposedly pristine Aborigine customs and beliefs (Berndt 1981); and (3) the Aborigines were not originally a band-level society, with the egalitarian and noncomplex social and political organization that that level of society connotes. Even though the following cursory examination of data does not do justice to them, a review of the literature indicates that these mitigating influences are at least partly applicable.

Several anthropologists have noted the range in quality of the research conducted among the Aborigines, which has contributed to some inaccurate views of the people (see Pilling 1968:138; Rohrlich-Leavitt, Sykes, and Weatherford 1975:110).

In comparative studies of primitive peoples the Australian aborigines have long held a special place and, perhaps for this very reason, a number of misconceptions concerning their society and culture have entered the anthropological literature. . . . (Meggitt 1968:176)

Although contact with Europeans has altered to one degree or another almost every group we know of, the impact appears to be deemphasized in some ethnographies of the Aborigines (though certainly not in all). This may be, in part, a result of attempts (or desires) to study a "primeval" group. That the changes induced by Europeans have not always been sufficiently taken into account when discussing traditional Aborigine culture and behavior has been noted by Berndt (1981:171):

I know very well . . . how much was lost, not only in the fields of my special interests but in every field of Aboriginal culture and not

only in the regions I am acquainted with but in others. The time
span involved is not really very long, relatively speaking. Yet so
much has gone, even from the level of "memory culture" when no
living person remembers the content of some things that were traditionally there, or even recalls that they *were* there. The new my-
thologies or the new ideologies that have been growing up in those
regions—almost all regions, although more conspicuously in some—
are helping to redefine the traditional picture, developing new, re-
framed traditions. Probably this was always a feature of the ongoing
scene, in the pre-European past as well as since. But the transfor-
mations that have been taking place in the last couple of decades
would appear to have no close precedents. The nearest parallel is
the cultural turmoil (as it was from the Aborigines' perspective) that
followed the first waves of invasion in the south. (original emphasis)

Even though the interior Australian Aborigines are often
classified as a mobile band-level society, and therefore polit-
ically and socially egalitarian and noncomplex (Service 1971
and others), their culture and behavior generally suggest otherwise. For example, they have a pronounced division of labor
(Berndt 1981:175–76; and others). They display a great deal of
social complexity compared to the Bushmen or Batek, as evidenced by their kinship system, which is organized into clans
(Hiatt 1968:101) and moieties (Elkin 1938:130; Meggitt
1968:176–81; Service 1971:15). Clans own artistic designs as
well as land (Hiatt 1968:101; Rose 1968:201). As a result of
these characteristics, some researchers have tentatively classified the Aborigines as tribal people (see Yengoyan 1968). This
seems more appropriate than their band classification, especially in comparison to groups like the Bushmen and Batek.
Incipient occupational stratification in the form of part-time
specialists, such as the medicine men described by Elkin
(1938:315–35), also suggests a tribal level of organization.
However, the Aborigines are still anomalous in terms of the
model because of their relatively noncomplex political organization.

None of this explains why the model does not work with
the Aborigines, but it does make the discrepancy less incon-
gruous than it first appears. For reasons that are as yet unknown, perhaps the Aborigine patterning of culture, behavior,
and cultural material will always remain disparate from what
the model would predict.

The reasons why Eskimos also apparently do not conform to the patterns predicted by the model are equally obscure, but some of the same factors may be operating in their case as with the Aborigines. Specifically, Eskimos may actually represent a tribal society (rather than a band) except in certain areas of their culture and behavior, probably in part as a result of the harsh environment they inhabit. Studies of the exceptions to a mode are often as productive and enlightening as are studies of groups that conform to the model. At any rate, more research is clearly needed.

Compartmentalization Versus Holism

The tendency to compartmentalize can be seen in the lowest forms of animals who distinguish edible from nonedible materials and safety from danger. Human language and cognition are categorizing mechanisms that have led to an increased fragmentation of the universe by humans.

... the primitive stage in cognition is one of a comparative lack of differentiation. Probably certain distinctions are inescapable; the difference between a loud noise and near silence, between a bright contour and a dark ground, etc. These inevitable discriminations divide the perceived world into a small number of very large (abstract) categories. Cognitive development is increasing differentiation. The more distinctions we make, the more categories we have and the smaller (more concrete) these are. (Brown 1958:19)

Nevertheless, despite the tendency toward differentiation, individuals must be part of a whole, or of something larger than themselves, in order to maintain a sense of well-being. It is only as part of a whole that an individual can find security; alone, he/she is both psychologically and physically vulnerable. Inevitably, then, there is a tension between the tendency to compartmentalize and the need to be part of a whole.

Man has an inward orientation toward himself as a totality, but he is pulled outward by his necessity to become a part of a collectivity and to serve its requirements. Simmel goes beyond the social psychological implications of his position to see this as a central problem in the evolution of society, which is "an attempt at saving the unity and totality of society from disruption by the autonomy of its parts. . . ." (Murphy 1980:135)

Compartmentalization and holism are reflected throughout the universe as we know it, because we all perceive the universe through a *Homo sapiens sapiens* brain. As a consequence, we see almost every object known to us—atoms, plants, rocks, and so on—as made up of parts, and these parts all interact to form a whole entity, be it an amoeba, a rock, or a flower (although this tendency to perceive parts of wholes may be more pronounced in some groups than others). A person, too, must be part of a greater whole in order to function properly. This necessity is reflected in culture in various ways. One way is in kinship systems, which attempt to classify an individual in relation to a greater whole, be it a nuclear family, extended family, lineage, or clan. Religion also puts humans into a wider context; they are merely one part of their total universe.

The [religious] believer who has communicated with his god is not merely a man who sees new truths of which the unbeliever is ignorant; he is a man who is *stronger*. He feels within him more force, either to endure the trials of existence, or to conquer them. It is as though he were raised above the miseries of the world, because he is raised above his condition as a mere man. . . . (Durkheim 1965:416; original emphasis)

Identifying with an ethnic group or a profession is another avenue to achieve the same end—a feeling of being less fragmented and less alone, of belonging to a greater whole. The segmentation-unity continuum, then, is simply a reflection of this compartmentalization/holism principle.

Compartmentalization is defined as separating parts of a whole into distinct categories (or compartments). In other words, it is extreme segmentation. Holism, the opposite of compartmentalization, is complete, undivided, consisting of all parts; it represents extreme unity. It is this principle—the relationship between compartmentalization and holism—that underlies the segmentation-unity continuum, and it is this relationship that underlies behavior (specifically activity area usage), culture, and cultural material. Although the compartmentalization/holism principle is consistent throughout time and space, it is reflected differently in different groups. These differences, which we perceive as distinct cultures, are the result of a group's history, interaction with neighbors, physical environment, and other factors.

Specifically why some groups may be closer than others to the segmentation end of the continuum in culture, behavior, and cultural material is still not completely understood because not all the variables involved have been identified. It should be kept in mind that "*any* processual outcome results from the operation of plural factors. . . . *All* . . . single-factor theories belong to the kindergarten stage of social science's development. *Any* factor is always interdependent with several others" (Parsons 1966:113; original emphasis). Keeping this in mind, I would suggest that two important variables are population density (especially aggregation) and sedentism.

The growth of a population in an area has been posited by many anthropologists as the impetus behind the development of a more complex social and political organization. According to a number of anthropologists, this development ultimately leads to stratification, hierarchies, and so on (see Cordy 1981:230–31; Harner 1970:67; and others; for a discussion of variables that result in complex societies, see Jones and Kautz 1981).

An increase in differentiation is characteristic of complex societies (cf. Durkheim 1933:41; Parsons 1966; and others). Service (1971:490–91) tied the segmentation of complex societies, or state-level societies in contrast to band-level ones, to their complex structure:

> It would seem that, in the course of cultural evolution, increasing size and density of the successively more evolved social bodies necessarily required increasing subdivision or segmentation—i.e., more parts—and increasing differentiation among them. (1971:491)

Julian Steward (1955:47–48) also characterized state-level societies as more segmented than, for example, band-level societies.

First there are localized groups, which may result from differentiation that has occurred during national development—for example, subcultures arising from local specialization in production or cultural ecological adaptations—or which may consist of ethnic minorities. . . . Second, there are "horizontal" groups, such as castes, classes, occupational divisions, and other segments, which hold status positions in an hierarchical arrangement and usually crosscut localities to some extent. These, too, may represent segments which either have been differentiated during national development or have been incorporated from the outside.

The potential for disputes in a society increases with the population density of an area, and especially with aggregation and sedentism, as more people begin to interact with one another on a more permanent basis (cf. Goldschmidt 1980:54).

At the same time simply being committed to continued residence has meant that each household is drawn into the problems and conflicts of their neighbors to an extent not seen among the nomadic families studied.

Nomadic mobility . . . has important sociological effects on group integration. For example, conflict which may arise among families can be resolved before violence occurs. . . . Disputants simply avoid one another. Yoruk society has no elaborate formal mechanisms to adjudicate disputes or to mediate hostilities. . . . In the nomadic society households which dislike each other rarely need see each other and can keep considerable distance between their tents while still following the same migratory schedule. The option of moving away probably obviated the need for more formal means of resolving conflicts. (Bates 1980:132–33)

The increased interaction results in the need for an arbiter, someone who has enough recognized power to settle disputes. The resulting incipient political stratification is concomitant with a change in the social organization. The individual with the political authority to make decisions (informal as that may be) usually has a slightly different social status from that of other group members in that he/she is the person consulted when problems arise. Perhaps the most dramatic example of the need for a more complex sociopolitical organization in large groups has been noted by Carneiro (1967:240–41), who describes:

the elaboration in Plains Indian social structure brought about by large periodic aggregations of population. During most of the year the several bands of a typical Plains tribe subsisted separately and acted independently of one another. Political organization within the band was minimal: there was a chief, but he had relatively little authority, and there was no council. Socio-ceremonial life was equally simple.

For the summer buffalo hunt, however, the dozen or more bands constituting a tribe came together and formed an aggregate of several thousand persons. This aggregate took on a tribal organization distinctly more complex than that of the band. The band chiefs now formed themselves into a council, and from among their members elected a paramount chief who exercised considerable authority. It was his responsibility to coordinate and direct the activities of the tribe as a whole. . . .

That the emergence of these structural features was a response to the organizational problems posed by supra-band aggregation is shown by the fact that every one of them—the tribal chief, the council, the men's societies, the police force, the sun dance organization—lapsed when the tribe broke up into its constituent units in the fall.

This mode of cultural transformation, which among the Plains Indians occurred abruptly, dramatically, and reversibly, takes place among all evolving societies, only more slowly, less obviously, and oftentimes, irreversibly.

Many authors have recognized a relationship between population increases and sedentism (Lee 1972a:338–39; and others). In addition, the need for a recognized arbitrator is accentuated when a group becomes sedentary because more people are forced to interact with one another on a permanent basis. "Data on the !Kung . . . suggest that *sedentarization alone may trigger population growth, since women may have children more frequently without any increase in work on their part and without reducing their ability to provide for each one*" (Lee 1972a:342; original emphasis). Hassan (1981:181) has noted that "significant increase in population brought about by one factor or more would thus encourage the development of a higher level of complexity, if the society is to remain viable" and that "the number of organizational traits is proportional to the root (or power) of the population size."

Leaders are necessary to settle disputes and generally to ensure the smooth running of sedentary groups. These political leaders, with their concomitant social status, become important and necessary for a variety of community decisions once people are living in villages. The relationship between population density and sociopolitical organization has been discussed by several authors, including Dumond (1972:306–9), Harner (1970:67–85), Hassan (1981:180–86), and Netting (1972:219, 236–37). According to Lee:

The effect of living in larger communities has been to stimulate a more intensive social life. When the size of the local group grows beyond the scale where everyone knows everyone else well, new modes of behavior and new forms of social organization must crystallize in order to regularize the added complexity. . . .

The major disadvantage of intense social life in larger groups is the increased frequency of conflict. Arguments and fights take place in Bushman camps of all sizes and seasons, but the larger camps seem particularly plagued with disputes. For example, at /ai/ai, a water hole with a large resident population (100 to 150), serious disputes broke out about once every two weeks during 1968–1969. The comparable rate for water hole Dobe and Mahopa, with resident populations averaging between 40 and 60, was three or four times a year. In the past, the *choma* initiation camps often failed because of disputes on procedural matters. The big camps would split up, and participants would disperse into smaller groupings in local areas.

Keeping very large groups together requires special efforts from individuals. They must maintain higher levels of cooperation and coordination of hunting and gathering activities than would be necessary in smaller domestic groupings. For this reason the largest aggregations of Bushmen and of other hunters such as the Pygmies . . . were inherently unstable; fights were likely to break out and lead to the breakup of the group. (Lee 1972b:343, 346–47)

Modern sedentary Bushmen camps are possible only as a result of the Herero pastoralists, who intervene as legal arbitrators and who maintain order in the camps.

Arguments are a frequent occurrence at /ai/ai, but whenever a dispute comes to blows or shows other signs of becoming nasty (as it did about once every two weeks during my fieldwork at /ai/ai), someone runs for the Herero. At this point one or more Hereros intervene to separate the combatants and mediate the dispute. Formerly, the Bushmen did their serious fighting with spears and poisoned arrows. . . . Thus the Bushmen can maintain an intensity of social life over long periods that would not have been possible under the traditional hunting and gathering conditions. Under the old order real conflict and threat of conflict tended to work against the Bushmen's desire for a more intense social life. It is the presence of the Hereros as mediators, backed up by the legal sanctions of the Batawana Tribal Authority . . . that provides the umbrella that enables

150 Bushmen to live together in relative harmony for the greater part of the year. (Lee 1972b:349)

Hassan (1981:251) has stated that one of the trends important to the development of urbanism was "incipient social hierarchical differentiation as a result of the development of incipient semiformal leadership to take charge of the responsibilities of social and economic inter- and intracommunal coordination."

According to the model, an increase in the stratification of the socio-political organization of a group results in specialization (the leader being a political specialist, even though it may be on a very informal and part-time basis) and in the development of incipient hierarchies in both the political and social realms. This stratification will eventually influence other aspects of culture, behavior, and cultural material.

Some groups are more segmented than others, then, at least partly because of differential population densities (especially aggregations) and the amount of sedentism present. These factors are operating today; they can be seen by studying some of the effects of contact with Europeans/Euroamericans on non-Western groups. For example among the !Kung Bushmen:

> Features of sedentary life that appear to be related to a decrease in women's autonomy and influence are: *increasing rigidity in sex-typing of adult work;* more permanent attachment of the individual to a particular place and group of people; *dissimilar childhood socialization for boys and girls;* decrease in the mobility of women as contrasted with men; changing nature of women's subsistence contribution; *richer material inventory with implications for women's work;* tendency for men to have greater access to and control over important resources such as . . . wage work; male entrance into extravillage politics; settlement pattern; and increasing household privacy. (Draper 1975:78; emphasis added)

This same trend toward segmentation has also been observed among the Navajos for the same reasons—an increase in population density, and a newly sedentary way of life, as well as the impact of the European/Euroamerican culture.

> While Navajos are isomorphic as a people when compared to other groups, there are some differences present between traditional, semi-

traditional, and semi-nontraditional Navajo families. . . . There appears to be a trend towards more differentiation of the culture, behavior, and material culture by less traditional families, although such differentiation is definitely and substantially less than that found in some non-Navajo groups.

Observations of a semi-traditional Navajo family who lived in a three bedroom Anglo-American manufactured house revealed the use of some monofunctional areas and artifacts. . . . The trend away from the use of multipurpose tools and activity areas was also observed at other semi-nontraditional families. . . . (Kent 1983:82–83)

In addition, Navajos, once seminomadic pastoralists, are becoming increasingly sedentary. Sedentism permits, among other things, the accumulation of sex-specific and monofunctional objects, whereas mobility restricts the number of objects one can possess by the amount one is able to transport and/or cache (see Kent 1983).

The trend toward segmentation cannot be totally explained by stating that Navajos are being influenced by the more segmented Euroamericans. They have been in contact with Euroamericans for at least 150 years, and the changes described are only now occurring (although aboriginally Navajos were an Athapaskan band-level society and have since undergone many changes, one being an increase in segmentation—in other words, we are seeing only one point in an ongoing process). The changes that are occurring today are the result not only of the impact of Euroamerican culture, but also of the rising population density on the reservation, the result being that the new dominant mode of habitation is now semi or complete sedentism. Thus, as is often the case, this culture change is the result of many factors rather than a single one.

Although it is speculative, the above discussion represents one productive way of explaining intergroup variability using the model. Actually, the identification of the exact ultimate reasons why one group becomes more segmented than another is not my primary concern. It is determining what happens after the increase in segmentation occurs that is of interest— that is, how change affects a group's culture, behavior, and cultural material. Rather than trying in the manner of positivists to explain causalities, I am concerned with understanding process and elucidating general interrelationships.

Functional relationships, in the usual sense, take place only in space; dialectical ones occupy both time and space. One might say: positivism destroys time to assert common-sense reality; dialectical reasoning destroys common-sense reality to assert time. In the process, *the locus of reality shifts from the things of the positivists, which are unidimensional and timeless, to relationships and processes, which convert the supposedly fixed in time into the temporally variable.* (Murphy 1980:96; emphasis added)

Many archaeologists can be described as positivists who attempt to identify the causes of culture change, rather than trying to understand the process of culture change (or what happens after a change occurs). In addition, many archaeologists profess to study culture change when, in fact, they are studying behavior change. They consider such behavior as settlement patterns, subsistence strategies, activity area usage, and so on as culture. They actually neglect many aspects of culture, which they claim are inaccessible through archaeology or unimportant for the ultimate goals of archaeology. One of the major goals of this study is to show that it *is* possible to discern aspects of culture, using a systematic model like the one proposed. It is important to illuminate cultural aspects (as well as others) of bygone groups in order to reach the ultimate goals of archaeology—understanding the past and the processes that were a part of it. It is time to expand Schiffer's (1976:4) statement that "the subject matter of archaeology is the relationships between human behavior and material culture in all times and places" to include culture. This cannot be done by emphasizing only particularistic views of behavior and cultural material, or even by searching for broad universal laws of behavior, which thus far have only stated the more than obvious (e.g., "The longer a site is occupied the more refuse is deposited," or "The diversity of maintenance activities performed at a site varies directly with the length of occupation"). It can be done by searching for predictable universal patterns that deal with the relationship and interrelationship of cultural material, behavior, and culture.

Although archaeologists may only rarely be able to get at something as abstract as the proposed general principle, it does not mean that they should completely ignore it when it can enhance our understanding of the past, as well as the present.

Determining the actual principles that underlie culture, behavior, and cultural material may be perhaps best left to ethnoarchaeologists and/or ethnographers, but the existence of principles (just like the existence of kinship systems and religion) should, nevertheless, be recognized by archaeologists.

The approach I am proposing differs from the more established ones in that it is concerned with the *processes* of phenomena like culture change, rather than their *causes*. However, it is not necessary (or even prudent or appropriate) for archaeologists to insist single-mindedly that only one approach be adhered to and others be ignored. It is important to encourage any approach that might potentially produce or interpret data in ways other than whatever is currently in vogue, for without such alternatives, archaeology will stagnate. In any case, the past is far too complex and our knowledge of it far to limited to let us think we can ever really understand it by using only one approach.

The segmentation-unity continuum is a descriptive device that can be used to examine cross-culturally the relationships among cultural material, behavior, and culture. The compartmentalization/holism principle underlies the model, with which one can better understand these general interrelationships. To recall the epigraph that began this chapter, the knowledge of some of the parts allows one to infer the whole. Of course, any such inference depends on accurate knowledge and awareness of the parts of the whole. Nevertheless, it is my opinion that knowlege of whether or not activity areas were sex specific and/or monofunctional at a site can lead to important inferences about past cultures. It will allow archaeologists to obtain cultural, instead of mostly behavioral and/or environmental, data from their excavations. These data can potentially permit conjectures concerning sex roles, specialization, and so on, which, when put into a time perspective, can be viewed in terms of culture change, cultural diversity, the patterning of small-scale societies without influence from Western European culture, and so on. The model permits the understanding of culture, behavior, and cultural material, which can lead to predictions about this patterning.

Although the model may be somewhat simplistic (I prefer to view it as parsimonious and scientifically elegant), I would be the last to suggest that the relationships among culture, behavior, and cultural material are simple. Nevertheless, my research suggests that a trend or pattern lies behind the rich and varied forms of culture, behavior, and cultural material. The pattern is deterministic only in the general sense that the human skeleton is deterministic as a frame for the many shapes, colors, and personalities of human beings. In other words, other factors may operate, as was the case with the traditional Navajo use of space within hogans, but the trend or pattern still underlies culture, behavior, and cultural material. Knowledge of this trend and the study of factors that condition the deviation from the predicted patterning offer a potentially productive avenue for studying the past, as well as the present and the future.

7

Epilogue
Summary and Conclusions

> It is necessary, of course, for a research worker to be as unbiased
> as possible insofar as he is aware of his assumptions, but we
> often take our culture's more basic assumptions so much for
> granted that we are not even aware of them. Relative objectivity
> can be achieved through discovering what these tendencies are,
> the ways in which one's culture allows one to comprehend
> another, and the limitations it places on this comprehension.
> (Wagner 1975:2)

In order to assess the validity of assumptions commonly employed by archaeologists concerning activity area usage, I observed the spatial patterning of three groups. The specific assumptions evaluated were tested as three hypotheses: (1) that activity areas can be discerned from the content and spatial patterning of artifact and faunal remain assemblages; (2) that most activity areas are sex specific; (3) that most activity areas are monofunctional. Corollaries of these hypotheses were: (a) that artifacts and faunal remains are abandoned at the locus at which they are used; (b) that the refuse abandoned at an activity area permits inferences regarding the area's function(s); (c) that men and women do not usually use the same activity loci; and (d) that activities relating to different functions are performed at separate areas.

Because of the inundation of bulky, mass-produced Euroamerican artifacts and the role of dogs at the archaeological sites investigated, the first hypothesis could not be evaluated. However, of more importance to archaeologists, the analysis revealed some of the factors conditioning the distribution of cultural material that will allow archaeologists to ascertain when objects will or will not tend to be located at the areas at which they were used.

The research demonstrated that the second and third hypotheses concerning the use of activity areas are not valid

223

cross-culturally and that assumptions stemming from them are not appropriate for all groups throughout time and space. However, once the uses of activity areas have been determined (using lithic, ceramic, botanical, spatial, and other analyses) the proposed model potentially allows archaeologists to understand the dynamics of inter- and intrasite variability on both synchronic and diachronic levels. In addition, the model of the interrelationship of culture, behavior, and cultural material allows an archaeologist to extrapolate information concerning prehistoric groups that has not yet been well explored by archaeologists (although exceptions do exist, e.g., Plog 1974). By ascertaining the frequencies of a prehistoric group's sex-specific and monofunctional artifacts and activity areas, and comparing them with that of other archaeological and/or ethnographic groups' frequencies, it is possible to postulate the relative emphasis placed on the differences between the sexes and differentiation of their division of labor, amount of specialization present, and so on. They can be placed on the segmentation-unity continuum in relation to different archaeological and ethnographic groups in order to study variability through time and geographical space. Thus, an archaeologist need not be limited to describing the material culture and behavior of a bygone people, but can make inferences about their culture and can then investigate cultural diversity, culture change, sex roles, specialization, and other phenomena.

It is hypothesized that a general principle underlies the segmentation-unity continuum and permeates culture, behavior, and cultural material (chapter 6). The principle of compartmentalization/holism, I suggest, is reflected in activity area usage. Language, with its tendency to categorize and compartmentalize, seems to have increased the tension of this binary opposition in human culture. Humans have attempted to reduce this tension through, among other things, kinship and religion (chapter 6). The relationship between compartmentalization and holism is isomorphic throughout time and space; however, it is reflected differently in heterogeneous cultures. These differences are due, in part, to the historical perspectives of groups, their interaction with neighboring peoples, their level of social and political complexity, and their local physical environment. Two particularly important factors in the development of segmentation within a group's culture are thought to be increases in population density (especially aggregation) and sedentism, which then lead to the development of more complex social and political organizations, in addition to other changes.

In conclusion, this research has demonstrated that the assumptions that archaeologists commonly employ concerning the use of activity areas best describe the spatial patterning present in their own culture (although such patterning is not necessarily limited to their own culture). Activity areas are not universally sex specific or monofunctional. The presence of copious amounts of durable, bulky mass-produced objects probably influences refuse disposal patterns. As a result, objects are apparently not always deposited where used, and this will hamper some, but not all, activity area delineations. However, this problem applies only to sites inundated with durable mass-produced objects, such as those present at most historic sites. Faunal remain spatial distributions, with occasional exceptions, appear to be the result of animal rather than human behavior and, thus, are not always reliable indicators of activity area location or usage. Weather, season, house type and size, and so on may influence the location of activity areas, but not the manner in which they are used, which appears to be the result of predictable patterning. The model of the interrelationship of culture, behavior, and cultural material allows archaeologists to explore areas hitherto not thought possible and to investigate such exciting areas as culture change and variability.

The general principle of compartmentalization/holism is hypothesized to be reflected behaviorally in the use of activity areas, as well as in the relative segmentation of a group's culture and use of cultural material. All of these levels are interrelated; none exists alone. Activity area usage can best be understood in terms of this interrelationship—behavior that is a reflection of culture, cultural material, and of the general principle of compartmentalization/holism. This research represents an attempt to go from observations to inference, from behaviors to general principle, from descriptions to understanding. It has revealed that the uses of activity areas are neither arbitrary nor universal, and why they are not. Consequently, activity area usage must be determined, not assumed. It is hoped that the approach presented in this study will offer anthropologists one more productive avenue by which to study and understand our past and present—a predictive model of intergroup variability appropriate to both the past and the present, as well as potentially to the future. It is by means of such an approach that archaeologists can begin to understand the complexities and processes of the past and their relationship to the present and future.

Appendixes

Appendix 1. Example of the Determination of Confidence Intervals

	Subsistence Oriented Artifacts	
Feature Type	fo[a]	fe[b]
Isolated artifacts	336	261.86
Hogans	54	72.67
Other feature types	135	— —
Total	525	— —

[a]fo, observed frequency
[b]fe, expected frequency.

NOTE: Confidence intervals determined as follows:
Isolates/Subsistence oriented artifacts

$fo\ \hat{p} = 336/525 = .640 \qquad 1 - .640 = .360$

$$\sqrt{\frac{.640\ (.360)}{525}} = .021$$

$$-1.96\ (.021) + .640 < p < .640 + 1.96\ (.021)$$

$$\underline{.599 < p < .681}\quad \text{(confidence interval)}$$

$fe\ \hat{p} = \dfrac{261.86}{525} = .499$

Hogan/Subsistence oriented artifacts

$fo\ \hat{p} = 54/525 = .013 \qquad 1 - .013 = .897$

$$\sqrt{\frac{.103\ (.897)}{525}} = .013$$

$$-1.96\ (.013) + .103 < p < .103 + 1.06\ (.013)$$

$$\underline{.078 < p < .129}\quad \text{(confidence interval)}$$

$fe\ \hat{p} = \dfrac{72.67}{525} = .138$

Appendix 2. Confidence Intervals for the Distribution of Artifact Categories Among Individual Feature Types

| Feature Type | Artifact Categories | | |
	Subsistence	Personal Adornment and Clothing	Toys
Isolate	.599–.681 $fe\,\hat{p}$ = .499	.350–.480 $fe\,\hat{p}$ = .499	.131–.535 $fe\,\hat{p}$ = .499
Hogan	.078–.129 $fe\,\hat{p}$ = .138	.112–.210 $fe\,\hat{p}$ = .138	−.044–.140 $fe\,\hat{p}$ = .138
Ash area	.142–.208 $fe\,\hat{p}$ = .264	.265–.387 $fe\,\hat{p}$ = .264	.217–.641 $fe\,\hat{p}$ = .264
Wood-chip area	.024–.060 $fe\,\hat{p}$ = .056	.045–.115 $fe\,\hat{p}$ = .056	.022–.360 $fe\,\hat{p}$ = .056
Corral	.022–.508 $fe\,\hat{p}$ = .035	.00–.036 $fe\,\hat{p}$ = .035	.00–.00 $fe\,\hat{p}$ = .035
Total Number Observed	525	224	21

NOTE: *Read columns down.* See Graph 1, following page.

Appendix 3. Confidence Intervals for the Distribution of Artifact Categories Within Individual Feature Types

| Feature Type | Artifact Categories | | |
	Subsistence	Personal Adornment and Clothing	Toys
Isolate	.513–.591 $fe\,\hat{p}$ = .430	.124–.182 $fe\,\hat{p}$ = .184	.004–.020 $fe\,\hat{p}$ = .017
Hogan	.249–.391 $fe\,\hat{p}$ = .430	.150–.276 $fe\,\hat{p}$ = .184	−.006–.01 $fe\,\hat{p}$ = .01
Ash area	.237–.335 $fe\,\hat{p}$ = .430	.182–.272 $fe\,\hat{p}$ = .184	.010–.046 $fe\,\hat{p}$ = .01
Wood-chip area	.212–.436 $fe\,\hat{p}$ = .430	.159–.371 $fe\,\hat{p}$ = .184	.002–.116 $fe\,\hat{p}$ = .01
Corral	.339–.637 $fe\,\hat{p}$ = .430	.007–.179 $fe\,\hat{p}$ = .184	.00–.00 $fe\,\hat{p}$ = .01
Total Number Observed	525	224	21

NOTE: *Read columns down.* See Graph 2, following page.

Artifact Categories

Medicinal Supplies	Trans-portation	Animal Husbandry	Miscella-neous	Total Number Observed
.109–.367 $fe\,\hat{p} = .499$	.463–.729 $fe\,\hat{p} = .499$	.570–1.002 $fe\,\hat{p} = .499$	.302–.404 $fe\,\hat{p} = .499$	609
.021–.217 $fe\,\hat{p} = .138$	.029–.201 $fe\,\hat{p} = .138$	.00–.00 $fe\,\hat{p} = .138$	.180–.270 $fe\,\hat{p} = .138$	169
.349–.651 $fe\,\hat{p} = .264$	.132–.368 $fe\,\hat{p} = .264$	−.064–.206 $fe\,\hat{p} = .264$	.281–.379 $fe\,\hat{p} = .264$	322
−.023–.071 $fe\,\hat{p} = .056$	−.019–.059 $fe\,\hat{p} = .056$	.00–.00 $fe\,\hat{p} = .056$	−.023–.181 $fe\,\hat{p} = .056$	68
.00–.00 $fe\,\hat{p} = .035$	−.018–.056 $fe\,\hat{p} = .035$	−.041–.327 $fe\,\hat{p} = .035$	.022–.066 $fe\,\hat{p} = .035$	43
42	52	14	343	1221

Artifact Categories

Medicinal Supplies	Trans-portation	Animal Husbandry	Miscella-neous	Total Number Observed
.006–.026 $\hat{p} = .034$	.033–.069 $fe\,\hat{p} = .043$	.008–.028 $fe\,\hat{p} = .012$	.168–.230 $fe\,\hat{p} = .281$	609
.005–.056 $\hat{p} = .034$	.009–.063 $fe\,\hat{p} = .043$	.00–.00 $fe\,\hat{p} = .012$	.382–.531 $fe\,\hat{p} = .281$	169
.038–.089 $\hat{p} = .034$	.017–.061 $fe\,\hat{p} = .043$	−.003–.009 $fe\,\hat{p} = .012$	.289–.391 $fe\,\hat{p} = .281$	322
.014–.044 $\hat{p} = .034$	−.014–.044 $fe\,\hat{p} = .043$	.00–.00 $fe\,\hat{p} = .012$	.281–.531 $fe\,\hat{p} = .281$	68
.00–.00 $\hat{p} = .034$	−.022–.068 $fe\,\hat{p} = .043$	.016–.110 $fe\,\hat{p} = .012$	.206–.492 $fe\,\hat{p} = .281$	43
42	52	14	343	1221

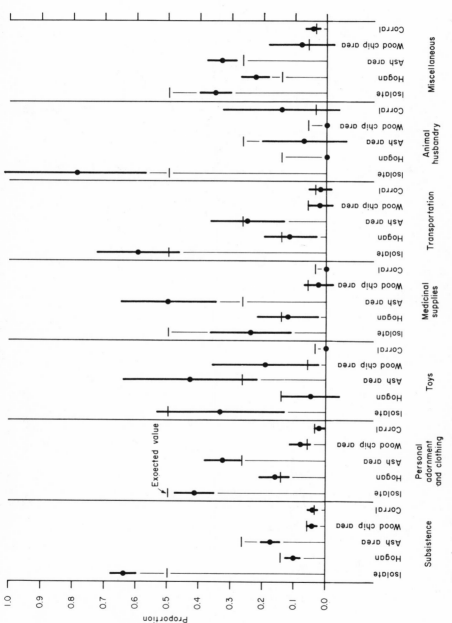

Graph 1. Representation of the distribution of feature types among artifact functional categories using confidence intervals.

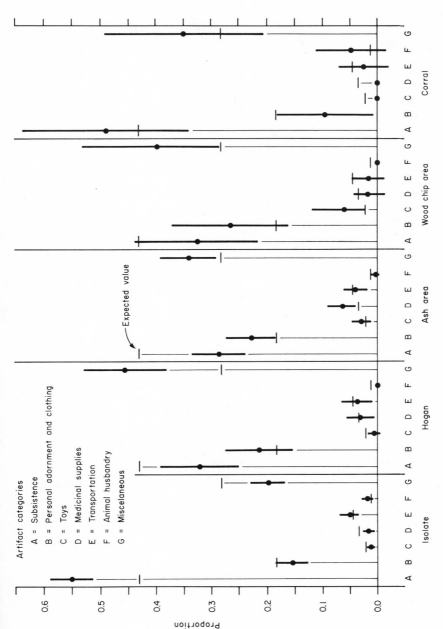

Graph 2. Representation of the distribution of artifact functional
categories within each feature type using confidence intervals.

Appendix 4. Chi-Square Test for Feature Types and Artifact Categories

| | Artifact Categories | | |
Feature Type	Subsistence	Personal Adornment and Clothing	Toys
Isolate	fe = 261.86 fo = 336.00	fe = 111.73 fo = 93.00	fe = 10.47 fo = 7.00
Hogan	fe = 72.67 fo = 54.00	fe = 31.00 fo = 36.00	fe = 2.91 fo = 1.00
Ash area	fe = 138.45 fo = 92.00	fe = 59.07 fo = 73.00	fe = 5.54 fo = 9.00
Wood-chip area	fe = 29.24 fo = 22.00	fe = 12.48 fo = 18.00	fe = 1.17 fo = 4.00
Corral	fe = 18.49 fo = 21.00	fe = 7.89 fo = 4.00	fe = 0.74 fo = 0.00
Total Number Observed	525	224	21

Appendix 5. Chi-Square Test for Feature Types and Skeletal Categories

| | Skeletal Section Categories | | | |
Feature Types	Skull and Midsection	Limb	Indeterminate and/or Unidentified	Total Number Observed
Isolate	fe = 16.68 fo = 7.00	fe = 11.67 fo = 19.00	fe = 6.66 fo = 9.00	35
Hogan	fe = 21.44 fo = 18.00	fe = 15.00 fo = 17.00	fe = 8.56 fo = 10.00	45
Ash area	fe = 113.41 fo = 137.00	fe = 79.93 fo = 68.00	fe = 45.26 fo = 33.00	238
Wood-chip area	fe = 61.47 fo = 51.00	fe = 43.00 fo = 45.00	fe = 24.53 fo = 33.00	129
Total Number Observed	213	149	85	447

NOTE: χ^2 = 26.75; df = 6; $\alpha.05$ = 12.59.

Artifact Categories

Medicinal Supplies	Trans- portation	Animal Husbandry	Miscella- neous	Total Number Observed
$fe = 20.95$ $fo = 10.00$	$fe = 25.94$ $fo = 31.00$	$fe = 6.98$ $fo = 11.00$	$fe = 171.08$ $fo = 121.00$	609
$fe = 5.81$ $fo = 5.00$	$fe = 7.20$ $fo = 6.00$	$fe = 1.94$ $fo = 0.00$	$fe = 47.48$ $fo = 77.00$	169
$fe = 11.08$ $fo = 21.00$	$fe = 13.71$ $fo = 13.00$	$fe = 3.69$ $fo = 1.00$	$fe = 90.46$ $fo = 113.00$	322
$fe = 2.34$ $fo = 1.00$	$fe = 2.90$ $fo = 1.00$	$fe = 0.78$ $fo = 0.00$	$fe = 19.10$ $fo = 27.00$	68
$fe = 1.48$ $fo = 0.00$	$fe = 1.83$ $fo = 1.00$	$fe = 0.49$ $fo = 2.00$	$fe = 12.08$ $fo = 15.00$	43
42	52	14	343	1221

NOTE: $\chi^2 = 137.60$; $df = 24$; $\alpha.01 = 42.98$.

References

Ackerman, Robert E., and Lillian A. Ackerman
  1973   Ethnoarcheological interpretations of territoriality and land use in southwestern Alaska. *Ethnohistory* 20(4):315–34.

Adams, William H.
  1976   *Silcott, Washington: Ethnoarchaeology of a rural American community.* Ph.D. dissertation, Washington State University.

Agenbroad, Larry
  1978   Cultural implications from the distributional analysis of a lithic site, San Pedro Valley, Arizona. In *Discovering past behavior: Experiments in the archaeology of the American Southwest*, edited by Paul Grebinger, pp. 55–71. Gordon and Breach, New York.

Anderson, Duane C.
  1974   Cherokee Sewer Site (13Ck405): Lithic analysis. *Journal of the Iowa Archaeological Society* 21:57–92.

Ascher, Robert
  1962   Ethnography for archaeology: A case from the Seri Indians. *Ethnology* 1(3):360–69.
  1968   Time's arrow and the archaeology of a contemporary community. In *Settlement archaeology*, edited by K. C. Chang, pp. 43–52. National Press Books, Palo Alto.

Bailey, Oran F., and Richard D. Graft
  1961   *Soil survey of Jackson County, Oklahoma.* Soil Survey Series 1958(4). U.S. Government Printing Office, Washington, D.C.

Bates, Daniel
  1980   Yoruk settlement in southeast Turkey. In *When nomads settle: Processes of sedentarization as adaptation and response*, edited by Philip Salzman, pp. 124–39. J. F. Bergin Publishers, Brooklyn.

Bauxar, J. Joseph
  1957a Yuchi ethnoarchaeology Part I: Some Yuchi identifications reconsidered. *Ethnohistory* 4(3):279–301.
  1957b Yuchi ethnoarchaeology: Parts II–V. *Ethnohistory* 4(4):369–437.

Berndt, Catherine H.
  1981   Interpretations and "facts" in aboriginal Australia. In *Woman the gatherer*, edited by Frances Dahlberg, pp. 153–203. Yale University Press, New Haven.

Binford, Lewis R.
  1976   Forty-seven trips: A case study in the character of some formation processes of the archaeological record. In *Contributions to an-*

thropology: The interior peoples of Northern Alaska, edited by Edwin Hall, Jr., pp. 352–81. Archaeological Survey of Canada 49. National Museum of Man, Mercury Series, Ottawa.

1978a Dimensional analysis of behavior and site structure: Learning from an Eskimo hunting stand. *American Antiquity* 43(3):330–61.

1978b *Nunamiut ethnoarchaeology.* Academic Press, New York.

1979a *Site structure as a clue to site function.* Paper presented at the Forty-fourth Annual Meeting of the Society for American Archaeology, Vancouver.

1979b Organization and formation processes: Looking at curated technologies. *Journal of Anthropological Research* 35(3):255–73.

1980 Willow smoke and dogs' tails: Hunter-gatherer settlement systems and archaeological site formation. *American Antiquity* 45(1):4–20.

1981 *Bones: Ancient men and modern myths.* Academic Press, New York.

Binford, Lewis R., and Jack Bertram
1977 Bone frequencies: And attritional processes. In *For theory building in archaeology: Essays on faunal remains, aquatic resources, spatial analysis and systematic modeling*, edited by Lewis R. Binford, pp. 77–153. Academic Press, New York.

Binford, Lewis R., and Sally Binford
1966 A preliminary analysis of functional variability in the Mousterian of LeVallois facies. *American Anthropologist* 68(2):238–95.

Binford, Lewis R., and Jeremy A. Sabloff
1982 Paradigms, systematics, and archaeology. *Journal of Anthropological Research* 38(2):137–53.

Birkedal, Terje G.
1976 *Basketmaker III residence units: A study of prehistoric social organization in the Mesa Verde Archaeological district.* Ph.D. dissertation, University of Colorado.

Blake, Michael
1976 *The Rocky Point Site (EdQx20): Spatial analysis and descriptive report.* Occasional Papers of the Archaeology Sites Advisory Board of British Columbia, 2.

Bonnichsen, Robson
1973 Millie's Camp: An experiment in archaeology. *World Archaeology* 4(3):277–91.

Bourdieu, P.
1973 The Berber house. In *Rules and meanings: The anthropology of everyday knowledge*, edited by Mary Douglas, pp. 98–110. Penguin Books, Harmondsworth.

Brain, C. K.
1969 *The contribution of Namib Desert Hottentots to an understanding of australopithecine bone accumulations.* Scientific Papers of the Namib Desert Research Station, 39.

Brauner, David R.
  1976   *Alpowai: The culture history of the Alpowa Locality.* Ph.D. dissertation, Washington State University.

Breternitz, Cory
  1982   *Identifying prehistoric activity areas: Analyses of temporal and functional variability among Dolores area structures* A.D. 575–900. M.A. thesis, Washington State University.

Brown, Roger
  1958   How shall a thing be called? *Psychological Review* 65(1):14–21.

Brugge, David M.
  1956   Navaho sweat houses. *El Palacio* 63(4):101–5.
  1963   *Navajo pottery and ethnohistory.* Navajoland Publications, Series 2. Navajo Tribal Museum, Window Rock, Arizona.
  1980   Historical sites in the San Juan Basin. Paper presented at the San Juan Advanced Seminar at the School of American Research, Santa Fe.

Bullen, Adelaide Kendall
  1947   Archaeological theory and anthropological fact. *American Antiquity* 13(2):128–34.

Bullock, Paul
  1970   Employment problems of the Mexican-American. In *Mexican-Americans in the United States: A Reader.* Schenkman Publishing Co., Cambridge, Mass.

Carneiro, Robert L.
  1967   On the relationship between size of population and complexity of social organization. *Southwestern Journal of Anthropology* 23:234–43.

Casteel, Richard W.
  1971   Differential bone destruction: Some comments. *American Antiquity* 36(4):466–69.

Chang, K. C., editor
  1968   *Settlement archaeology.* National Press Books, Palo Alto.

Clark, David L.
  1972   A provisional model of an Iron Age society and its settlement system. In *Models in archaeology,* edited by David Clark, pp. 801–69, Methuen and Co., London.

Clark, J. Desmond, and Hiro Kurashina
  1981   A study of the work of a modern tanner in Ethiopia and its relevance for archaeological interpretation. In *Modern material culture: The archaeology of us,* edited by Richard A. Gould and Michael B. Schiffer, pp. 303–21. Academic Press, New York.

Collier, Malcolm C.
  1966   *Local organization among the Navaho.* Human Relations Area Files, New Haven.

Cooley, Maurice
  1958   Physiography of the Glen–San Juan Canyon area, Part I. *Plateau* 31(2):21–33.

Cordell, Linda
  1979   Prehistoric: Eastern Anasazi. In *Handbook of North American Indians, Southwest* (vol. 9), edited by Alfonso Ortiz, pp. 131–51. Smithsonian Institution, Washington, D.C.
Cordy, Ross H.
  1981   A study of prehistoric social change: The development of complex societies in the Hawaiian Islands. Academic Press, New York.
Crader, Diana C.
  1974   The effects of scavengers on bone material from a large mammal: An experiment conducted among the Bisa of the Luangwa Valley, Zambia. In *Ethnoarchaeology*, edited by Christopher Donnan and C. William Clewlow, Jr., pp. 161–73. University of California Institute of Archaeology, Monograph IV. Los Angeles.
Cranstone, B. A.
  1971   The Tifalmin: A "Neolithic" people in New Guinea. *World Archaeology* 3(2):132:42.
Cunningham, Clark
  1973   Order in the Atoni house. In *Right and left: Essays on dual symbolic classification*, edited by Rodney Needham, pp. 204–38. University of Chicago Press, Chicago.
Crystal, Eric
  1974   Man and the Menhir: Contemporary megalithic practice of the Sa'dan Toraja of Sulawesi, Indonesia. In *Ethnoarchaeology*, edited by Christopher Donnan and C. William Clewlow, Jr., pp. 117–28. University of California Institute of Archaeology, Monograph IV. Los Angeles.
David, Nicholas
  1971   The Fulani compound and the archaeologist. *World Archaeology* 3(2):111–31.
Davis, Dave D.
  1978   Lithic assemblage variability in relation to early hominid subsistence strategies at Oldowai Gorge. In *Lithics and subsistence: The analysis of stone tool use in prehistoric economics*, edited by Dave D. Davis, pp. 35–86. Vanderbilt University Press, Nashville.
DeBoer, Warren R., and Donald W. Lathrap
  1979   The making and breaking of Shipibo-Conibo ceramics. In *Ethnoarchaeology: Implications of ethnographic archaeology*, edited by Carol Kramer, pp. 102–38. Columbia University Press, New York.
Deetz, James
  1968   The inference of residence and descent rules from archaeological data. In *New perspectives on archaeology*, edited by Sally Binford and Lewis R. Binford, pp. 41–48. Aldine Publishing Company, Chicago.
DeGarmo, Glen
  1975   *Coyote Creek Site 01: A methodological study of a prehistoric*

pueblo population. Ph.D. dissertation, University of California, Los Angeles.

Dolgin, Janet L., David S. Kemnitzer, and David M. Schneider
1977   "As people express their lives, so they are. . . ." In *Symbolic anthropology: A reader in the study of symbols and meanings,* edited by Janet Dolgin, David Kemnitzer, and David M. Schneider, pp. 3–44. Columbia University Press, New York.

Donley, Linda W.
1982   House power: Swahili space and symbolic markers. In *Symbolic and structural archaeology,* edited by Ian Hodder, pp. 63–73. Cambridge University Press, Cambridge.

Douglas, Mary
1972   Symbolic orders in the use of domestic space. In *Man, settlement, and urbanism,* edited by Peter Ucko, Ruth Tringham, and G. W. Dimbleby, pp. 513–21. Schenkman Publishing Co., Cambridge, Mass.

Downs, James F.
1972   *The Navajo.* Holt, Rinehart and Winston, New York.

Draper, Patricia
1975   !Kung women: Contrasts in sexual egalitarianism in foraging and sedentary contexts. In *Toward an anthropology of women,* edited by Rayna Reiter, pp. 77–109. Monthly Review Press, New York.

Dumond, Don E.
1972   Population growth and political centralization. In *Population growth: Anthropological implications,* edited by Brian Spooner, pp. 286–310. M.I.T. Press, Cambridge, Mass.

Durkheim, Emile
1933   *The division of labor in society.* Free Press of Glencoe, London.
1965   *Elementary forms of religious life.* Free Press, New York.

Ebert, James I.
1979   An ethnoarchaeological approach to reassessing the meaning of variability in stone tool assemblages. In *Ethnoarchaeology: Implications of ethnography for archaeology,* edited by Carol Kramer, pp. 59–74. Columbia University Press, New York.

Elkin, A. P.
1938   *The Australian Aborigines: How to understand them.* Angus and Robertson, Sydney.

Endicott, Karen L.
1979   *Batek Negrito sex roles,* M.A. thesis, Australian National University.

Feirstein, Bruce
1982   *Real men don't eat quiche: A guidebook to all that is truly masculine.* Pocket Books, New York.

Fewkes, Jesse Walter
1900   Tusayan migration traditions. *Bureau of American Ethnology* 19(2):577–633.

Flannery, Kent V., and Marcus C. Winter
  1976   Analyzing household activities. In *The early Mesoamerican village*, edited by Kent V. Flannery, pp. 34–47. Academic Press, New York.
Flenniken, J. Jeffrey
  1980   *Replicative systems analysis: A model applied to the vein quartz artifacts from the Hoko River Site*. Ph.D. dissertation, Washington State University.
Flenniken, J. Jeffrey, and Alan L. Stanfill
  1979   *A preliminary technological examination of 20 archaeological sites located during the cultural resource survey of the Whitehorse Ranch Public Land Exchange*. Bureau of Land Management, Vail District, Oregon. Laboratory of Lithic Technology, Washington State University, Pullman.
Ford, Richard
  1980   Plant remains. In *Prehistory and history of the Ojo Amarillo: Archaeological investigations of Block II, Navajo Indian Irrigation Project, San Juan County, New Mexico*, edited by David Kirkpatrick, pp. 1277–98. Cultural Resources Management Division Report 276, New Mexico State University, Las Cruces.
Foster, George
  1960   Life-expectancy of utilitarian potter in Tzintzuntzan, Michoacán, Mexico. *American Antiquity* 25(4):606–9.
Franciscan Fathers
  1910   *An ethologic dictionary of the Navaho language*. Franciscan Fathers, Saint Michaels.
Friedrich, Margaret Hardin
  1970   Design structure and social interaction: Archaeological implications of an ethnographic analysis. *American Antiquity* 35(3):332–43.
Fuller, Buckminster
  1970   *Operating Manual for Spaceship Earth*. Pocket Books, New York.
Furst, Peter T.
  1972   The Olmec were-jaguar motif in the light of ethnographic reality. In *Contemporary archaeology*, edited by Mark P. Leone, pp. 333–53. Southern Illinois University Press, Carbondale.
Geertz, Clifford
  1973   *The interpretation of cultures*. Basic Books, New York.
Gifford, Diane
  1978   Ethnoarchaeological observations of natural processes affecting cultural materials. In *Explorations in ethnoarchaeology*, edited by Richard A. Gould, pp. 77–101. University of New Mexico Press, Albuquerque.
Gillespie, William B.
  1976   *Culture change at the Ute Canyon Site: A study of the pithouse kiva transition in the Mesa Verde Region*. M.A. thesis, University of Colorado.

Glassie, Henry
 1975   *Folk housing in Middle Virginia: A structural analysis of historic artifacts.* University of Tennessee Press, Knoxville.
Goldschmidt, Walter
 1980   Career reorientation and institutional adaptation in the process of natural sedentarization. In *When nomads settle: Processes of sedentarization as adaptation and response,* edited by Philip Salzman, pp. 44–61. J. F. Bergin Publishers, Brooklyn.
González, Nancie L.
 1969   *The Spanish-Americans of New Mexico.* University of New Mexico Press, Albuquerque.
Goodyear, Albert C.
 1974   *The Brand site: A techno-functional study of a Dalton site in northeast Arkansas.* Arkansas Archaeological Survey Publications in Archaeology, Research Series 7.
Gould, Richard A.
 1974   Some current problems in ethnoarchaeology. In *Ethnoarchaeology,* edited by Christopher Donnan and C. William Clewlow, Jr., pp. 29–48. University of California Institute of Archaeology, Monograph IV. Los Angeles.
 1978a   From Tasmania to Tucson: New directions in ethnoarchaeology. In *Explorations in ethnoarchaeology,* edited by Richard A. Gould, pp. 1–10. University of New Mexico Press, Albuquerque.
 1978b   Beyond analogy in ethnoarchaeology. In *Explorations in ethnoarchaeology,* edited by Richard A. Gould, pp. 249–93. University of New Mexico Press, Albuquerque.
 1978c   The anthropology of human residues. *American Anthropologist* 80(4):815–35.
Graebner, Alan
 1975   Growing up female. In *The Nacirema: Readings in American culture,* edited by James Spradley and Michael Rynkiewick, pp. 23–30. Little, Brown and Co., Boston.
Grebler, Leo, Joan W. Moore, and Ralph C. Guzman
 1970   *The Mexican-American people: The nation's second largest minority.* Free Press, New York.
Griffin, John W.
 1974   *Investigations in Russel Cave.* National Park Service Publications in Archaeology 13. U.S. Government Printing Office, Washington, D.C.
Haile, Berard
 1954   *Property concepts of the Navaho Indians.* Catholic University of American Anthropologist Series 17.
Hall, Edward T.
 1963   Proxemics: A study of man's spatial relationships. In *Man's image in medicine and anthropology,* edited by Iago Galdston, pp. 422–45. International Universities Press, New York.
 1966   *The hidden dimension.* Doubleday and Co., Garden City.

1968   Proxemics. *Current Anthropology* 9(2–3):83–108.

Hammack, Laurens
1969a   Highway salvage archaeology in the Forestdale Valley, Arizona. *The Kiva* 34(2–3):58–69.
1969b   Highway salvage archaeology in the Upper Tonto Basin, Arizona. *The Kiva* 34(2–3):132–39.

Hardin, Margaret A.
1979   The cognitive basis of productivity in a decorative art style: Implications of an ethnographic study for archaeologists' taxonomies. In *Ethnoarchaeology: Implications of ethnography for archaeology*, edited by Carol Kramer, pp. 75–101. Columbia University Press, New York.

Harner, Michael
1970   Population pressure and the social evolution of agriculturalists. *Southwestern Journal of Anthropology* 26(1):67–86.

Hassan, Fekri A.
1981   *Demographic archaeology.* Academic Press, New York.

Hayden, Brian, and Aubrey Cannon
1982   The corporate group as an archaeological unit. *Journal of Anthropological Archaeology* 1(2):132–58.

Hayes, Alden
1964   *The archaeological survey of Wetherill Mesa, Mesa Verde National Park, Colorado.* National Park Service Archaeological Research Series 7-A.

Haynes, Gary
1980   Evidence of carnivore gnawing on Pleistocene and recent mammalian bones. *Paleobiology* 6:341–51.

Heider, Karl G.
1967   Archaeological assumptions and ethnographic facts: A cautionary tale from New Guinea. *Southwestern Journal of Anthropology* 23:52–64.

Hester, James J.
1972   *Blackwater Locality No. 1: A stratified early man site in eastern New Mexico.* Publication of the Fort Burgwin Research Center 8.

Hiatt, L. R.
1968   Ownership and use of land among the Australian Aborigines. In *Man the hunter*, edited by Richard Lee and Irven DeVore, pp. 99–102.

Hill, James N.
1970   *Broken K Pueblo: Prehistoric social organization in the American Southwest.* Anthropological Papers of the University of Arizona 18.

Hodder, Ian
1979   *Refuse and models of within-site spatial patterns.* Paper presented at the Forty-fourth Annual Meeting of the Society for American Archaeology, Vancouver.

Hodder, Ian, editor
1978   *The spatial organization of culture.* University of Pittsburgh Press, Pittsburgh.
1982   *Symbolic and structural archaeology.* Cambridge University Press, Cambridge.

Hodder, Ian, and Clive Orton
1976   *Spatial analysis in archaeology.* Cambridge University Press, Cambridge.

Hole, Frank
1978   Pastoral nomadism in Western Iran. In *Explorations in ethnoarchaeology,* edited by Richard A. Gould, pp. 127–67. University of New Mexico Press, Albuquerque.
1979   Rediscovering the past in the present: Ethnoarchaeology in Luristan Iran. In *Ethnoarchaeology: Implications of ethnography for archaeology,* edited by Carol Kramer, pp. 192–218. Columbia University Press, New York.

Hsu, Francis L.
1979   The cultural problem of the cultural anthropologist. *American Anthropologist* 81(3):517–32.

Hugh-Jones, Christine
1979   *From the Milk River: Spatial and temporal practices in Northwest Amazonia.* Cambridge University Press, Cambridge.

Jett, Stephen, and Virginia Spencer
1981   *Navajo architecture: Forms, history, distribution.* University of Arizona Press, Tucson.

Jones, Grant, and Robert Kautz, editors
1981   *The transition to statehood in the New World.* Cambridge University Press, Cambridge.

Jones, Rhys
1978   Why did the Tasmanians stop eating fish? In *Explorations in ethnoarchaeology,* edited by Richard A. Gould, pp. 11–47. University of New Mexico Press, Albuquerque.

Kahl, Joseph A.
1957   *The American class structure.* Rinehart and Co., New York.

Kaplan, Abraham
1964   *The conduct of inquiry.* Chandler Publishing Co., San Francisco.

Keeley, Lawrence
1980   *Experimental determination of stone tool uses: A microwear analysis.* University of Chicago Press, Chicago.

Kelley, Klara
1982   Ethnoarchaeology of the Black Hat Navajos: Historical and ahistorical determinants of site features, Journal of Anthropological Research 38(1):45–74.

Kent, Susan
1980a   Site 2-1-01. In *Prehistory and history of the Ojo Amarillo: Archaeological investigations of Block II, Navajo Indian Irrigation Project, San Juan County, New Mexico,* edited by David Kirkpa-

trick, pp. 393–404. Cultural Resources Management Report 276, New Mexico State University, Las Cruces.

1980b   Site 2-1-03. In *Prehistory and history of the Ojo Amarillo: Archaeological investigations of Block II, Navajo Indian Irrigation Project, San Juan County, New Mexico,* edited by David Kirkpatrick, pp. 487–581. Cultural Resources Management Report 276, New Mexico State University, Las Cruces.

1980c   Site 2-54-28. In *Prehistory and history of the Ojo Amarillo: Archaeological investigations of Block II, Navajo Indian Irrigation Project, San Juan County, New Mexico,* edited by David Kirkpatrick, pp. 421–58. Cultural Resources Management Report 276, New Mexico State University, Las Cruces.

1980d   Site 2-C6-14. In *Prehistory and history of the Ojo Amarillo: Archaeological investigations of Block II, Navajo Indian Irrigation Project, San Juan County, New Mexico,* edited by David Kirkpatrick, pp. 625–47. Cultural Resources Management Report 276, New Mexico State University, Las Cruces.

1980e   Site 2-C6-18. In *Prehistory and history of the Ojo Amarillo: Archaeological investigations of Block II, Navajo Indian Irrigation Project, San Juan County, New Mexico,* edited by David Kirkpatrick, pp. 459–86. Cultural Resources Management Report 276, New Mexico State University, Las Cruces.

1980f   Site 2-65-02. In *Prehistory and history of the Ojo Amarillo: Archaeological investigations of Block II, Navajo Indian Irrigation Project, San Juan County, New Mexico,* edited by David Kirkpatrick, pp. 805–32. Cultural Resources Management Report 276, New Mexico State University, Las Cruces.

1980g   Ethnographic theory and archaeological fact. *Southwestern Lore* 46(4):1–9.

1981   The dog: An archaeologist's best friend or worst enemy—the spatial distribution of faunal remains. *Journal of Field Archaeology* 8:367–72.

1982a   Two data sets are better than one: A case study of the use of ethnographic data in an attempt to understand archaeological data. Paper presented at the Forty-seventh Annual Meeting of the Society for American Archaeology, Minneapolis.

1982b   Hogan, sacred circles and symbols: Navajo use of space. In *Navajo religion and culture: Selected views—Papers in Honor of Leland C. Wyman,* edited by David Brugge and Charlotte Frisbie. Museum of New Mexico Press, Santa Fe.

1983   The differentiation of Navajo culture, behavior, and material culture: A comparative study in culture change. *Ethnology* 22(1):81–91.

in press   The differential acceptance of culture change: An archaeological test case. *Historical Archaeology* 17(2).

Kleindienst, Maxine R., and Patty Jo Watson

1956   Action archeology: The archeological inventory of a living community. *Anthropology Tomorrow* 5:75–78.

Kluckhohn, Clyde, W. W. Hill, and Lucy Wales Kluckhohn
   1971   *Navaho material culture.* Belknap Press of Harvard University
          Press, Cambridge, Mass.
Kluckhohn, Clyde, and Dorothea Leighton
   1962   *The Navaho.* Doubleday and Co., Garden City.
Kluckhohn, Florence R.
   1961   The Spanish-Americans of Atrisco. In *Variations in value orien-
          tations*, edited by Florence Kluckhohn and Fred Strodtbeck, pp.
          175–257. Greenwood Press, Westport.
Kramer, Carol
   1979   Introduction. In *Ethnoarchaeology: Implications of ethnography
          for archaeology*, edited by Carol Kramer, pp. 1–20. Columbia Uni-
          versity Press, New York.
   1982   *Village ethnoarchaeology: Rural Iran in archaeological perspec-
          tive.* Academic Press, New York.
Kroeber, Alfred, and Clyde Kluckhohn
   1963   *Culture: A critical review of concepts and definitions.* Vintage
          Books, New York.
Kutsche, Paul, and John R. Van Ness
   1981   *Cañones: Values, crisis, and survival in a northern New Mexico
          village.* University of New Mexico Press, Albuquerque.
Lamphere, Louise
   1977   *To run after them: Cultural and social bases of cooperation in a
          Navajo community.* University of Arizona Press, Tucson.
Lange, Frederick W., and Charles R. Rydberg
   1972   Abandonment and post-abandonment behavior at a rural Central
          American house-site. *American Antiquity* 37(3):419–32.
Lee, Richard B.
   1972a Population growth and the beginnings of sedentary life among
          the !Kung Bushmen. In *Population growth: Anthropological im-
          plications*, edited by Brian Spooner, pp. 329–42. M.I.T. Press, Cam-
          bridge, Mass.
   1972b The intensification of social life among the !Kung Bushmen. In
          Population growth: Anthropological implications, edited by Brian
          Spooner, pp. 343–50. M.I.T. Press, Cambridge, Mass.
   1979   *The !Kung San: Men, women, and work in a foraging society.*
          Cambridge University Press, Cambridge.
Leighton, Dorothea, and Clyde Kluckhohn
   1948   *Children of the people.* Harvard University Press, Cambridge,
          Mass.
Leone, Mark P.
   1982   Some opinions about recovering mind, *American Antiquity* 27
          (4):742–60.
Little, Elbert L., Jr.
   1971   *Atlas of U.S. trees: Important hardwoods* (vol. 1). U.S. Depart-
          ment of Agriculture Forest Service Miscellaneous Publications
          1146.
   1976   *Atlas of U.S. trees: Minor western hardwoods* (vol. 3). U.S. De-

partment of Agriculture Forest Service Miscellaneous Publications 1314.

Longacre, William
    1968   Some aspects of prehistoric society in East-Central Arizona. In *New perspectives in archaeology*, edited by Sally Binford and Lewis R. Binford, pp. 89–102. Aldine Publishing Co., Chicago.
    1974   Kalinga pottery-making: The evolution of a research design. In *Frontiers of anthropology*, edited by Murray J. Leaf, pp. 51–67. D. Van Nostrand Co., New York.

Longacre, William, and James E. Ayres
    1968   Archaeological lessons from an Apache wickiup. In *New perspectives in archaeology*, edited by Sally Binford and Lewis R. Binford, pp. 151–59. Aldine Publishing Co., Chicago.

Lyman, Richard Lee
    1976   *A cultural analysis of faunal remains from the Alpowa Locality.* M.A. thesis, Washington State University.

Lyon, Patricia J.
    1970   Differential bone destruction: An ethnographic example. *American Antiquity* 35(2):213–15.

McGregor, John C.
    1965   *Southwestern archaeology*, 2d ed. University of Illinois Press, Urbana.

Matson, Frederick R.
    1974   The archaeological present: Near Eastern village patterns at work. *American Journal of Archaeology* 78(4):345–47.

Mead, Margaret
    1967   *Male and female.* William Morrow and Co., New York.

Meggers, Betty J., and Clifford Evans
    1957   *Archaeological investigations at the mouth of the Amazon.* Bureau of American Ethnology Bulletin 167.

Meggitt, M. J.
    1968   "Marriage classes" and demography in Central Australia. In *Man the hunter*, edited by Richard Lee and Irven DeVore, pp. 176–84. Aldine Publishing Co., Chicago.

Mellaart, James
    1967   *Catal Hüyük: A neolithic town in Anatolia.* McGraw-Hill Book Co., New York.

Moore, H. L.
    1982   The interpretation of spatial patterning in settlement residues. In *Symbolic and structural archaeology*, edited by Ian Hodder, pp. 74–79. Cambridge University Press, Cambridge.

Murphy, Robert
    1980   *The dialectics of social life: Alarms and excursions in anthropological theory.* Columbia University Press, New York.

Murray, David W.
    1977   Ritual communications: Some consideration regarding meaning in Navajo ceremonials. In *Symbolic anthropology: A reader in*

the study of symbols and meanings, edited by Janet L. Dolgin, David S. Kemnitzer, and David M. Schneider, pp. 195–220. Columbia University Press, New York.

Murray, Priscilla
1980 Discard location: The ethnographic data. *American Antiquity* 45:490–502.

Nance, J. D.
1971 Functional interpretations from microscopic analysis. *American Antiquity* 36(3):361–66.

Nelson, Margaret C.
1981 *Chipped stone analysis in the reconstruction of prehistoric subsistence practices: An example from Southwestern New Mexico.* Ph.D. dissertation, University of California, Santa Barbara.

Netting, Robert McC.
1972 Sacred power and centralization: Aspects of political adaptation in Africa. In *Population growth: Anthropological implications,* edited by Brian Spooner, pp. 219–44. M.I.T. Press, Cambridge, Mass.

Ochsenschlager, Edward L.
1974 Modern potterns at Al-Hiba with some reflections on the excavated early dynastic pottery. In *Ethnoarchaeology,* edited by Christopher Donnan and C. William Clewlow, Jr., pp. 149–57. University of California Institute of Archaeology Monograph IV. Los Angeles.

O'Connell, James
1979 *Site structure and dynamics among modern Alyawara hunters.* Paper presented at the Forty-fourth Annual Meeting of the Society for American Archaeology, Vancouver.

Ohel, Milla
1977 Patterned concentrations on living floors at Olduvai, Beds I and II: Experimental study. *Journal of Field Archaeology* 4:423–33.

Oswalt, Wendell H.
1974 Ethnoarchaeology. In *Ethnoarchaeology,* edited by Christopher Donnan and C. William Clewlow, Jr., pp. 3–11. University of California Institute of Archaeology Monograph IV. Los Angeles.

Parsons, Talcott
1966 *Societies: Evolutionary and comparative perspectives.* Prentice-Hall, Englewood Cliffs.

Pastron, A. G., and C. W. Clewlow, Jr.
1974 Ethnoarchaeological observation on human burial decomposition in the Chihuahua Sierra. In *Ethnoarchaeology,* edited by Christopher Donnan and C. William Clewlow, Jr., pp. 177–81. University of California Institute of Archaeology Monograph IV. Los Angeles.

Pearson, Michael P.
1982 Mortuary practices, society, and ideology: An ethnoarchaeological study. In *Symbolic and structural archaeology,* edited by Ian Hodder, pp. 99–113. Cambridge University Press, Cambridge.

Pilling, Arnold R.
 1968 Southeastern Australia: Level of social organization. In *Man the hunter*, edited by Richard Lee and Irven DeVore, pp. 138–45. Aldine Publishing Company, Chicago.

Plog, Fred T.
 1974 *The study of prehistoric culture change.* Academic Press, New York.

Portnoy, Alice
 1981 A microarchaeological view of human settlement space and function. In *Modern material culture: The archaeology of us*, edited by Richard A. Gould and Michael Schiffer, pp. 213–33. Academic Press, New York.

Price, T. Douglas
 1978 The spatial analysis of lithic artifact distribution and association on prehistoric occupational floors. In *Lithics and subsistence: The analysis of stone tool use in prehistoric economics*, edited by Dave D.Davis, pp. 1–33. Vanderbilt University Publication in Anthropology 20.

Rapoport, Amos
 1969 *House form and culture.* Prentice-Hall, Englewood Cliffs.

Redfield, Robert
 1960 *The little community.* University of Chicago Press, Chicago.

Reher, Charles A., and Dan C. Witter
 1977 Archaic settlement and vegetation diversity. In *Settlement and subsistence along the lower Chaco River: The CGP Survey*, edited by Charles A. Reher, pp. 113–26. University of New Mexico Press, Albuquerque.

Robbins, L. H.
 1973 Turkana material culture viewed from an archaeological perspective. *World Archaeology* 5(2):209–14.

Roberts, John M.
 1965 *Zuni daily life.* Human Relations Area Files Press, New Haven.

Rohn, Arthur H.
 1977 *Culture change and continuity on Chapin Mesa.* Regents Press of Kansas, Lawrence.

Rohrlich-Leavitt, Ruby, Barbara Sykes, and Elizabeth Weatherford
 1975 Aboriginal woman: male and female anthropological perspectives. In *Toward an anthropology of women*, edited by Rayna Reiter, pp. 110–26. Monthly Review Press, New York.

Romney, A. Kimball, and Clyde Kluckhohn
 1961 The Rimrock Navaho. In *Variations in value orientations*, edited by Florence R. Kluckhohn and Fred Strodtbeck, pp. 319–39. Greenwood Press, Westport.

Rosaldo, Michelle Z.
 1974 Woman, culture, and society: A theoretical overview. In *Woman, culture, and society*, edited by Michelle Z. Rosaldo and Louise Lamphere, pp. 17–42. Stanford University Press, Stanford.

Rose, Frederick G.
  1968   Australian marriage land-owning groups, and initiations. In *Man the hunter*, edited by Richard Lee and Irven DeVore, pp. 200–208. Aldine Publishing Co., Chicago.

Sahlins, Marshall
  1976   *Culture and practical reason.* University of Chicago Press, Chicago.

Sallade, Janet, and David Braun
  1982   Spatial organization of peasant agricultural subsistence territories: Distance factors and crop locations. In *Ethnography by archaeologists: 1978 proceedings of the American Ethnological Society*, edited by Elisabeth Tooker, pp. 19–41. American Ethnological Society, Washington, D.C.

Schiffer, Michael B.
  1972   Archaeological context and systemic context. *American Antiquity* 37(2):156–65.
  1976   *Behavioral archeology.* Academic Press, New York.
  1978   Methodological uses in ethnoarchaeology. In *Explorations in ethnoarchaeology*, edited by Richard A. Gould, pp. 229–47. University of New Mexico Press, Albuquerque.

Schiffer, Michael B., Theodore Downing, and Michael McCarthy
  1981   Waste not, want not: An ethnoarchaeological study of refuse in Tucson, Arizona. In *Modern material culture: The archaeology of us*, edited by Richard A. Gould and Michael B. Schiffer, pp. 67–86. Academic Press, New York.

Service, Elman R.
  1971   *Profiles in ethnology*, rev. ed. Harper and Row Publishers, New York.

Sharon, Douglas, and Christopher Donnan
  1974   Shamanism in Moche iconography. In *Ethnoarchaeology*, edited by Christopher Donnan and C. William Clewlow, Jr., pp. 51–77. University of California Institute of Archaeology Monograph IV. Los Angeles.

Shepardson, Mary, and Blodwen Hammond
  1970   *The Navajo Mountain community: Socialization and kinship terminology.* University of California Press, Berkeley and Los Angeles.

Solecki, Ralph
  1979   Contemporary Kurdish winter-time inhabitants of Shanidar Cave, Iraq. *World Archaeology* 10(3):318–30.

South, Stanley
  1979   Pattern recognition in historical archaeology. *American Antiquity* 43(2):223–30.

Stanislawski, Michael B.
  1969   The ethno-archaeology of Hopi pottery making. *Plateau* 42(1):27–33.

1973   Ethnoarchaeology and settlement archaeology. *Ethnohistory* 20(4):375–92.

1974   The relationship of ethnoarchaeology, traditional, and systems archaeology. In *Ethnoarchaeology*, edited by Christopher Donnan and C. William Clewlow, Jr., pp. 15–26. University of California Institute of Archaeology Monograph IV. Los Angeles.

1978   If pots were mortal. In *Explorations in ethnoarchaeology*, edited by Richard A. Gould, pp. 201–27. University of New Mexico Press, Albuquerque.

Sterud, Eugene
1979   Prehistoric populations of the Dinaric Alps: An investigation of interregional interaction. In *Social archaeology: Beyond subsistence and dating*, edited by Charles L. Redman, et al., pp. 381–409. Academic Press, New York.

Steward, Julian
1937   Ecological aspects of Southwestern society. *Anthropos* 32:87–104.
1955   *Theory of culture.* University of Illinois Press, Urbana.

Stiles, Daniel
1977   Ethnoarchaeology: A discussion of methods and applications. *Man* 12(1):87–103.

Swedlund, Alan, and Steven Sessions
1976   A developmental model of prehistoric population growth on Black Mesa, northeastern Arizona. In *Papers on the archaeology of Black Mesa, Arizona*, edited by George Gumerman and Robert Euler, pp. 136–48. Southern Illinois University Press, Carbondale.

Thomas, David H.
1972   A computer simulation model of Great Basin Shoshonean subsistence and settlement patterns. In *Models in archaeology*, edited by David L. Clarke, pp. 671–704. Methuen and Co., London.

Thompson, D. E.
1974   Architectural continuities in the North Central Highlands of Peru. In *Ethnoarchaeology*, edited by Christopher Donnan and C. William Clewlow, pp. 81–89. University of California, Institute of Archaeology, Monograph IV. Los Angeles.

Thompson, Raymond H.
1956   The subjective element in archaeological inference. *Southwestern Journal of Anthropology* 12(3):327–32.

Tönnies, Ferdinand
1887   *Community and society* [Gemeinschaft und Gesellschaft], translated and edited by Charles P. Loomis, 1963. Harper and Row Publishers, New York.

Topper, Martin D.
1972   *The daily life of a traditional Navajo household: An ethnographic study in human daily activity.* Ph.D. dissertation, Northwestern University.

Trigger, Bruce
1968   The determinants of settlement patterns. In *Settlement archae-*

ology, edited by K. C. Chang, pp. 53–78. National Press Books, Palo Alto.

Tschopik, Harry
1941   Navaho pottery making. *Papers of the Peabody Museum* XVII(1).

Wagner, Roy
1975   *The invention of culture.* Prentice-Hall, Englewood Cliffs.

Ward, Albert E., Emily K. Abbink, and John R. Stein
1977   Ethnohistorical and chronological basis of the Navajo material culture. In *Settlement and subsistence along the Lower Chaco River: The CGP Survey,* edited by Charles A. Reher, pp. 217–78. University of New Mexico Press, Albuquerque.

Warner, W. Lloyd, and Paul S. Lunt
1941   *The social life of a modern community.* Yale University Press, New Haven.

Watson, O. Michael
1970   *Proxemic behavior: A cross-cultural study.* Mouton, The Hague.
1972   *Symbolic and expressive uses of space: An introduction to proxemic behavior.* Addison-Wesley Module in Anthropology 20. Reading, Mass.

Watson, Patty Jo
1979   *Archaeological ethnography in Western Iran.* Viking Fund Publications in Anthropology No. 57.
1978   Architectural differentiation in some Near Eastern communities, prehistoric and contemporary. In *Social archaeology: Beyond subsistence and dating,* edited by Charles L. Redman, et al., pp. 131–58. Academic Press, New York.

Watson, Patty Jo, Steven A. LeBlanc, and Charles L. Redman
1971   *Explanation in archaeology: An explicitly scientific approach.* Columbia University Press, New York.

White, Carmel, and Nicholas Peterson
1969   Ethnographic interpretations of the prehistory of Western Arnhem Land. *Southwestern Journal of Anthropology* 25(1):45–67.

White, J. Peter
1967   Ethno-archaeology in New Guinea: Two examples. *Mankind* 6(9):409–14.

Willey, Gordon R., editor
1956   *Prehistoric settlement patterns in the New World.* Viking Fund Publications in Anthropology 23.

Yellen, John E.
1977a   *Archaeological approaches to the present: Models for reconstructing the past.* Academic Press, New York.
1977b   Cultural patterning in faunal remains: Evidence from the !Kung Bushmen. In *Experimental archaeology,* edited by Daniel Ingersoll, John E. Yellen, and William Macdonald, pp. 271–331. Columbia University Press, New York.

Yengoyan, Aram A.
1968   Demographic and ecological influences on Aboriginal Australian

marriage sections. In *Man the hunter*, edited by Richard Lee and Irven DeVore, pp. 185–99. Aldine Publishing Co., Chicago.

Yoffee, Norman
1979   The decline and rise of Mesopotamian civilization: An ethnoarchaeological perspective on the evolution of social complexity. *American Antiquity* 44(1):5–35.

Index

Abbink, Emily K., 159
Ackerman, Robert E., and Lillian A. Ackerman, 6
activity areas: assumptions on, 2; conclusion on, 225; creation/obliteration of, 184; cross-cultural comparison of, 203; crowding and, 65, 78; defined, 1, 55; function and location of, 65; individual mood and, 64, 78, 96, 128; non-artifactual indicators for, 170; relation to disposal, 173; seasons/weather and, 65, 78, 81, 95, 127; statistics for, 167; use variability and, 196, 225. *See also* interpretive model; monofunctional areas; sex-specific areas; spatial patterning
Adams, William H., 4
Agenbroad, Larry, 8
Anasazi, the, 202
Anderson, Duane C., 7
archaeological sites: overview, on, 138–39; site 2-1-01, 139; site 2-1-03, 141; site 2-54-28, 148; site 2-C6-14, 150; site 2-C6-18, 153. *See also* artifact assemblage
archaeology: methodology, 221; reconstruction, 4, 201, 203, 224; metaphor, 187; segmentation and, 200–205. *See also* archaeological sites; artifacts
artifact assemblage, 156; for animal husbandry, 159, 168; Euroamerican manufactured, 156, 160, 171–75; lithic, 5, 160, 174, 203; medicinal, 144, 158, 168;

miscellaneous, 159, 168–69; personal, 144, 157, 167; subsistence, 145, 150, 157, 166–67; for toys, 144, 157, 168; transportation, 145, 159, 168. *See also* artifact deposition; artifacts; provenience
artifact deposition: alternatives to, 173; approach to study of, 165; assumptions on, 2, 164, 169, 184; factors for, 171, 172, 176; primary/secondary, 170; recycling/reuse and, 156. *See also* artifact assemblage; artifacts; provenience
artifacts: aboriginal ceramic, 161; after use, 62, 66, 67; chi-square tests with, 232–33; clusters of, 165; at dismantled hogan, 83; diversity and continuum for, 198; mass–produced, 170–71, 174; monofunctional, 198; multipurpose, 189; patterning assumptions for, 2, 8; religious, 145, 150, 154; sex specific, 199. *See also* artifact assemblage; artifact deposition; faunal remains; provenience
Ascher, Robert, 3, 4, 11
ash areas, 167, 168, 170, 173, 177
Australian Aborigines, 210
automobiles, 159
Ayers, James E., 4

Bailey, Oran F., 40
basket weaving, 56, 59, 60, 65, 67, 100, 174
Batek Dé 'Negritos, 208

253